PRESENTS

SUPER SECRET
RESTAURANT COLLECTION

A Succulent Serving of
Original Kitchen Clones
from America's Favorite Restaurant Chains

BY

TODD WILBUR

Illustrated by the author

A PLUME BOOK

Visit us on Web at: www.TopSecretRecipes.com.

PLUME
Published by the Penguin Group
Penguin Group (USA) Inc., 375 Hudson Street, New York, New York 10014, U.S.A.
Penguin Books Ltd, 80 Strand, London WC2R 0RL, England
Penguin Books Australia Ltd, 250 Camberwell Road, Camberwell, Victoria 3124, Australia
Penguin Books Canada Ltd, 10 Alcorn Avenue, Toronto, Ontario, Canada M4V 3B2
Penguin Books India (P) Ltd, 11 Community Centre, Panchsheel Park, New Delhi –
110 017, India
Penguin Books (N.Z.) Ltd, Cnr Rosedale and Airborne Roads, Albany, Auckland 1310,
New Zealand
Penguin Books (South Africa) (Pty) Ltd, 24 Sturdee Avenue, Rosebank, Johannesburg
2196, South Africa

Penguin Books Ltd, Registered Offices: 80 Strand, London WC2R 0RL, England

First published by Plume, a member of Penguin Group (USA) Inc.

First Printing, April 2006
10 9 8 7 6 5 4 3 2 1

Some of the recipes in this edition are selected from *Top Secret Restaurant Recipes*,
published by Plume.

For Ajay and Roxie

CONTENTS

CLASSIC RECIPES SECTION

BONUS RECIPES SECTION

INTRODUCTION

If you are new to *Top Secret Recipes*, you are about to experience a cookbook concept unlike any other. This book is a collection of original recipes, created from scratch through a process of reverse-engineering popular brand-name foods, using common ingredients and simplified steps, so that you can easily recreate the taste of the famous products at home.

In the 10 years since *Top Secret Restaurant Recipes* was released I received thousands of e-mails and letters filled with cloning requests for chain restaurant appetizers and entrees and desserts that I hadn't thought about before, or that I never got around to dissecting for the first book. I'm happy to say that this latest collection is assembled with replica recipes from those mouth-watering suggestions. There are more full-service restaurant clone recipes included in his book than in any previous *Top Secret Recipes* volume.

To add to the collection, I've included 26 classic restaurant recipes from the original book. These are favorites such as Hooter's Buffalo Wings, Olive Garden Toscana Soup, Planet Hollywood Chicken Crunch, and Applebee's Oriental Chicken Salad. Full-service restaurant clone recipes are the focus of the book, but, just for fun, I've also included 30 bonus recipes that have never been published in any *Top Secret Recipes* book. These are brand-new original clone recipes for fast food items, snacks and retail products, from companies like Starbucks, Boston Market, Kraft, Sonic Drive-In, Wendy's and Baja Fresh.

To make the book easy-to-use, we've comb-bound it so it will lay flat in your kitchen, and we've added tabs so that you can quickly flip to the section of your choice.

In a full house, where the kitchen is the hub of activity, the activity of preparing tasty meals can be a rewarding event in which all can participate. The reason I first created these *Top Secret Recipes* is that I found cooking home duplicates of favorite famous dishes adds an extra sprinkling of joy to the process. It's a real kick digging into a dish you made at home that comes out tasting just like a menu item from a famous restaurant chain. And now, with these clone recipes to assist you, a combination of taste-alike versions of your favorite courses from different chains can be served in one meal creating a dining experience you couldn't have in any one restaurant.

These days we spend nearly half of the money designated for food on dining outside of our homes. Emeril Lagasse, Rachael Ray and Martha Stewart are more popular than ever, but on any given day 44 percent of adults are filling their bellies in a diner, cafe, coffeehouse, bistro, sub shop, dinnerhouse, pizza joint, cafeteria, or buffet somewhere in America rather than preparing food in their own shiny home kitchens. Speed and convenience are obviously major factors that play into our decision to pay someone to make food for us, but what about the cost? Out of curiosity, I priced each ingredient for a dozen recipes in this book and then broke those totals down by serving. If you're into saving a little coin, you'll see from this list how making food at home will usually cost much less than dining out:

Dish	Original	Clone
Applebee's Honey Grilled Salmon	$10.99	$6.38
Applebee's White Chocolate & Walnut Blondie	$4.99	$2.05
Cheesecake Factory Chicken Madeira	$14.95	$9.69
Claim Jumper Meatloaf	$12.95	$3.84
IHOP Country Griddle Cakes	$5.99	$1.15
Margaritaville Key Lime Pie	$5.25	$1.47
Olive Garden Sicilian Scampi	$8.95	$5.98
Olive Garden Chicken Scampi	$12.50	$5.01
Outback Steakhouse Grilled Shrimp on the Barbie	$8.49	$5.12
P. F. Chang's Chocolate Torte	$4.50	$2.70

P. F. Chang's Mai Tai	$6.50	$2.07
Romano's Macaroni Grill Penne Rustica	$11.99	$5.59

I first started hammering out these recipes immediately following the release of *Top Secret Restaurant Recipes*, so what you have here is the culmination of work that spans a decade. The process is time-consuming and tedious, and I resisted releasing this book before it contained the very best collection of clone recipes I could muster. Within the mix are many recipes that required repeated tooling over 6 months or more before I finally struck gold. If a recipe doesn't pierce the bull's-eye, I keep shooting until I score. If the final product isn't a direct hit, that recipe doesn't make the cut. Because of this strict process, I believe in my formulas, and I'm confident that you will find the results rewarding.

If you'd like additional input on these recipes, check out the *Top Secret Recipes* website (www.TopSecretRecipes.com) where fellow kitchen cloners have added their comments and suggestions for many of these formulas. The important thing is to enjoy the creative freedom you now have with this collection. Cooking at home means having the liberty to experiment with a variety of ingredients, and the ability to customize recipes to suit varying tastes and dietary requirements. I encourage you to make these recipes uniquely yours.

Until next time, I'll be down here in the top secret underground lab, dissecting away, to come up with another big batch of recipes that helps you create kitchen clones of America's favorite brand-name foods. Happy cloning!

APPLEBEE'S MUD SLIDE

MENU DESCRIPTION: *"Bury your sweet tooth with smooth Kahlua, creamy vanilla ice cream, whipped cream and rich Hershey's chocolate syrup."*

Sure, there's a little Kahlua in there, but this famous Applebee's drink is more dessert than cocktail, really. And the presentation will make you look like a pro because you spiral the chocolate syrup around the inside the glass before adding the drink. It looks cool and it's easy to do . . . even after you've had a couple. Grab a straw and prepare to crave another when this one's gone. No wonder this drink also comes in a larger size.

2 cups vanilla ice cream
2 ounces Kahlua coffee liqueur
Hershey's chocolate syrup (in a
    squirt bottle)

canned whipped cream

1. Measure 2 cups of ice cream into your blender. Add the Kahlua and blend until smooth.
2. Prepare a 16-ounce wine glass by swirling chocolate syrup around the inside of the glass. Hold the wine glass by the stem with one hand and twirl the wine glass as you squeeze the chocolate. Slowly move the chocolate up toward the rim of the glass so that the chocolate makes a continuous spiral around the inside of the glass.

3. Pour the drink from the blender into the glass. Add a pile of whipped cream to the top of the drink and drizzle additional chocolate syrup over the whipped cream. Add a straw and serve.

• MAKES 1 DRINK.

• • • •

STRAW

WHIPPED CREAM

BLENDED ICE CREAM & KAHLÚA

SWIRLED INSIDE GLASS

CHOCOLATE SYRUP

16 OUNCE WINE GLASS

SIDE

PROJECT: APPLEBEE'S MUDSLIDE

CATEGORY: COCKTAIL   JOB NO. A640347637-M

APPLEBEE'S
PERFECT APPLE MARGARITA

Here's a great twist on the traditional margarita. Sour apple schnapps and apple juice join forces with tequila and sweet and sour mix in a martini glass that's rimmed with cinnamon sugar. Hey, it's like drinking apple pie! This recipe makes one drink, but it's easy to double up. That's a good thing, since it seems like one is never enough.

2 tablespoons granulated sugar
¼ teaspoon ground cinnamon
1 ounce Sauza Hornitos tequila
1 ounce DeKuyper Sour Apple
    Pucker schnapps

2 ounces sweet-and-sour mix
2 ounces cold apple juice

GARNISH
olive
lime wedge

1. Mix sugar and cinnamon together in a small bowl, then pour the mixture onto a saucer or small plate. Moisten a napkin or clean towel with water. Run the wet napkin around the rim of the martini glass. Invert the glass and dip the moistened rim into the cinnamon/sugar. Set the glass aside for now.
2. Drop a handful of ice into a cocktail shaker.

3. Add the tequila, schnapps, sweet-and-sour, and apple juice. Shake vigorously.
4. Strain drink into the prepared martini glass, spear an olive and small lime wedge on a toothpick and drop it in the drink, and serve it up along with the shaker if there's any left over.

- SERVES 1.

• • • •

APPLEBEE'S ONION PEELS

MENU DESCRIPTION: *"Crisp-fried tender onion strips served with a creamy horseradish dipping sauce."*

This signature appetizer from Applebee's is the chain's reaction to overwhelming success of Outback's Bloomin' Onion and Chili's Awesome Blossom. But, while accurate kitchen cloning of a Bloomin' Onion requires a special slicing device, cloning Onion Peels requires only the most basic kitchen prep and tools: Slice the onion, separate the slices, dip the slices in batter and fry. Just remember to make the essential horseradish dipping sauce in advance so that the ingredients can mingle and really get to know one another as they chill out in the fridge.

CREAMY HORSERADISH DIPPING SAUCE

½ cup mayonnaise
1 tablespoon prepared
    horseradish
2 teaspoons white vinegar
1 teaspoon water
1 teaspoon paprika
1 teaspoon ketchup
¼ teaspoon medium grind black
    pepper

⅛ teaspoon dried oregano
⅛ teaspoon cayenne pepper
dash garlic powder
dash onion powder

6 to 10 cups vegetable shortening
    (as required by fryer)
1 large white onion

BATTER

½ cup all-purpose flour
½ cup Progresso plain
   breadcrumbs

½ teaspoon salt
½ teaspoon ground black pepper
1 ½ cups milk

1. Make horseradish dipping sauce by combining ingredients in a medium bowl with a whisk. Mix until creamy then cover and chill the sauce.
2. Heat the shortening to 350 degrees in a deep fryer.
3. Slice the stem end and the root end off onion, then, with the onion resting on a flat side, cut down through the onion, slicing it in half. Slice each half 4 to 5 more times in a spoke fashion to create wedges of onion. Separate the onion pieces.
4. Create batter by combining all dry ingredients in a medium bowl. Whisk in milk until batter is smooth then let the batter sit for 5 minutes. It should thicken. Whisk batter again.
5. When the oil is hot dip each onion piece in the batter, let some of the batter drip off then drop the coated onion piece carefully into the hot oil. Fry 8 to 12 peels at a time for 1 to 2 minutes or until light brown. Drain on a rack or paper towels. Repeat until the onion is used up, stacking the newer batches on top of the old ones to keep them warm. When they're all done, serve the fried onion slices on a plate or in a paper-lined basket with horseradish dipping sauce on the side.

- SERVES 4 TO 6.

TIDBITS

While shortening works best for this recipe, you may also fry these with vegetable oil or canola oil.

• • • •

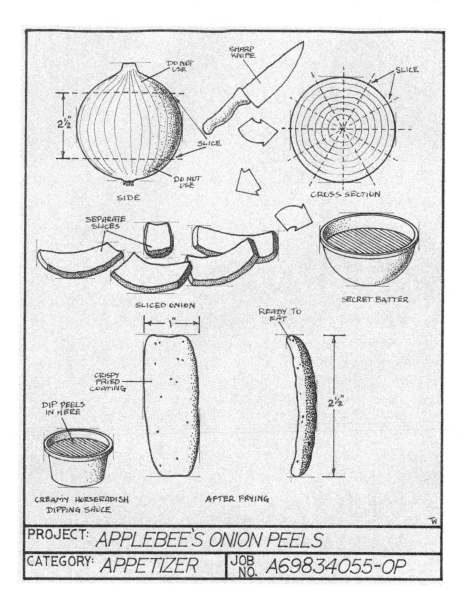

SHARP KNIFE

DO NOT USE

SLICE

SLICE

2½

SIDE

DO NOT USE

CROSS SECTION

SEPARATE SLICES

SLICED ONION

SECRET BATTER

1"

CRISPY FRIED COATING

READY TO EAT

2½"

DIP PEELS IN HERE

CREAMY HORSERADISH DIPPING SAUCE

AFTER FRYING

PROJECT:	*APPLEBEE'S ONION PEELS*	
CATEGORY: *APPETIZER*	JOB NO.	*A69834055-OP*

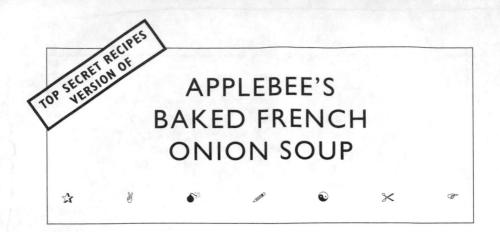

APPLEBEE'S BAKED FRENCH ONION SOUP

It may not be listed on the menu, but this is Applebee's most la-dled soup each and every day. Just be sure you have some oven-safe soup bowls on hand before you jump into this clone, since you're going to pop the dish under the broiler to brown and melt the cheese on top. Under the gooey melted provolone of the original version you get from Applebee's is a unique round crouton that's made from bread that looks like a hamburger bun. In fact, that's exactly what we'll use for our clone. The round shape of the bread is perfect for topping the soup.

3 tablespoons vegetable oil
6 medium white onions, sliced
8 cups beef broth (Swanson is
    best)
1 cup water
2½ teaspoons salt

½ teaspoon garlic powder
¼ teaspoon ground black pepper
5 plain hamburger buns
10 slices provolone cheese
10 teaspoons shredded Parmesan
    cheese

1. Add 3 tablespoons oil to a large soup pot or saucepan over medium/high heat. Add the sliced onions and sauté for 20 minutes until the onions begin to soften and start to become translucent. You don't want them to brown.
2. Add the beef broth, water, salt, garlic powder and black

pepper to the pan and bring mixture to a boil. When soup begins to boil, reduce heat and simmer for 45 minutes.

3. To make the croutons cut off the top half of each top of the hamburger bun so that the bread is the same thickness as the bottom half of each bun. Throw the top crusts away. Now you should have 10 round pieces of bread—5 bottom buns, and 5 top buns with the tops cut off. Preheat oven to 325 degrees. Place the bread in the oven directly on the rack and bake for 15 to 20 minutes or until each piece is golden brown and crispy. Set these croutons aside until you need them.

4. When the soup is done, spoon about 1 cup into an oven-safe bowl. Float a crouton on top of the soup, then place a slice of provolone cheese on top of the crouton. Sprinkle ½ teaspoon of shredded parmesan cheese over the provolone.

5. Place the bowl into your oven set to high broil. Broil the soup for 5 to 6 minutes or until the cheese is melted and starting to brown (you may need to broil longer if you are making more than one bowl at a time). Sprinkle an additional ½ teaspoon of shredded parmesan cheese over the top of the soup and serve. Repeat process to prepare remaining servings.

• MAKES 10 SERVINGS.

• • • •

APPLEBEE'S
SANTA FE CHICKEN SALAD

MENU DESCRIPTION: *"Grilled chipotle chicken breast with gua-*
camole and sour cream on a bed of greens tossed with two cheeses,
pico de gallo, tortilla strips and our Mexi-ranch dressing."

Create a robust chipotle marinade that fills your chicken fillets
with flavor. As you wait for the chicken to marinate you have
plenty of time to throw together clones of the Mexi-ranch
dressing and fresh pico de gallo. Now most of the work is done,
and you're standing in front of the gate to salad heaven. When
you're ready to enter, simply grill the chicken, assemble your
salads and open wide.

You should know that if you don't have buttermilk for the
dressing, and don't want to buy a whole carton to use just a single
tablespoon, simply substitute regular milk. You'll find ground
chipotle pepper where all the spices are in the market (I use Mc-
Cormick). If you can't track down ground chipotle, use ground
cayenne pepper. Just be sure to measure roughly half the amount,
since cayenne packs more heat than chipotle.

MARINADE

2 cups water
⅓ cup soy sauce
3 tablespoons granulated sugar
2 tablespoons salt
2 tablespoons apple cider vinegar

1 tablespoon ground chipotle
 pepper (or 1 ½ teaspoons
 ground cayenne pepper)
2 teaspoons hickory smoke
 flavoring

2 teaspoons paprika

2 teaspoon garlic powder

1 teaspoon onion powder

1 teaspoon ground black pepper

4 skinless chicken breast fillets

MEXI-RANCH DRESSING

½ cup mayonnaise

2 tablespoons minced onion

2 tablespoons diced tomato

1 tablespoon buttermilk

1 tablespoon white vinegar

2 teaspoons minced fresh cilantro

1 teaspoon canned chopped mild
   green chiles

¾ teaspoon paprika

½ teaspoon granulated sugar

¼ teaspoon salt

pinch dried dill weed

pinch ground cumin

pinch cayenne pepper

PICO DE GALLO

2 medium tomatoes, diced

⅓ cup diced red onion

1 jalapeno, seeded and diced

2 teaspoons lime juice

2 teaspoons minced fresh cilantro

¼ teaspoon salt

¼ teaspoon ground black
   pepper

8 cups chopped iceberg lettuce

8 cups chopped romaine lettuce

1 cup chopped red cabbage

1 cup fancy shredded Cheddar
   cheese

1 cup fancy shredded Monterey
   Jack cheese

4 handfuls tortilla strips or chips

½ cup sour cream

½ cup guacamole

1. You want to marinate the chicken for 2 hours in advance, so make the marinade first by combing all the ingredients for the marinade in a medium bowl. Stir well until the sugar has dissolved. Drop the chicken breasts into the marinade, then cover and chill for 2 hours. You don't want to marinate for much more than 2 hours or the chicken could get tough.
2. While the chicken marinates, make the Mexi-ranch dressing by combining the ingredients in a medium bowl. Cover and chill so the flavors will develop as the chicken marinates.

3. You'll also make the pico de gallo in advance so that it can rest a bit in the fridge. Combine all the ingredients in a medium bowl, then cover and chill this as well.
4. When the chicken has marinated for 2 hours, fire up the grill to medium/high heat. Grill the chicken breasts for 4 to 7 minutes per side or until chicken is done. Take the chicken off the grill then let it rest for a bit while you prepare the salads.
5. Build each salad in a large bowl by first tossing 2 cups chopped iceberg lettuce and 2 cups chopped romaine lettuce with ¼ cup chopped red cabbage and about ¼ cup of the dressing.
6. Combine the shredded cheeses then add, about ½ cup to each salad on the lettuce. Sprinkle a handful of tortilla strips or crumbled chips on next.
7. Slice each chicken breast into strips and arrange each one on each of the salads. Sprinkle about ¼ cup of pico de gallo over the top.
8. Finish off each salad by adding a 2-tablespoon scoop of sour cream on one side of each salad, then a 2-tablespoon scoop of guacamole on the other side of the salad.

• SERVES 4.

• •   •   •

2 teaspoons paprika
2 teaspoon garlic powder
1 teaspoon onion powder

1 teaspoon ground black pepper

4 skinless chicken breast fillets

MEXI-RANCH DRESSING

½ cup mayonnaise
2 tablespoons minced onion
2 tablespoons diced tomato
1 tablespoon buttermilk
1 tablespoon white vinegar
2 teaspoons minced fresh cilantro
1 teaspoon canned chopped mild
   green chiles

¾ teaspoon paprika
½ teaspoon granulated sugar
¼ teaspoon salt
pinch dried dill weed
pinch ground cumin
pinch cayenne pepper

PICO DE GALLO

2 medium tomatoes, diced
⅓ cup diced red onion
1 jalapeno, seeded and diced
2 teaspoons lime juice

2 teaspoons minced fresh cilantro
¼ teaspoon salt
¼ teaspoon ground black
   pepper

8 cups chopped iceberg lettuce
8 cups chopped romaine lettuce
1 cup chopped red cabbage
1 cup fancy shredded Cheddar
   cheese

1 cup fancy shredded Monterey
   Jack cheese
4 handfuls tortilla strips or chips
½ cup sour cream
½ cup guacamole

1. You want to marinate the chicken for 2 hours in advance, so make the marinade first by combing all the ingredients for the marinade in a medium bowl. Stir well until the sugar has dissolved. Drop the chicken breasts into the marinade, then cover and chill for 2 hours. You don't want to marinate for much more than 2 hours or the chicken could get tough.
2. While the chicken marinates, make the Mexi-ranch dressing by combining the ingredients in a medium bowl. Cover and chill so the flavors will develop as the chicken marinates.

3. You'll also make the pico de gallo in advance so that it can rest a bit in the fridge. Combine all the ingredients in a medium bowl, then cover and chill this as well.

4. When the chicken has marinated for 2 hours, fire up the grill to medium/high heat. Grill the chicken breasts for 4 to 7 minutes per side or until chicken is done. Take the chicken off the grill then let it rest for a bit while you prepare the salads.

5. Build each salad in a large bowl by first tossing 2 cups chopped iceberg lettuce and 2 cups chopped romaine lettuce with ¼ cup chopped red cabbage and about ¼ cup of the dressing.

6. Combine the shredded cheeses then add, about ½ cup to each salad on the lettuce. Sprinkle a handful of tortilla strips or crumbled chips on next.

7. Slice each chicken breast into strips and arrange each one on each of the salads. Sprinkle about ¼ cup of pico de gallo over the top.

8. Finish off each salad by adding a 2-tablespoon scoop of sour cream on one side of each salad, then a 2-tablespoon scoop of guacamole on the other side of the salad.

- SERVES 4.

• • • •

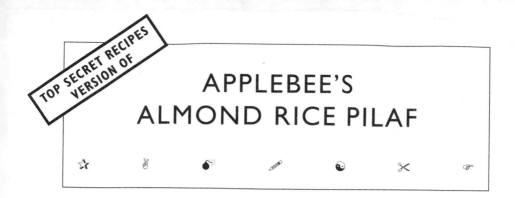
APPLEBEE'S ALMOND RICE PILAF

You're grilling some steaks or baking some chicken and don't know what to serve on the side? Try out this simple clone for a dish that's served along with several of Applebee's entrees. Since the recipe requires converted rice (because instant rice is gross) you have to plan ahead about 25 minutes to give the rice time to cook. It's worth the wait. The secret to an authentic, great-tasting rice pilaf is sautéing the uncooked rice kernels in butter first, before adding the liquid—in this case chicken broth. Then, as the rice is cooking, you have plenty of time to sauté the almonds, celery, and onions that are tossed into the rice at the end.

3 tablespoons butter
1 cup uncooked converted rice
2¼ cups chicken broth
⅛ teaspoon salt

⅓ cup sliced or slivered almonds
¼ cup diced celery
¼ cup diced onion
1 teaspoon dried parsley

1. Melt 2 tablespoons butter over medium heat in a medium saucepan. Be sure to use a saucepan with a lid. Add 1 cup uncooked converted rice and sauté rice for 2 to 4 minutes in the butter or until some of the rice begins to turn light brown. As the rice is cooking heat chicken broth on high in microwave for 3 to 4 minutes or until the broth begins to bubble. When the rice begins to brown, quickly add the hot stock and salt to the pan. Cover the pan, reduce heat to low and simmer rice for 20 minutes.

2. As rice cooks, melt remaining 1 tablespoon butter in a medium skillet over medium heat. Add almonds and sauté for 1 to 2 minutes or until the almonds begin to brown. Add celery and onions and sauté for another couple of minutes or until the onions begins to turn translucent.
3. When the rice has cooked for 20 minutes, remove it from the heat. Add almonds, celery, onion and parsley to the rice, then let it sit, covered, for 5 minutes or until the remaining liquid is absorbed.

- SERVES 4.

•   •   •   •

APPLEBEE'S
CHICKEN FAJITA ROLLUP

MENU DESCRIPTION: *"A large flour tortilla topped with melted Monterey Jack and Cheddar cheeses, grilled chipotle chicken, shredded lettuce and pico de gallo. Rolled, sliced and served with a Mexi-ranch dipping sauce"*

Take Applebee's delicious chicken chipotle fajita recipe, roll it up in a large flour tortilla with lettuce, cheeses and fresh pico de gallo and you've got a meal to wrap your hands around. The Mexi-ranch dipping sauce is the perfect creamy compliment for this recipe and you can use what's left over for a dressing on your next salad. The sauce is actually just a kicked-up ranch dressing recipe that includes a small amount of buttermilk in the ingredients list. But if you don't want to buy a whole carton of buttermilk to use just a tablespoon for this recipe, that's okay. Substitute the regular moo juice you've got sitting in the fridge. For the spicy marinade it's best to use ground chipotle pepper (dried smoked red jalapeno) made by McCormick. If you can't find that stuff, cut the amount in half and use cayenne pepper. For the cheeses, many major brands make a Cheddar/Jack blend that will work great here if you'd rather not buy the cheeses separately. That's helpful if you're about to tip the limit for the express lane checkout line.

MARINADE

2 cups water
⅓ cup soy sauce

3 tablespoons granulated sugar
2 tablespoons salt

2 tablespoons white vinegar
1 tablespoon ground chipotle
    pepper(or 1 ½ teaspoons
    ground cayenne pepper)
2 teaspoons hickory smoke
    flavoring

2 teaspoons paprika
2 teaspoon garlic powder
1 teaspoon onion powder
1 teaspoon ground black pepper

4 skinless chicken breast fillets

MEXI-RANCH DIPPING SAUCE

½ cup mayonnaise
2 tablespoons minced onion
2 tablespoons diced tomato
1 tablespoon buttermilk
1 tablespoon white vinegar
2 teaspoons minced fresh cilantro
1 teaspoon canned chopped mild
    green chiles

¾ teaspoon paprika
½ teaspoon granulated sugar
¼ teaspoon salt
pinch dried dill weed
pinch ground cumin
pinch cayenne pepper

PICO DE GALLO

2 medium tomatoes, diced
⅓ cup diced red onion
1 jalapeno, seeded and
    diced
2 teaspoons lime juice
2 teaspoons minced fresh
    cilantro
¼ teaspoon salt

¼ teaspoon ground black pepper

4 large flour tortillas
1 cup fancy shredded Cheddar
    cheese
1 cup fancy shredded Monterey
    Jack cheese
4 cups shredded iceberg lettuce

1. The chicken needs to marinate for 2 hours, so make the marinade first by combining the ingredients in a medium bowl. Stir well until the sugar has dissolved. Add four chicken breasts to the marinade, cover and chill for 2 hours. Don't let the chicken marinate for much more than that or it could get tough.

2. While the chicken marinates, prepare the dipping sauce by

combining the ingredients in a medium bowl. Stir well then cover and chill. This will allow all the flavors to develop nicely while parked in the fridge.

3. The pico de gallo will also develop nicely in the fridge. Combine all those ingredients, then cover and chill it as well.

4. When you're ready to make your roll-ups, preheat your grill to medium/high heat. Grill the chicken breast for 4 to 7 minutes per side or until done.

5. Build each roll-up by first laying a large flour tortilla in a large skillet over low-heat. Sprinkle about ½ cup of the combined cheeses over the surface of the tortilla while it heats up in the pan. When the cheese begins to melt, remove the tortilla from the pan. Sprinkle about 1 cup of shredded lettuce in a strip across the center of the tortilla, followed by about 3 tablespoons of pico de gallo. Slice one grilled chicken breast into bite-size chunks and arrange the chicken on the lettuce. Fold the ends of the tortilla over the filling, then roll the tortilla from the bottom. Make a diagonal cut across the center of the roll-up and serve with a small dish of the dipping sauce on the side.

• SERVES 4.

•   •   •   •

HEAT TORTILLA & CHEESE IN THIS

10"

MARINATED SLICED CHICKEN BREAST

CHICKEN MARINADE

PICO DE GALLO

SHREDDED JACK & CHEDDAR

SHREDDED LETTUCE

10-INCH FLOUR TORTILLA

① ② ③ ④

SLICE

TOP
6½"

2½"

GOOD STUFF IN THERE

2"

SIDE

PROJECT:	*APPLEBEE'S CHICKEN FAJITA ROLLUP*	
CATEGORY: *SANDWICH*	JOB NO.	*A2165973340-CFR*

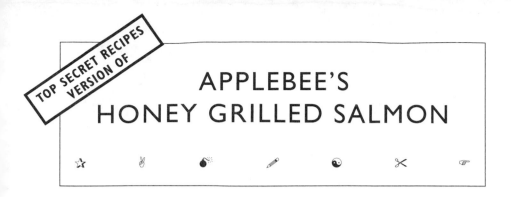

APPLEBEE'S
HONEY GRILLED SALMON

MENU DESCRIPTION: *"Flame-grilled Atlantic Salmon with Applebee's Honey Pepper Sauce served with a side of almond rice pilaf, seasoned vegetables and toasted garlic bread."*

It's all about the sauce. This sweet, tangy and slightly spicy sauce goes perfectly with salmon, but can also be used on chicken or ribs. Just be sure to watch the sauce closely as it cooks in case it starts to bubble over. If it sounds like I'm speaking from experience, you're right—oh, what a beautiful mess I made on one attempt. So cook the sauce slowly, and watch it closely as it thickens. If it gets too thick, you can always add a bit of water to thin it out. I suggest serving this salmon with almond rice pilaf as they do in the restaurant. You'll find that clone recipe on page 13.

HONEY PEPPER SAUCE

¾ cup honey
⅓ cup soy sauce
¼ cup dark brown sugar,
    packed
¼ cup pineapple juice
juice of 1 lemon (about 2
    tablespoons)
2 tablespoons white vinegar
2 teaspoons olive oil

1 teaspoon ground black pepper
½ teaspoon cayenne pepper
½ teaspoon paprika
¼ teaspoon garlic powder

4 8-ounce salmon fillets (without
    skin)
vegetable oil

1. Make the sauce by combining all ingredients in a medium saucepan over medium/low heat. Stir occasionally until sauce begins to boil, then simmer uncovered for 15 minutes or until syrupy. Watch the sauce closely to be sure it doesn't bubble over.
2. Preheat barbecue grill to medium heat. Rub each salmon fillet with vegetable oil, then add a light sprinkling of salt and pepper. Grill the salmon for 4 to 7 minutes per side or until done. Serve salmon with a small cup of the honey pepper sauce on the side.

- SERVES 4.

• • • •

APPLEBEE'S
TEQUILA LIME CHICKEN

MENU DESCRIPTION: *"A tender boneless chicken breast marinated with lime juice and tequila flavors and grilled. Served on a bed of crisp tortilla strips. Topped with a Mexi-ranch and Jack-Cheddar sauce. Served with Southwest rice and pico de gallo."*

Because of the huge success of this dish, Applebee's has recently changed the name to "Fiesta Lime Chicken," and trademarked the name. Most people still know this dish by its original title, so that's what I'm going with for this book. When making your clone, just be sure not to marinate the chicken for much longer than the 2 to 3 hours specified, or the acid in the lime juice may toughen your chicken. The bed of crispy corn tortilla strips can be easily made by simply crumbling store-bought tortilla chips, or, if you want strips more closely resembling those served at the restaurant, just follow the Tidbits below. Serve this dish with your choice of rice, and some salsa or pico de gallo on the side.

MARINADE

1 cup water
.⅓ cup teriyaki sauce
2 tablespoons lime juice
2 teaspoons minced garlic
1 teaspoon liquid mesquite smoke

½ teaspoon salt
¼ teaspoon ground ginger
¼ teaspoon tequila

4 skinless chicken breast fillets

MEXI-RANCH SAUCE

¼ cup mayonnaise
¼ cup sour cream
1 tablespoon milk
2 teaspoons minced tomato
1½ teaspoons white vinegar
1 teaspoon minced canned
　　jalapeno slices (nacho slices)
1 teaspoon minced onion
¼ teaspoon dried parsley
¼ teaspoon Tabasco pepper sauce
⅛ teaspoon salt
⅛ teaspoon dried dill weed

⅛ teaspoon paprika
⅛ teaspoon cayenne pepper
⅛ teaspoon ground cumin
⅛ teaspoon chili powder
dash garlic powder
dash ground black pepper

1 cup shredded Cheddar/
　　Monterey Jack cheese blend
2 cups crumbled tortilla chips or
　　fried tortilla strips (see Tidbits)

1. Prepare marinade by combining marinade ingredients in a medium bowl. Add the chicken to the bowl, cover and chill for 2 to 3 hours.
2. Make the Mexi-ranch dressing by combining all of the ingredients in a medium bowl. Mix well until smooth, then cover the dressing and chill it until it's needed.
3. When you are ready to prepare the entree, preheat the oven to high broil. Also, preheat your barbecue or indoor grill to high heat. When the grill is hot cook the marinated chicken breasts for 3 to 5 minutes per side, or until they're done.
4. Arrange the cooked chicken in a baking pan. Spread a layer of Mexi-ranch dressing over each piece of chicken (you'll have plenty left over), followed by ¼ cup of the shredded cheese blend. Broil the chicken for 2 to 3 minutes, or just until the cheese has melted.
5. Spread a bed of ½ cup of the tortilla strips or crumbled tortilla chips on each of four plates. Slide a chicken breast onto the chips on each plate and serve with your choice of rice, and pico de gallo or salsa.

• SERVES 4.

Crumbling store-bought tortilla chips is the easy way to make the bed of crunchy chips that the tequila lime chicken rests on. But, you can make tortilla strips like those served at the restaurant by cutting a stack of eight 6-inch corn tortillas in half. Stack the halves on top of each other and slice the tortillas into thin strips. Fry the tortilla strips in batches in 2 cups of preheated oil in a large skillet for 3 to 5 minutes or until crispy. Salt lightly and cool on paper towels.

• • • •

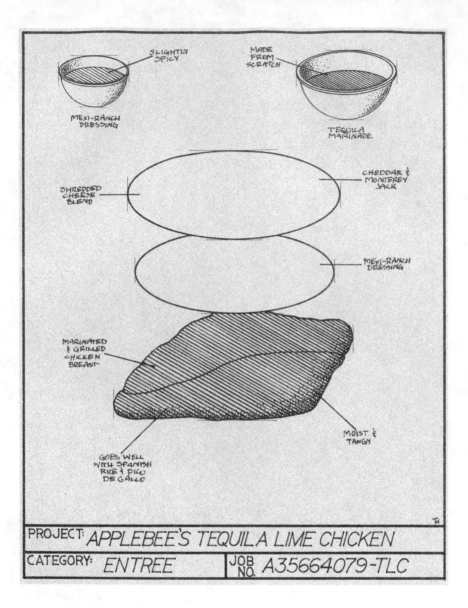

SLIGHTLY SPICY

MADE FROM SCRATCH

MEXI-RANCH DRESSING

TEQUILA MARINADE

SHREDDED CHEESE BLEND

CHEDDAR & MONTEREY JACK

MEXI-RANCH DRESSING

MARINATED & GRILLED CHICKEN BREAST

MOIST & TANGY

GOES WELL WITH SPANISH RICE & PICO DE GALLO

PROJECT: APPLEBEE'S TEQUILA LIME CHICKEN

CATEGORY: ENTREE

JOB NO. A35664079-TLC

APPLEBEE'S WHITE CHOCOLATE & WALNUT BLONDIE

MENU DESCRIPTION: *"Dare to indulge with a white chocolate and walnut blondie under a scoop of ice cream and chopped walnuts. Served warm and topped at your table with a rich, sizzling maple butter sauce."*

For Applebee's regulars, this dessert is a hands-down favorite. In a hot skillet comes a delicious slice of white chocolate and walnut cake (it's similar to a brownie in texture) topped with a scoop of ice cream and warm maple butter sauce bubbling as it hits the pan. Commence with the salivating. To recreate this pile of pleasure at home you start by making the cake from scratch. For the white chocolate, get a couple of 4-ounce bars or one 8-ounce bar and chop it into chunks. White chocolate chunks work best in this recipe, but you can certainly use white chocolate chips in a pinch. While the blondie cake is baking, whip up the sauce—it will be fluffy at first. When you're ready to serve the dessert, zap the sauce in the microwave until it's hot and creamy. Arrange the decadence in a hot skillet and serve it sizzling to happy, drooling mouths.

BLONDIE

4 egg whites	¼ cup granulated sugar
½ cup butter, softened (1 stick)	1 teaspoon vanilla extract
½ cup light brown sugar, packed	2¼ cups all-purpose flour

1 teaspoon baking soda
½ teaspoon baking powder
¼ teaspoon salt
½ cup milk

8 ounces white chocolate (cut into
    chunks)
½ cup chopped walnuts

SAUCE

½ cup butter, softened (1 stick)
½ cup powdered sugar
¼ cup cream cheese, softened
2 tablespoons maple syrup

¼ teaspoon salt

8 scoops vanilla ice cream
½ cup chopped walnuts

1. Preheat oven to 325 degrees.
2. To make the blondie cake whip the egg whites until they are stiff and form peaks. Add softened butter, ½ cup packed brown sugar, ¼ cup granulated sugar, and vanilla and mix with an electric mixer until smooth. In a separate bowl sift together flour, baking soda, baking powder and ¼ teaspoon salt. Add the dry ingredients to the wet ingredients and mix well until smooth. Mix in milk, white chocolate chunks, and walnuts. Pour ingredients into a greased 9x13-inch baking pan and bake for 40 to 45 minutes or until cake is golden brown on top. Slice cake into 8 equal slices when cool.
3. While cake bakes, combine all ingredients for the sauce in a medium bowl with an electric mixer.
4. To prepare dessert, heat a small skillet on your stove over high heat for about 5 minutes. A cast iron skillet is the best. (You can also serve the dessert on a plate, but you'll miss out on the showy sizzle.) Arrange the cake in the center of the skillet or plate. Heat up the sauce for 30 to 60 seconds in the microwave until hot. Place a scoop of vanilla ice cream on the cake, then drizzle some of the sauce over the top, followed by a tablespoon of chopped walnuts. Serve immediately.

• SERVES 8.

CHOPPED WALNUTS

WARM MAPLE BUTTER SAUCE

SCOOPED VANILLA ICE CREAM

BLONDIE CAKE

WHITE CHOCOLATE

WALNUTS

SIZZLES IN THIS

CAST IRON WORKS BEST

SERVE IT IN THIS

HOT SKILLET

PROJECT: *APPLEBEE'S WHITE CHOC. & WAL. BLONDIE*

CATEGORY: *DESSERT*

JOB NO. *A7409767-WCWB*

BENIHANA
GINGER SALAD DRESSING

Before your meal at the Benihana chain of hibachi grill restaurants you are served a side salad doused in this tangy, slightly sweet, fresh ginger dressing. When spooned over a simple iceberg lettuce salad this easy clone transforms your bowl of greens into a great start for any meal. Making the dressing is as simple as dumping the ingredients into a blender, whizzing it up, and popping it into the cooler to chill. I've seen many attempts to duplicate this coveted formula, but I think the original clone recipe presented here comes closer to the real thing than any other recipe out there.

½ cup minced onion
½ cup peanut oil
⅓ cup rice vinegar
2 tablespoons water
2 tablespoons minced fresh ginger
2 tablespoons minced celery
2 tablespoons ketchup

4 teaspoons soy sauce
2 teaspoons granulated sugar
2 teaspoons lemon juice
½ teaspoon minced garlic
½ teaspoon salt
¼ teaspoon ground black pepper

Combine all ingredients in a blender. Blend on high speed for about 30 seconds or until all of the ginger is pureed.

- MAKES 1¾ CUPS.

• • • •

BENIHANA
JAPANESE ONION SOUP

MENU DESCRIPTION: *"It takes half a day to make this perfect combination of onion, celery, carrot and garlic."*

Before a skilled chef appears tableside to perform his culinary prestidigitation on the hot hibachi grill at Benihana, you're treated to a tasty bowl of chicken broth-based soup with fried onions, sliced mushrooms and green onions floating cheerfully on top. The restaurant menu claims this soup takes a half a day to make, but we can clone it in a fraction of that time using canned chicken broth (I use Swanson brand). This soup works great as a prelude to your favorite Asian dishes or other Benihana clones since it's so light and won't fill up anyone before the main course. I've included a simple technique here for making the breaded fried onions from scratch (for the most accurate clone), but you can skip that step by substituting French's canned French Fried Onions that are sold in most markets.

4 cups canned chicken broth
2 cups water
1 white onion (see Tidbits)
½ carrot, coarsely chopped (about ¼ cup)
½ celery stalk, coarsely chopped (about ¼ cup)
1 small clove garlic, sliced

½ teaspoon salt
1 cup vegetable oil
1 cup milk
1 cup all-purpose flour
6 medium mushrooms, thinly sliced
4 green onions, diced (green part only)

1. Combine chicken broth and water in a large saucepan over high heat. Slice the white onion in half, and then coarsely chop one half (save the other half for later). Add coarsely chopped onion, carrot, celery, garlic, and salt to the saucepan and bring to a boil. Reduce heat and simmer for 10 minutes, or until the onions start to become translucent.
2. As the broth simmers, heat up 1 cup of vegetable oil in a small saucepan over medium heat. Slice the remaining white onion into very thin slices. Separate the slices, dip the slices into the milk, then into the flour. Fry the breaded onions, a handful at a time in the oil until golden brown. Drain on a paper towel.
3. When the soup has simmered for 10 minutes, strain the vegetables out of the broth and toss them out. Pour the broth back into the pan and keep it hot over low heat.
4. To serve soup, ladle about 1 cup of broth into a bowl. Drop a few pieces of fried onion into the soup, followed by 6 to 8 mushroom slices (about 1 mushroom each) and a couple pinches of diced green onion. When the fried onions sink to the bottom of the bowl (a couple of minutes), serve the soup.

• MAKES 6 SERVINGS.

TIDBITS

You will only need ½ of a white onion if you opt to use the canned French's French Fried Onions for this recipe—the small can will be enough—rather than frying your own. You also won't need the vegetable oil, milk or flour listed in the ingredients.

• • • •

BENIHANA
MANDARIN ORANGE
CHEESECAKE

This charismatic cheesecake is a specialty at the world's largest Benihana restaurant located in the Hilton hotel and casino in Las Vegas. But don't expect to find this amazing dessert on the menu at any of the other 69 Benihana eateries, since it's custom-made just for the Sin City location and probably unlike any cheesecake you've had. Check it out: The lightly orange-flavored, fluffed-up cream cheese sits on layer of soft white cake, the edge is frosted and coated with crunchy hazelnut crumbs, and the top is covered with wedges of mandarin oranges in an orange-flavored gelatin. Every element of this top secret kitchen clone is made from scratch, and the finished product is well worth the work you put in. For the cake layer, we whip up just enough of a simple white cake batter to fit into the bottom of a 9-inch springform pan. The cheese layer in our clone is created with a special custom combination of gelatin, Dream Whip, and cream cheese so that no baking is required to firm it up. You could, of course, use a store-bought white frosting for the edge of the cake, but since you only need a small amount of frosting the clone recipe here makes it cheaper. The hazelnuts are candied with sugar and reduced to crumbs in a food processor (you can find a ½-cup bag of chopped hazelnuts in most supermarkets that is perfect for this). And two 15-ounce cans of mandarin orange wedges is just the right amount for garnishing the top. Just be sure to save ½-cup of the liquid from the cans of orange wedges to create the gel that holds the topping in place.

CAKE

¼ cup all-purpose flour
¼ teaspoon baking powder
pinch of salt
2 tablespoons butter, softened

¼ cup granulated sugar
2 tablespoons milk
⅛ teaspoon vanilla extract
1 egg

CREAM CHEESE LAYER

1 envelope unflavored gelatin
¾ cup granulated sugar
1 cup boiling water
1 envelope Dream Whip
½ cup low-fat milk
3 8-ounce pkgs. cream cheese,
   softened

1 teaspoon vanilla extract
¼ teaspoon orange extract
¼ teaspoon lemon juice
5 drops yellow food coloring
1 drop red food coloring

TOPPING

2 15-ounce cans mandarin
   oranges (in light syrup)
1 teaspoon unflavored gelatin

NUT CRUST

1 tablespoon water
2 tablespoons granulated sugar
½ cup chopped hazelnuts
   (2.25 ounce bag)

ICING

¼ cup vegetable shortening
½ cup powdered sugar
1 tablespoon milk
⅛ teaspoon vanilla extract

1. To make cake layer, combine flour, baking powder and salt in a small bowl. Cream together butter and sugar with an electric mixer in a medium bowl. Add dry ingredients to the butter and mix well. Mix in milk, vanilla and 1 egg. Pour into a well-greased 9-inch springform pan (or line it with parchment paper). Slam pan down on the counter a few times to

even out the batter. Bake in a preheated 350 degree oven for 15 minutes or until the cake is light brown on top.

2. For the cream cheese layer, combine gelatin with ¾ cup sugar in a medium bowl. Add boiling water and stir until gelatin is dissolved. Set this aside.

3. Prepare Dream Whip by whipping together 1 envelope of Dream Whip and ½ cup milk with an electric mixer in another medium bowl. Whip it good until the topping makes stiff peaks.

4. In another bowl, whip the cream cheese with vanilla, orange extract, lemon juice and food coloring in a large bowl until smooth. Slowly add the gelatin mixture while beating.

5. Add half (about 1 cup) of the Dream Whip to the cream cheese mixture and beat until smooth.

6. Pour this mixture over the cake layer in the springform pan. Chill for 2 hours or until firm.

7. Drain the liquid from the cans of mandarin oranges, saving ½ cup. Heat the ½ cup liquid in the microwave on high for 1 to 1½ minutes or until hot. Dissolve 1 teaspoon unflavored gelatin in the liquid. Combine liquid with orange wedges and pour over the top of the firmed-up cheesecake that's still in the springform pan. Chill the cake for at least 2 more hours.

8. For the crunchy nut crust, combine 1 tablespoon water with 2 tablespoons sugar in a small saucepan over medium heat. When sugar is dissolved and liquid begins to boil, add the hazelnuts and stir until nuts are coated. Stir often until the water has cooked off, then continue to stir until the sugar begins to caramelize and turn light brown. Be careful not to burn the nuts. The nuts are done when they are light brown and glazed with candied sugar. Pour the nuts onto a plate and let them cool completely. When the candied nuts are cool, chop them up in a food processor until they are the consistency of crumbs.

9. Make the icing by combining shortening with powdered sugar, milk and vanilla.

10. When the mandarin orange gelatin has firmed up on top of

the cake, remove the cake from the springform pan. Use a spatula to spread the icing around the edge of the cake. Press the hazelnut crumbs onto the icing around the edge of the cake (you've got more than enough hazelnut crumbs and much of it will fall off as you press it on the sides). Chill the cake for at least another hour before serving. To serve, cut cake into 12 slices.

- MAKES 12 SERVINGS.

• • • •

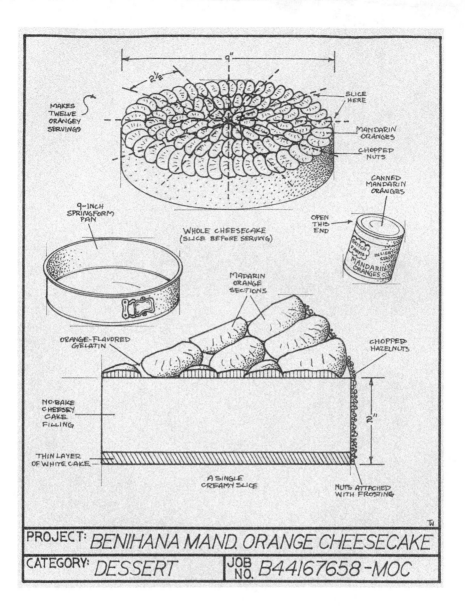

9"

2½"

MAKES
TWELVE
ORANGEY
SERVINGS

SLICE
HERE

MANDARIN
ORANGES

CHOPPED
NUTS

CANNED
MANDARIN
ORANGES

9-INCH
SPRINGFORM
PAN

WHOLE CHEESECAKE
(SLICE BEFORE SERVING)

OPEN
THIS
END

DUTCH
FARMS
MANDARIN
ORANGES
IN LIGHT
SYRUP

MADARIN
ORANGE
SECTIONS

ORANGE-FLAVORED
GELATIN

CHOPPED
HAZELNUTS

NO-BAKE
CHEESEY
CAKE
FILLING

2"

THIN LAYER
OF WHITE CAKE

A SINGLE
CREAMY SLICE

NUTS ATTACHED
WITH FROSTING

TW

PROJECT: *BENIHANA MAND. ORANGE CHEESECAKE*

CATEGORY: *DESSERT*   **JOB NO.** *B44167658-MOC*

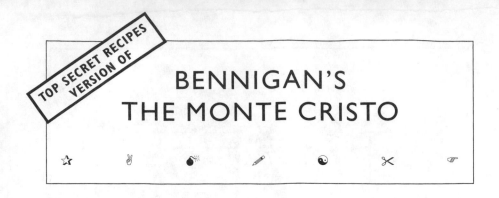

BENNIGAN'S
THE MONTE CRISTO

MENU DESCRIPTION: *"A delicious combination of ham and turkey, plus Swiss and American cheeses on wheat bread. Lightly battered and fried until golden. Dusted with powdered sugar and served with red raspberry preserves for dipping."*

It sounds crazy, but tastes great: A triple-decker ham, turkey, and cheese sandwich is dipped in a tempura-style batter; fried to a golden brown; then served with a dusting of powdered sugar and a side of raspberry preserves. For over ten years tons of cloning requests for this one have stacked up at *TSR* Central, so it was time for a road trip. There are no Bennigan's in Las Vegas, and since the Bennigan's chain made this sandwich famous, I headed out to the nearest Bennigan's in San Diego. Back home, with an ice chest full of original Monte Cristo sandwiches well-preserved and ready to work with, I was able to come up with this simple clone for a delicious sandwich that is crispy on the outside, and hot, but not greasy, on the inside (the batter prevents the shortening from penetrating). This recipe makes one sandwich, which may be enough for two. If you want to make more, you'll most likely have to make more batter so that any additional sandwiches get a real good dunking.

8 to 12 cups vegetable shortening

SANDWICH

3 slices whole wheat sandwich
   bread
1 slice Swiss cheese (deli-style)
3 ounces sliced turkey (deli-style)

1 slice American cheese
   (deli-style)
3 ounces sliced ham (deli-style)

BATTER

2 egg yolks
1 cup ice water

1 cup all purpose flour
1 teaspoon baking soda

ON TOP

powdered sugar

ON THE SIDE

raspberry preserves

1. Heat 8 to 12 cups of shortening in a deep fryer or large saucepan to 375 degrees. You will need the hot shortening to be at least 4 inches deep.
2. Make the sandwich by arranging the slice of Swiss cheese on a piece of wheat bread. Arrange the turkey breast on the Swiss cheese. Place a piece of wheat bread on the turkey. Place the slice of American cheese on the wheat bread. Arrange the ham slices on the American cheese. Top off the sandwich with the third slice of bread. Make sure the meat is not hanging over the edge of the sandwich. Press down on the sandwich with the palm of your hand to flatten it a bit.
3. Make the batter by beating the egg yolks. Stir in the ice water. Measure the flour and baking soda into a sifter, and sift the mixture into the ice water and egg yolk. Stir with a large spoon, but don't mix it too well. You should still have many visible lumps in the batter.
4. Slice the sandwich in half from corner to corner. Dip one half of the sandwich in the batter, while holding it together with your fingers (the batter will hold the sandwich together in the shortening). Coat the sandwich well, but let any excess

batter fall off. Drop the battered sandwich half into the oil. If your pan or fryer can fit the other half of the sandwich, batter that piece and drop it into the fryer as well. If your fryer is small, you may only be able to fry only one half at a time. Fry the sandwich for 6 to 8 minutes, turning it over halfway through cooking time. It should be golden brown when done.

5. Remove the sandwich halves to paper towels to drain. When you can touch the sandwich, slice each half in half making four pieces. Dust the sandwich with powdered sugar and serve it with a small bowl of raspberry preserves.

- MAKES 1 SANDWICH.

• • • •

DIP IN BATTER

BEFORE FRYING

SLICE HERE

AFTER FRYING

SERVED WITH GUSTO
(AND RASPBERRY PRESERVES)

WHOLE WHEAT BREAD

SLICED HAM

AMERICAN CHEESE

WHOLE WHEAT BREAD

SLICED TURKEY

SWISS CHEESE

WHOLE WHEAT BREAD

PROJECT: *BENNIGAN'S THE MONTE CRISTO*

CATEGORY: *SANDWICH*　　**JOB NO.** *B2241169691-TMC*

BUFFALO WILD WINGS
BUFFALO WINGS
AND SAUCES

MENU DESCRIPTION: *"Here they are in all their lip-smacking, award-winning glory: Buffalo, New York-style chicken wings spun in your favorite signature sauce."*

Since Buffalo, New York was too far away, Jim Disbrow and Scott Lowery satisfied their overwhelming craving in 1981 by opening a spicy chicken wing restaurant close to home in Kent, Ohio. With signature sauces and a festive atmosphere, the chain has now evolved from a college campus sports bar with wings to a family restaurant with over 300 units. While frying chicken wings is no real secret—simply drop them in hot shortening for about 10 minutes—the delicious spicy sauces make the wings special. There are 12 varieties of sauce available to coat your crispy chicken parts at the chain, and three of the traditional hot sauces are cloned here. These sauces are very thick, almost like dressing or dip, so we'll use an emulsifying technique that will ensure a creamy final product where the oil won't separate from the other ingredients. These are clones for the most popular sauces: Spicy Garlic, Medium, and Hot. I've also added another big seller, Caribbean Jerk, to the list, followed by the cooking and coating technique for the wings. The first three sauce recipes might look the same at first glance, but each has slight variations. The bottom line is that you can make your sauce hotter or milder by adjusting the level of cayenne pepper. You can find Frank's pepper sauce by the other hot sauces at the market. If you can't find that brand, you can also use Crystal brand Louisiana hot sauce.

SPICY GARLIC WING SAUCE

1 cup Frank's cayenne pepper
    sauce
1/3 cup vegetable oil
1 teaspoon granulated sugar
1 teaspoon garlic powder
1/2 teaspoon coarse ground black
    pepper

1/2 teaspoon cayenne pepper
1/2 teaspoon Worcestershire sauce
1 egg yolk
2 teaspoons water
2 teaspoons cornstarch

MEDIUM WING SAUCE

1 cup Frank's cayenne pepper
    sauce
1/3 cup vegetable oil
1 teaspoon granulated sugar
1/2 teaspoon cayenne pepper
1/2 teaspoon garlic powder

1/2 teaspoon Worcestershire sauce
1/8 teaspoon coarse ground black
    pepper
1 egg yolk
2 teaspoons water
2 teaspoons cornstarch

HOT WING SAUCE

1 cup Frank's cayenne pepper
    sauce
1/3 cup vegetable oil
1 teaspoon granulated sugar
1 1/2 teaspoons cayenne pepper
1/2 teaspoon garlic powder

1/2 teaspoon Worcestershire sauce
1/8 teaspoon coarse ground black
    pepper
1 egg yolk
2 teaspoons water
2 teaspoons cornstarch

1. Combine all ingredients except egg yolk, water and cornstarch for the sauce of your choice in a small saucepan. Heat sauce over medium heat until boiling, then reduce heat and simmer for 5 minutes. Remove pan from the heat and allow it to cool, uncovered, for 10 minutes.

2. While the sauce cools, vigorously whisk egg yolk with 2 teaspoons water in a medium bowl for about 2 minutes or until color is pale yellow. Whisk in cornstarch until dissolved.
3. Drizzle the hot sauce mixture into the egg yolk mixture in a steady stream while rapidly whisking. This will create a thick, creamy emulsion that will prevent the oil from separating. Cover the sauce and chill it until it's needed.

• MAKES 1½ CUPS.

CARIBBEAN JERK SAUCE

The chain sells each of its 12 signature sauces in the restaurant because many of them work great as a baste or side sauce for a variety of home cooked masterpieces. This sauce is a favorite for that reason (ranking at the top of the list with Spicy Garlic as the chain's best-seller), so I thought it would be a useful clone that doesn't require you to fill up the fryer to make chicken wings. You can use this sauce on grilled chicken, pork, ribs, salmon or anything you can think of that would benefit from the sweet, sour and spicy flavors that come from an island-style baste.

3 tablespoons margarine
2 tablespoons minced green onion
    (white and light green parts
    only)
1 cup water
¾ cup ketchup
½ cup plus 2 tablespoons dark
    brown sugar
¼ cup apple cider vinegar
2 tablespoons white vinegar
2 tablespoons Frank's cayenne
    pepper sauce
2 teaspoons ground black pepper

2 teaspoons Worcestershire sauce
2 teaspoons lemon juice
1½ teaspoons cayenne pepper
1 teaspoon dried parsley flakes
1 teaspoon cornstarch
½ teaspoon salt
½ teaspoon garlic powder
½ teaspoon dried thyme
¼ teaspoon onion powder
⅛ teaspoon ground cloves
⅛ teaspoon ground nutmeg
⅛ teaspoon ground allspice
⅛ teaspoon rubbed sage

1. Melt margarine over medium/low heat. Add minced green onions and cook for 5 minutes. You just want to sweat the onions to soften them up. You're not looking to brown them.
2. Remove the pan from the heat, and whisk in the remaining ingredients. Put the pan back on the stove and bring the mixture to a boil over medium heat. Reduce heat and simmer for 45 minutes or until the sauce darkens and thickens. Cover sauce, then cool and chill until it's needed.

• MAKES 2 CUPS.

WINGS
20 chicken wing pieces
6 to 12 cups vegetable shortening

ON THE SIDE
celery sticks

1. Heat shortening in your fryer to 350 degrees.
2. Drop the wings into the shortening and fry for 10 to 12 minutes, or until the wings are turning light brown. Remove wings to a rack or paper towels to drain for 1 minute.
3. Put the wings into a plastic container with a lid. Add ¼ cup to ⅓ cup of your sauce of choice to the container, put the lid on and give it a good shake. Pour wings out onto a plate and add celery on the side. Oh, and get the napkins ready.

• SERVES 2 TO 4 AS AN APPETIZER.

• • • •

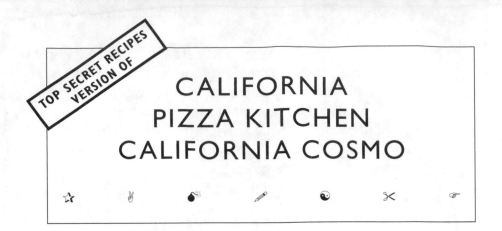

CALIFORNIA PIZZA KITCHEN CALIFORNIA COSMO

MENU DESCRIPTION: *"Our Original! Featuring Ciroc Snap Frost vodka, an all grape vodka, combined with red grape juice and accented with the sweet orange flavor of Cointreau and frozen red seedless grapes."*

While other vodkas are made from potatoes, wheat, molasses, corn, or rye, Ciroc is the first vodka to be distilled from late harvest French grapes. These super sweet grapes and the 5-step distilling process makes this vodka unique and extra smooth, with a subtle fruity flavor that goes great with grape juice and the orange flavor of Cointreau. Plan ahead for this drink by piercing three red seedless grapes on a toothpick and popping them into the freezer for at least an hour. Or, if you're like me, you'll have a dozen or so of these garnishes sitting in a small bag in the freezer ready to go when guests show up for happy hour.

1 ¼ ounces Ciroc Vodka
½ ounce Cointreau
2 ounces red grape juice

GARNISH
3 red seedless grapes on a
toothpick, frozen

1. Fill an 8-ounce martini glass with ice to chill the glass.
2. Fill a cocktail shaker with ice.

3. Measure Ciroc Vodka, Cointreau and grape juice into the shaker. Cover and shake vigorously.
4. Dump the ice out of the martini glass, and strain the cocktail into the glass.
5. Garnish with three grapes that have been pierced onto a toothpick and frozen. Serve it up, or sip it yourself.

• MAKES 1 COCKTAIL.

•   •   •   •

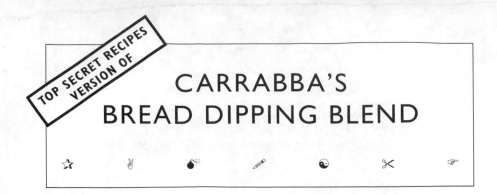

CARRABBA'S
BREAD DIPPING BLEND

When you sit down for Italian-style grub at one of the more than 168 nationwide Carrabba's restaurants, you're first served a small plate with a little pile of herbs and spices in the middle to which the waiter adds olive oil. Now you're set up to dip your sliced bread in the freshly flavored oil. To craft a version of this tasty blend at home you'll need a coffee bean grinder or a small food processor to finely chop the ingredients.

1 tablespoon minced fresh basil	½ teaspoon minced fresh rosemary
1 tablespoon chopped fresh parsley	½ teaspoon ground sea salt or
1 tablespoon minced fresh garlic	kosher salt
1 teaspoon dried thyme	¼ teaspoon crushed red pepper
1 teaspoon dried oregano	
1 teaspoon ground black pepper	½ teaspoon olive oil
(freshly ground is best)	⅛ teaspoon fresh lemon juice

1. Combine all the ingredients, except oil and lemon juice in a small food processor or coffee bean grinder. Chop briefly until all ingredients are about the same size.
2. Stir in oil and lemon juice.
3. To serve, combine about 1 teaspoon blend to 3 to 4 tablespoons extra virgin olive oil on a small dish. Dip sliced bread in mixture.

- MAKES ABOUT ¼ CUP BLEND.

• • • •

CARRABBA'S HOUSE SALAD DRESSING (CREAMY PARMESAN)

When Johnny Carrabba and his uncle Damian Mandola opened the first Carrabba's restaurant in 1986, they used a collection of their own traditional family recipes to craft a terrific Italian menu. You'll even find the names of friends and family in several of those dishes including Pollo Rosa Maria, Chicken Bryan, Scampi Damian and Insalata Johnny Rocco. Now we can easily recreate the taste of the delicious dressing that's tossed into the salad served before each Carrabba's entree. And we need only six ingredients. For the grated Parmesan cheese, go ahead and use the stuff made by Kraft that comes in the green shaker canisters. And if you don't have any buttermilk, you can substitute regular milk. Since it's so thick, this dressing is best when tossed into your salad before serving it, just like the real thing.

½ cup mayonnaise
¼ cup grated Parmesan cheese
¼ cup buttermilk

1 ½ teaspoons minced garlic
½ teaspoon minced fresh parsley
½ teaspoon lemon juice

Whisk together all ingredients in a small bowl.

• MAKES 1 CUP.

• • • •

CARRABBA'S CHICKEN MARSALA

MENU DESCRIPTION: *"Fire-roasted chicken breast topped with mushrooms, prosciutto and our Florio Marsala wine sauce."*

To reverse-engineer this big-time favorite entree, I ordered the dish to go, with the sauce on the side, so that I could separately analyze each component. After some trial and error in the underground lab, I found that recreating the secret sauce from scratch is easy enough with a couple small cans of sliced mushrooms, a bit of prosciutto, some Marsala wine, shallots, garlic and a few other good things. Cooking the chicken requires a very hot grill. The restaurant chain grills chicken breasts over a blazing real wood fire, so crank your grill up high enough to get the flames nipping at your cluckers (no, that's not an euphemism). If your grill has a lid, keep it open so you can watch for nasty flare-ups.

MARSALA SAUCE

⅓ cup butter
1 slice prosciutto, diced
2 teaspoons minced shallots
2 teaspoons minced garlic
2 4-ounce cans sliced mushrooms
　　(drained)

¼ cup Marsala wine
¼ teaspoon ground black pepper
1 cup chicken broth
2 teaspoons cornstarch
1 teaspoon minced fresh parsley
2 tablespoons heavy cream

CHICKEN SEASONING

1 ¼ teaspoons salt
1 teaspoon ground black pepper
½ teaspoon dried oregano
½ teaspoon dried thyme
½ teaspoon dried parsley
¼ teaspoon marjoram

¼ teaspoon garlic powder
¼ teaspoon onion powder

4 skinless chicken breasts fillets
olive oil

1. Melt butter over low heat in a medium saucepan.
2. Turn heat up to medium/high to sauté the prosciutto in the melted butter for about 2 to 3 minutes (be careful not to burn the butter). Add shallots and garlic and sauté for about 30 seconds. Add Marsala wine, simmer for another 30 seconds or so, then add drained mushrooms and black pepper. Simmer over medium/high heat for 5 minutes.
3. Dissolve cornstarch in chicken broth. Add broth to the saucepan and simmer for an additional 5 minutes.
4. Add parsley and cream to the sauce and simmer for 3 to 4 minutes or until thick. Remove pan from the heat, then cover it until needed.
5. Preheat barbecue grill on high heat. Combine ingredients for chicken seasoning in a small bowl. Use your thumb and fingers to crush the herbs and spices in the bowl to make a finer blend.
6. Wrap each chicken breast in plastic wrap and pound with a kitchen mallet until uniform in thickness. Brush each chicken breast generously with olive oil. Sprinkle seasoning blend over both sides of each chicken breast and grill for 6 to 8 minutes per side or until done. Give chicken a one-quarter turn on each side while cooking to make criss-cross grill marks.
7. Serve entree by arranging each chicken breast on a plate. Spoon one quarter of the Marsala sauce over each serving of chicken and dig in.

*   SERVES 4.

•   •   •   •

THE
CHEESECAKE FACTORY
MINI CRABCAKES

MENU DESCRIPTION: *"Served with remoulade sauce."*

The secret to great crab cakes starts with great crab. Freshly cooked blue crab is the crab of choice for these crustacean cakes, but you can often find high quality canned backfin blue crab in some stores. One such brand comes in 16-ounce cans from Phillips Seafood and is sold at Costco, Sam's Club, Wal-Mart and Von's stores. Once you've got the crab grabbed you need to pick up some panko. Panko is Japanese style breadcrumbs usually found near the other Asian foods in your market. The Factory uses a little bit of panko to coat each of these small crab cakes for a great, lightly crunchy texture. One order of this appetizer at the restaurant gets you 3 crab cakes; this recipe makes 6 cakes from ½-pound of crab. If you have a 1-pound can of crabmeat, you can save the leftover ½-pound for another recipe or double-up on this one. Any surplus crab cakes will keep for 24 hours in the fridge before you need to get them in a pan. Oh, and one other thing to remember when making crab cakes: Be gentle. Don't stir the crab too much into the other ingredients. Rather, fold the mixture gingerly with a spatula to combine. You want any big chunks of tasty crab to stay as big chunks of tasty crab in the finished product.

2 tablespoons mayonnaise

2 tablespoons minced green onion
(green part only)

2 tablespoons minced red bell
pepper

½ beaten egg

1 teaspoon minced fresh parsley

1 teaspoon Old Bay seasoning

½ teaspoon yellow prepared
mustard

½ pound lump crab meat

3 tablespoons plain breadcrumbs
(such as Progresso)

¼ cup panko (Japanese
breadcrumbs)

vegetable oil

REMOULADE SAUCE

½ cup mayonnaise

2 teaspoons capers

2 teaspoons chopped dill pickle
slices (hamburger pickles)

1 teaspoon lemon juice

½ teaspoon minced fresh parsley

½ teaspoon paprika

½ teaspoon chili powder

¼ teaspoon cayenne pepper

¼ teaspoon ground cumin

⅛ teaspoon salt

1. Measure all the ingredients for the crab cakes—except the breadcrumbs, crab, panko and vegetable oil—into a large bowl. Use a whisk to blend ingredients together. Carefully fold the crab and breadcrumbs into the whisked ingredients. Be sure not to over stir the mixture or those tasty lumps of crab will fall apart. The best crab cakes have nice big chunks of crab in 'em.

2. Rub a light coating of oil in six cups of a non-stick standard size muffin tin, then use your hands or a spoon to fill the cups with equal amounts of the crab mixture. Press down a bit on each crab cake so that the top is flat. Don't press too hard or the crab cakes may be hard to get out. Cover the muffin tin with plastic wrap and pop it in the fridge for an hour or so. This step will help the cakes stay together when they're browned in the oil.

3. Make the remoulade sauce by combining all the ingredients in a small bowl. Cover and chill the sauce until you're ready to serve up the crab cakes.

4. After the crab cakes have chilled through, heat up about ¼-inch of vegetable oil in large skillet over medium/low heat. Fill a shallow bowl with the panko breadcrumbs.
5. Carefully turn the crab cakes out onto a plate. Gently roll each crab cake around in the panko breadcrumbs. Each crab cake should be wearing a light coating of panko.
6. Test the oil by dropping a pinch of panko into the pan. It should sizzle. Sauté the crab cakes in the hot oil for 1½ to 3 minutes on each side or until the cakes are golden brown.
7. Drain crab cakes on paper towels or a rack very briefly, then serve them up hot with the remoulade sauce alongside in a little dish.

- MAKES 6 SMALL CRAB CAKES.

•　•　•　•

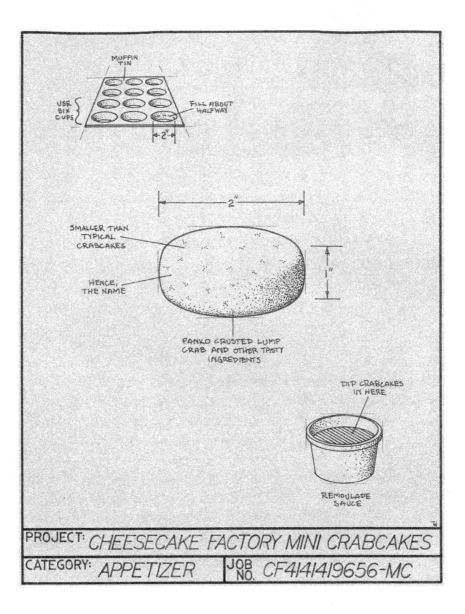

MUFFIN TIN

USE SIX CUPS

FILL ABOUT HALFWAY

2"

2"

SMALLER THAN TYPICAL CRABCAKES

HENCE, THE NAME

1"

PANKO CRUSTED LUMP CRAB AND OTHER TASTY INGREDIENTS

DIP CRABCAKES IN HERE

REMOULADE SAUCE

PROJECT: *CHEESECAKE FACTORY MINI CRABCAKES*

CATEGORY: *APPETIZER*   JOB NO. *CF4141419656-MC*

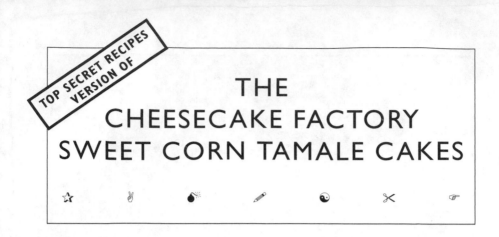

THE
CHEESECAKE FACTORY
SWEET CORN TAMALE CAKES

MENU DESCRIPTION: *"Topped with sour cream, salsa, avocado and salsa verde."*

Nestled between slick full-page ads on page 7 of the huge 19-page spiral-bound menu from The Cheesecake Factory, is a long list of fabulous appetizers that includes this southwestern-style crowd pleaser. Hand-formed tamale cakes are arranged on fresh salsa verde, topped with sour cream and a creamy Southwestern sauce, with a fresh avocado and cilantro garnish. It's happiness on a plate. And, while the ingredients list below may seem intimidating at first, the three sauces are very simple to make, and your crew will be rewarded and impressed by your effort. (The flavors in the sauces develop after sitting for a bit so you can prepare them all in advance and let them chill in the fridge until chow time.) If you get anything short of a standing ovation for this dish, it's important to encourage kudos by waving the pages of this recipe in front of your diners while casually wiping your brow. Sometimes you have to milk it.

SALSA VERDE

2 tomatillos, chopped (remove
    papery skin)
1 4-ounce can mild green
    chilies

1 green onion, chopped
2 tablespoons fresh cilantro
1 ¼ teaspoons granulated
    sugar

¼ teaspoon ground cumin
¼ teaspoon salt

⅛ teaspoon ground
 black pepper

TOMATO SALSA

1 medium tomato, diced
1 tablespoon minced Spanish
 onion
1 tablespoon minced, fresh
 cilantro

¼ teaspoon lime juice
½ small fresh jalapeno, minced
dash salt
dash ground black pepper

SOUTHWESTERN SAUCE

½ cup mayonnaise
1 teaspoon white vinegar
1 teaspoon water
¾ teaspoon granulated sugar
½ teaspoon chili powder

¼ teaspoon paprika
⅛ teaspoon cayenne pepper
⅛ teaspoon onion powder
dash salt
dash garlic powder

CAKES

1½ cups frozen sweet corn
½ cup butter, softened (1 stick)
3 tablespoons granulated sugar

⅛ teaspoon salt
½ cup masa harina (corn flour)
2 tablespoons all-purpose flour

GARNISH

¼ cup sour cream
½ avocado, chopped

2 tablespoons coarsely chopped,
 fresh cilantro

1. Prepare salsa verde by combining all ingredients (tomatillos, green chilies, green onion, cilantro, sugar, cumin, salt, and pepper) in a food processor on high speed. Cover and chill.
2. Prepare tomato salsa by combining all ingredients (diced tomato, onion, cilantro, lime juice, jalapeno, salt, and pepper) in a small bowl. Cover and chill.

3. Prepare southwestern sauce by combining all ingredients (mayonnaise, vinegar, water, sugar, chili powder, paprika, cayenne, onion powder, salt, and garlic powder) in a small bowl. Cover and chill.
4. Preheat oven to 400 degrees.
5. Prepare the tamale cakes by chopping 1 cup of the frozen corn in a food processor until it's coarsely pureed. Combine pureed corn with softened butter, sugar, and salt. Blend well with electric mixer until smooth.
6. Add masa and flour and blend well. Mix in the remaining ½ cup of frozen corn kernels by hand.
7. Measure ½ cup portions of the mixture and form it into 3-inch wide patties with your hands. Arrange the patties on a baking sheet and bake for 25 to 30 minutes or until the cakes are browned on the bottom. Carefully flip all cakes with a spatula and bake for an additional 5 to 7 minutes or until other side is browned.
8. While the cakes are baking, spoon a portion of the salsa verde onto a plate or platter (you may want to heat up your plate in the oven for a bit to help warm the sauce). You'll need to use enough salsa verde to coat the entire plate—it should be about ¼-inch deep. Arrange the tamale cakes side-by-side on the salsa verde. Spoon a dollop of sour cream onto each tamale cake. Drizzle the southwestern sauce over the cakes in a criss-cross pattern (use a squirt bottle if you've got one—see "Tidbits"). Spoon some tomato salsa over the cakes, followed by the chopped avocado. Finish off the plate by sprinkling the coarsely chopped cilantro leaves over the top.

TIDBITS

Save your empty plastic mustard or ketchup bottles to use in recipes such as this one. Use the squirt bottle to drizzle the southwestern sauce over your dish to give it that slick professional look. And if you want to cut out some of the fat in the sauce, you can easily substitute light mayo for the regular stuff.

You'll find tomatillos in the produce section, usually near the tomatoes or peppers. Be sure to remove the papery skin before using them.

Masa harina, or corn flour is found in the baking aisle by the other flours or where the Mexican foods are stocked.

- SERVES 4.

• • • •

BAKED UNTIL GOLDEN BROWN

VERY TASTY ON ITS OWN

ADD SAUCES & GARNISHES... AND OOH BABY!

SWEET CORN

MASA & BUTTER MIXTURE

3/4"

CROSS SECTION

SOUTHWESTERN SAUCE

CHOPPED AVOCADO

SALSA VERDE

SOUR CREAM

FRESH CILANTRO

TOMATO SALSA

GARNISHES

PROJECT: C.F. SWEET CORN TAMALE CAKES

CATEGORY: APPETIZER   JOB NO. CF683234195-SCTC

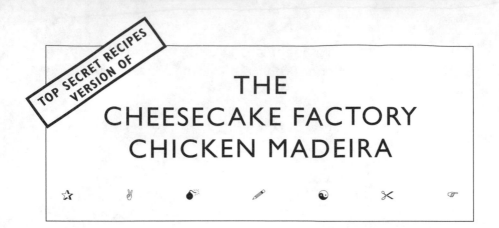

THE
CHEESECAKE FACTORY
CHICKEN MADEIRA

MENU DESCRIPTION: *"Our most popular chicken dish! Sautéed chicken breast topped with fresh asparagus and melted mozzarella cheese, covered with fresh mushroom madeira sauce. Served with mashed potatoes."*

What makes this chicken dish The Cheesecake Factory's "most popular" is the sweet and tangy madeira wine reduction sauce spooned over the top. Man, I could slurp that rich nectar straight from a glass (mushrooms might clog up a straw). It's that good. And—get this—it's easy. Even though the real stuff appears to include veal stock, we can concoct a great knockoff using canned beef broth. Get sliced mozzarella cheese from your deli section and be sure to pound the chicken breasts very thin using plastic wrap to cover each one before you whack on it. Also, in typical Cheesecake Factory style, their entree is huge, including two chicken fillets and a giant pile of mashed potatoes on the side. This recipe makes a total of four chicken fillets, which divides into two servings if you're at the restaurant. At home though, this is probably the perfect amount for a gaggle of four.

1 tablespoon olive oil	8 asparagus spears
4 skinless chicken breast fillets	4 mozzarella cheese slices

MADEIRA SAUCE

2 tablespoons olive oil
2 cups sliced fresh
   white mushrooms
3 cups madeira wine

2 cups beef broth
1 tablespoon butter
¼ teaspoon ground
   black pepper

1. Heat up 1 tablespoon olive oil in a large skillet over medium heat. Cover each chicken breast with plastic wrap then use a mallet to flatten the chicken to about ¼-inch thick. Sprinkle each fillet with salt and pepper.
2. Sauté the chicken fillets for 4 to 6 minutes per side, or until the chicken has browned just a bit. Remove chicken fillets from the pan and wrap them together in foil to keep the fillets warm while you make the sauce. Don't clean the pan. You want all that cooked-on goodness to stay in the skillet to help make the sauce.
3. With the heat still on medium, add two tablespoons of oil to the skillet. Add the sliced mushrooms and sauté for about two minutes. Add the madeira wine, beef broth, butter and pepper. Bring sauce to a boil, then reduce heat and simmer for about 20 minutes or until sauce reduces to about one-quarter of its original volume. When the sauce is done it will have thickened and turned a dark brown color.
4. As the sauce is simmering, bring a medium saucepan filled about halfway with water to a boil. Add a little salt to the water. Toss the asparagus into the water and boil for 3 to 5 minutes, depending on the thickness of your asparagus spears. Drop the asparagus in a bowl of ice water to halt the cooking. The asparagus should be slightly tender when done, not mushy.
5. Set oven to broil. Prepare the dish by arranging the cooked chicken fillets on a baking pan. Cross two asparagus spears over each fillet, then cover each with a slice of mozzarella cheese. Broil the fillets for 3 to 4 minutes or until light brown spots begin to appear on the cheese.

6. To serve, arrange one or two chicken breasts on each plate, then spoon 3 or 4 tablespoons of madeira sauce over the chicken.

*   MAKES 2 TO 4 SERVINGS.

•   •   •   •

THE CHEESECAKE FACTORY BANG-BANG CHICKEN & SHRIMP

MENU DESCRIPTION: *"A spicy Thai dish with the flavors of curry, peanut, chile, and coconut. Sautéed with vegetables and served over rice."*

This dish ranks very high among the most frequent entree clone requests from this growing chain's huge menu, and anyone who is a fan of Thai dishes falls in love with it. I dig recipes that include scratch sauces that can be used with other dishes. The curry and peanut sauces here are good like that. They can, for example, be used to sauce up grilled skewers of chicken or other meats, or as a flavorful drizzle onto lettuce wraps. But even though I've included the peanut sauce recipe from scratch here, you can take the quick route and save a little prep time by picking up a premade peanut sauce found near the other Asian foods at the market. Since the sauce is used sparingly in a drizzle over the top of this dish it won't make a big difference which way you go. This recipe produces two Cheesecake Factory-size servings—anyone who's been there knows that means "off-the-hook big." If your diners aren't prepared to process the gargantuan gastronomy and you're all out of doggie bags, you can easily split this recipe into four more sensible portions.

CURRY SAUCE

2 teaspoons chili oil
¼ cup minced onion
2 tablespoons minced garlic
2 teaspoons minced ginger
1 cup chicken broth
½ teaspoon ground cumin
½ teaspoon ground coriander
½ teaspoon paprika
¼ teaspoon salt

¼ teaspoon ground black
    pepper
¼ teaspoon ground mace
¼ teaspoon turmeric
3 cups coconut milk
2 medium carrots, julienned
1 small zucchini, julienned
½ cup frozen peas

PEANUT SAUCE

¼ cup creamy peanut butter
2 tablespoons water
4 teaspoons granulated sugar
1 tablespoon soy sauce
½ teaspoon chili oil
1 teaspoon rice vinegar
1 teaspoon lime juice

2 skinless chicken breast fillets
16 large raw shrimp, shelled
¼ cup cornstarch
½ cup vegetable oil

4 cups cooked white rice

GARNISH

1½ cups flaked coconut
½ teaspoon dried parsley,
    crumbled

2 tablespoons chopped peanuts
2 green onions, julienned

1. Make the curry sauce by heating the chili oil in a large sauce-pan over medium heat. When the oil is hot add the onion, garlic, and ginger. Sauté for about 30 seconds then add the chicken broth. Add the spices (cumin, coriander, paprika, salt, black pepper, mace, and turmeric) and stir well. Simmer for 5 minutes then add the coconut milk. Bring mixture back up to a boil, then reduce heat and simmer for 20 minutes or until sauce begins to thicken. Add the julienned carrots and zucchini, and the frozen peas. Simmer mixture for 10 minutes or until carrots become tender.
2. Make peanut sauce by combining peanut butter, water, sugar,

soy sauce, rice vinegar, lime juice, and chili oil in a small sauce-pan over medium heat. Heat just until mixture begins to bubble, then cover the pan and remove it from the heat.

3. Toast the flaked coconut by preheating your oven to 300 de-grees. Spread coconut on a baking sheet and toast it in the oven. Stir the coconut around every 10 minutes or so that it browns evenly, but watch it closely in the last 5 minutes so it doesn't get too dark. After 25 to 30 minutes the coconut should be light brown. Take it out of the oven and let it cool.

4. Cut the chicken breasts into bite-size pieces. Coat the chicken and shrimp with cornstarch. Heat the vegetable oil in a wok or large skillet over medium heat. Add the coated chicken to the pan and sauté it for a couple minutes, turning as it cooks. Add the shrimp to the pan. Cook the shrimp and chicken for a couple minutes, until it's done, then remove everything to a rack or towel to drain.

5. Build the two plates (or you can divide the meal into four portions) by filling a soup bowl with 1 or 2 cups of white rice. Press down on the rice. Invert the bowl onto the center of a plate, tap it a bit, and then lift off the bowl leaving a formed pile of rice in the center of each plate. Arrange an equal portion of chicken and shrimp around the rice. Spoon the curry sauce and vegetables over the chicken and shrimp, being careful not to get any sauce on top of the rice.

6. Drizzle peanut sauce over the dish concentrating most of it on the rice. Sprinkle ½ teaspoon of crumbled, dried parsley over the center of the rice. Add a tablespoon of chopped peanuts on the parsley, and then place a pile of julienned green onions on top. Sprinkle ½ cup to ¾ cup of toasted co-conut over the chicken and shrimp and serve it up.

• MAKES 2 TO 4 SERVINGS.

•   •   •   •

THE CHEESECAKE FACTORY ORIGINAL CHEESECAKE

MENU DESCRIPTION: *"Our famous Original cheesecake recipe! Creamy and light, baked in a graham cracker crust. Our most popular cheesecake!"*

Oscar and Evelyn Overton's wholesale cheesecake company was successful quickly after it first started selling creamy cheesecakes like this clone to restaurant chains in the early 1970's. When some restaurants balked at the prices the company was charging for high-end desserts, Oscar and Evelyn's son David decided it was time to open his own restaurant, offering a wide variety of quality meal choices in huge portions, and, of course, the famous cheesecakes for dessert. Today the chain has over 87 stores across the country, and consistently ranks number one on the list of highest grossing single stores for a U.S. restaurant chain.

Baking your cheesecakes in a water bath is part of the secret to producing beautiful cheesecakes at home with a texture similar to those sold in the restaurant. The water surrounds your cheesecake to keep it moist as it cooks, and the moisture helps prevent ugly cracking. You'll also start the oven very hot for just a short time, then crank it down to finish. I also suggest lining your cheesecake pan with parchment paper to help get the thing out of the pan when it's done without a hassle.

CRUST

1 ½ cups graham cracker crumbs
¼ teaspoon ground cinnamon
⅓ cup melted margarine

4 8-ounce pkgs. cream cheese

1 ¼ cups granulated sugar
½ cup sour cream
2 teaspoons vanilla extract
5 eggs

TOPPING

½ cup sour cream
2 teaspoons granulated sugar

OPTIONAL GARNISH

canned whipped cream

1. Preheat oven to 475 degrees. Place a large pan or oven-safe skillet (that the cheesecake pan will fit inside) filled with about ½-inch of water into the oven while it preheats. This will be your water bath.
2. Combine 1 ½ cups graham cracker crumbs and ¼ teaspoon cinnamon into a medium bowl. Mix in ⅓ cup melted margarine. Press the crumb into a 9-inch spring form pan that has been lined on the bottom and side with parchment paper. Use the bottom of a drinking glass to press the crumb mixture flat into the bottom of the pan and about ⅔ the way up the side. Wrap a large piece of foil around the bottom of the pan to keep the cheesecake dry when placed in the water bath in the oven. Put the crust in your freezer until the filling is done.
3. Use an electric mixer to combine the cream cheese with the sugar, sour cream, and vanilla. Blend mixture for a couple minutes or until the ingredients are smooth and creamy. Be sure to scrape down the sides of the bowl. Whisk the eggs in a medium bowl and then add them to the cream cheese mixture. Blend the mixture just enough to integrate the eggs.
4. Remove the crust from the freezer and pour the filling into it.
5. Carefully place the cheesecake into the preheated water bath. Bake for 12 minutes at 475 degrees, then turn the oven

down to 350 degrees and bake for 50 to 60 minutes or until the top of the cheesecake turns a light brown or tan color. Remove the cheesecake from the oven to cool.

6. When the cheesecake has cooled, combine ½ cup sour cream and 2 teaspoons sugar. Spread the sweetened sour cream over the entire top surface of the cheesecake. Cover and chill the cheesecake in the refrigerator for at least 4 hours. To serve, slice the cheesecake into 12 equal portions. Apply a pile of canned whipped cream to the top of each slice and serve.

• MAKES 12 SERVINGS.

• • • •

SWEETENED
SOUR
CREAM

9"

2½"

SLICE

9-INCH
SPRINGFORM
PAN

WHOLE CHEESECAKE

WHIPPED
CREAM

SWEETENED
SOUR
CREAM

CREAMY
CREAM
CHEESE
CUSTARD

2¼"

ONE SLICE

GRAHAM
CRACKER
CRUST

PROJECT: *C. F. ORIGINAL CHEESECAKE*

CATEGORY: *DESSERT*   JOB NO. *CF54986409-0C*

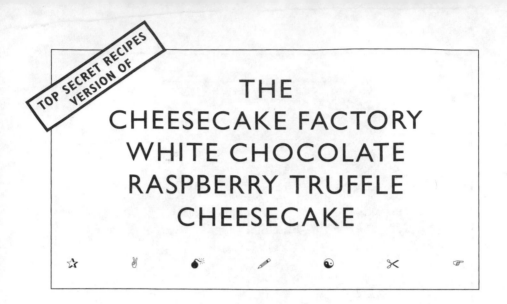

THE CHEESECAKE FACTORY WHITE CHOCOLATE RASPBERRY TRUFFLE CHEESECAKE

MENU DESCRIPTION: *"Our creamy cheesecake with chunks of white chocolate and swirls of imported seedless raspberries throughout. Baked in a chocolate crust and finished with white chocolate shavings and whipped cream."*

I'm not sure why "truffle" is in the name of this great dessert, but who cares when you've got raspberry preserves swirled throughout the cream cheese filling upon a layer of white chocolate chunks and crumbled chocolate cookie wafer crust. Yum. No wonder this cheesecake is the number one pick from the chain's massive list of flavored cheesecake choices.

CRUST

1 ½ cups chocolate cookie
    crumbs or 20 crumbled Oreo
    cookies (with filling removed)
⅓ cup margarine, melted

½ cup raspberry preserves
¼ cup water

4 8-ounce pkgs. cream cheese
1 ¼ cups granulated sugar
½ cup sour cream
2 teaspoons vanilla extract
5 eggs
4 ounces white chocolate,
    chopped into chunks

OPTIONAL GARNISH

2 ounces shaved white chocolate
canned whipped cream

1. Preheat oven to 475 degrees. Place a large pan or oven-safe skillet filled with about ½-inch of water into the oven while it preheats. This will be your water bath.
2. Combine the raspberry preserves with ¼ cup water in a medium microwave-safe bowl. Heat for 1½ minutes on high in your microwave. Stir until smooth. Strain to remove the raspberry seeds (toss 'em out), then let the strained preserves sit to cool, then put the bowl in the refrigerator until later.
3. Measure 1½ cups chocolate cookie crumbs (or crush 20 Oreo cookie wafers—with the filling scraped out—in a resealable plastic bag) into a medium bowl. Mix in ⅓ cup melted margarine. Press the crumb into a 9-inch spring form pan that has been lined on the bottom and side with parchment paper. Use the bottom of a drinking glass to press the crumb mixture flat into the bottom of the pan and about ⅔ the way up the side. Wrap a large piece of foil around the bottom of the pan to keep the cheesecake dry when placed in the water bath. Put the crust in your freezer until the filling is done.
4. Use an electric mixer to combine the cream cheese with the sugar, sour cream, and vanilla. Mix on medium speed for a couple minutes or until the ingredients are smooth and creamy. Be sure to scrape down the sides of the bowl. Whisk the eggs in a medium bowl and then add them to the cream cheese mixture. Blend the mixture just enough to integrate the eggs.
5. Remove the crust from the freezer and sprinkle 4 ounces of white chocolate chunks onto the bottom of the crust. Pour half of the cream cheese filling into the crust. Drizzle the raspberry preserves over the entire surface of the filling. Use a butter knife to swirl the raspberry into the cream cheese.

Just a couple passes is fine, you don't want to blend the raspberry and cream cheese together too much. Pour the other half of the filling into the crust.

6. Carefully place the cheesecake into the water bath in the oven. Bake for 12 minutes at 475 degrees, then turn the oven down to 350 degrees and bake for 50 to 60 minutes or until the top of the cheesecake turns a light brown or tan color. Remove the cheesecake from the oven to cool. When the cheesecake is cool, use the foil from the bottom to cover the cheesecake and chill it in the refrigerator for at least 4 hours.

7. Before serving, sprinkle the entire top surface of cheesecake with 2 ounces of shaved white chocolate. To serve, slice the cheesecake into 12 equal portions. Apply a pile of canned whipped cream to the top of each slice and serve.

- MAKES 12 SERVINGS.

•   •   •   •

9"

2½"

SLICE

SHAVED
WHITE
CHOCOLATE

9-INCH
SPRINGFORM
PAN

WHOLE CHEESECAKE

WHIPPED
CREAM

SHAVED
WHITE
CHOCOLATE

RASPBERRY
SAUCE

2¼"

WHITE
CHOCOLATE
CHUNKS

ONE SLICE

CHOCOLATE
COOKIE
CRUST

PROJECT: *C.F. WHITE CHOC. RASP. TRUFFLE*

CATEGORY: *DESSERT*   **JOB NO.** *CF6540997-WCRT*

CHEVYS
FRESH SALSA

Whip out the food processor and fire up the grill because you'll need these essential tools to clone one of the best restaurant salsas in the business. The key to recreating the flavor of the real deal is to fire roast the tomatoes and the jalapenos, and to add a little mesquite-flavored liquid smoke. The restaurant chain uses a mesquite grill, so these steps are crucial to getting the same smoky flavor as the addictive restaurant version. Chevys uses chipotle peppers, which are smoked red jalapenos. But unless you grow your own jalapenos, it may be difficult to find the riper red variety in your local supermarket. For this recipe, the green jalapeno peppers will work fine if you can't find the red ones. Adjust the number of jalapenos you use based on the size of the peppers that are available: If you have big jalapenos you need only 6, and you'll need around 10 if your peppers are small.

6 medium tomatoes
6 to 10 jalapenos (use more if
    small, fewer if large)
¼ of a medium Spanish onion
2 cloves garlic
2 tablespoons chopped fresh
    cilantro

2 tablespoons white vinegar
2 teaspoons salt
1 ½ teaspoons liquid mesquite
    smoke

1. Preheat your barbecue grill to high temperature.
2. Remove any stems from the tomatoes, then rub some oil

over each tomato. Leave the stems on the jalapenos and rub some oil on them, too.

3. Place the tomatoes on the grill when it's hot. After about 10 minutes, place all of the jalapenos onto the grill. In about 10 minutes you can turn the tomatoes and the peppers. When almost the entire surface of the peppers has charred black you can remove them from the grill. The tomatoes will turn partially black, but when the skin begins to come off they are done. Put the peppers and tomatoes on a plate and let them cool.

4. When the tomatoes and peppers have cooled, remove most of the skin from the tomatoes and place them into a food processor. Pinch the stem end from each of the peppers remove any skin that has burned, and place the peppers into the food processor with the tomatoes.

5. Add the remaining ingredients to the food processor and puree on high speed for 5 to 10 seconds or until the mixture has a smooth consistency.

6. Place the salsa into a covered container and chill for several hours or overnight so that the flavors develop.

•   MAKES APPROXIMATELY 2 CUPS.

•   •   •   •

CHEVY'S
MANGO SALSA

This zippy mango salsa clone from America's "Fresh Mex" chain is great sprinkled over fajitas, burritos, tacos, salads, sandwiches . . . you name it. The salsa is so good on its own you may be tempted to eat it straight from the bowl with a spoon. A little bit of fresh habanero pepper brings the heat to this concoction, but if you can't track down fresh peppers use a couple drops of your favorite bottled habanero sauce.

1 peeled mango, seeded and
   diced (about 2 cups)
¼ cup minced white onion
2 tablespoons minced red bell
   pepper

1 teaspoon minced fresh cilantro
1 teaspoon fresh lime juice
½ teaspoon finely minced
   habanero pepper
⅛ teaspoon salt

Combine all ingredients in a medium bow. Cover and chill before serving.

• MAKES 2⅓ CUPS.

• • • •

CHEVYS CHILE CON QUESO

☆　✌　💣　✎　☯　✂　☞

This top secret clone of the cheesy appetizer from this 107-unit Mexican food chain is perfect to whip out for your festive fiestas. This recipe will make enough of the spicy cheese concoction for plenty of party-time double dipping. The Anaheim chile has a mild spiciness, so we'll toss a jalapeno in there for an extra spicy kick. If you can't find an Anaheim pepper, use any mild green chilies that are available, as long as you get about ½ cup of diced pepper in the mix.

one 16-ounce box Velveeta, diced
¾ cup whole milk
1 green Anaheim pepper, seeded and diced (about ½ cup)
¼ cup diced white onion
1 jalapeno pepper, seeded and diced
2 teaspoons minced cilantro

juice of 1 lime
¼ teaspoon dried oregano
¼ teaspoon ground black pepper (freshly ground is best)
pinch of salt
pinch of dried thyme
2 medium tomatoes, seeded and diced (about ⅔ cup)

GARNISH
¼ cup ranchero cheese, crumbled

tortilla chips for dipping

1. Combine Velveeta and milk in a medium saucepan over medium/low heat. Stir often as cheese melts. Be careful not to burn it.
2. When cheese is melted add all remaining ingredients except the tomatoes. Continue to cook over medium/low heat for 7 minutes, stirring often to prevent burning. Stir in tomatoes and remove the queso from the heat.
3. Pour queso into a serving dish, top with crumbled ranchero cheese and serve with tortilla chips for dipping.

• MAKES ABOUT 2 CUPS.

TIDBITS

Ranchero cheese is a crumbly Mexican cheese that can be found near the cream cheese in your supermarket.

•   •   •   •

CHEVYS
GARLIC MASHED POTATOES

This easy-to-clone dish comes alongside many of the tasty entrees at this Mexican restaurant chain, or it can be ordered up,
pronto, on the side. It's a nice clone to have around since it goes
well with so many of your homemade dishes, Mexican or otherwise. Get yourself four large russet potatoes and start peeling,
but you don't need to peel all the skin off. Leave a little skin on
there for texture. And when you boil the potatoes, toss the
whole garlic cloves right in the pot. That way the garlic begins to
flavor the potatoes as they boil, and when you mash the potatoes
the cooked garlic gets mashed up too. Cool, eh?

6 to 7 cups water
4 medium/large russet potatoes
6 cloves garlic
6 tablespoons butter (¾ stick)

½ cup heavy cream
¾ teaspoon salt
¼ teaspoon ground black pepper

1. Peel potatoes, but leave some skin on. Slice the potatoes into
   quarters.
2. Boil the potatoes and garlic for 30 minutes in the water in a
   large saucepan or pot. Make sure the water completely covers
   the potatoes. When potatoes are tender drain them. Don't
   lose the garlic—keep it with the potatoes.
3. Pour potatoes and garlic back into the pan. Commence
   with the thorough mashing. Mashing is fun. Stir in butter,

cream, salt and pepper and reheat over medium/low heat until hot.

- SERVES 6 TO 8.

• • • •

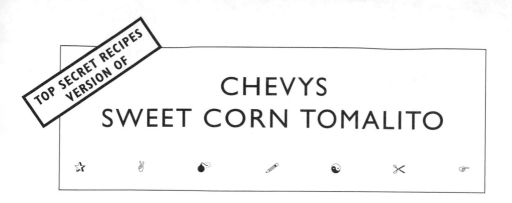

CHEVYS
SWEET CORN TOMALITO

Other Mexican food chains such as Chi-Chi's and El Torito call it "Sweet Corn Cake." But at Chevy's, the corn-filled, pudding-like stuff that's served with most entrees is known as "Tomalito." That masa harina in there (corn flour) is what's used to make tamales, and it can be found in your supermarket either with the corn meal and flour, or wherever the other Mexican/Spanish items are stocked. Everything else here is basic stuff. While other corn cake recipes may require canned corn or canned cream-style corn, Chevys' "no cans in the kitchen" commandment requires that we use frozen corn for a proper clone. Of course, you may also use corn that's been cut fresh from the cob, if you're up for the task.

4 cups frozen corn, thawed
⅓ cup butter, softened (⅔ stick)
½ cup granulated sugar
¾ cup milk

½ cup masa harina
½ cup corn meal
½ teaspoon baking powder
½ teaspoon salt

1. Preheat oven to 325 degrees.
2. Cream softened butter together with sugar in a large bowl with an electric mixer until smooth. Add milk and masa and mix well.
3. Use a blender or food processor to puree 2 cups of corn until smooth. Add pureed corn to butter/masa mixture and

mix well. Add corn meal, baking powder, salt, and remaining corn and mix until combined.

4. Pour mixture into an ungreased 8x8-inch baking pan. Cover with foil and place it into a 9x13-inch baking pan. Add hot water to the larger baking pan until it's about ⅓ full. Bake for 1½ to 2 hours or until corn cake is firm in the center. Let it sit covered for 10 minutes before serving. To serve, scoop out ½ cup portions with a large spoon.

- MAKES 8 SERVINGS.

• • • •

CHEVY'S
FLAN

Abiding by this large Mexican food chain's "no cans in the kitchen" edict, we'll craft our clone of the delicious flan dessert with fresh whole milk, rather than canned sweetened condensed milk required by most flan recipes out there. The canned stuff has a bit of a funky taste to it, plus it's much too sweet to be an accurate Chevys knockoff. When you're ready to clone this one, be sure to get some parchment paper (it's near the wax paper in the supermarket). When laid over the top of the baking pan, the parchment paper helps the flan cook faster and more evenly than if left uncovered. Aluminum foil doesn't seem to work as well since it tends to reflect the heat away from your ramekins of sweet, creamy goodness.

2½ cups granulated sugar
½ teaspoon ground cinnamon
¼ cup hot water
3 cups whole milk

4 eggs
3 egg yolks
1 teaspoon vanilla extract

1. Preheat oven to 300 degrees.
2. Combine cinnamon with 2 cups granulated sugar in a medium saucepan over medium/low heat. When sugar begins to melt, stir often until all sugar has dissolved and solution is light brown. Add water to pan and stir until smooth. Pour about ¼ cup sugar solution into each of six 6-ounce ramekins (custard cups). Swirl the sugar around the inside

edge of each of the ramekins. Arrange the ramekins in a 9x13-inch baking pan.

3. Heat milk in another medium saucepan over medium heat until it starts to bubble.

4. As milk heats up whisk together eggs, egg yolks, vanilla and remaining ½ cup sugar in a large bowl. Mix until sugar has dissolved.

5. When milk starts to bubble remove it from the heat. Carefully pour about ¼ cup of hot milk into the egg mixture while stirring. This will temper the eggs so they don't cook while adding the rest of the hot milk. Slowly add the remaining milk while mixing.

6. Fill the ramekins to the top with the custard mixture. Remove any foam from the top of each ramekin. Add water to the pan so that it goes halfway up the sides of the ramekins. Place a piece of parchment paper over the ramekins and bake for 75 to 90 minutes or until custard is firm and a knife inserted into the middle of the custard comes out clean.

7. Cool flan and cover each one with plastic wrap. Chill thoroughly before serving. To serve, simply cut around the inside edge of the ramekin with a knife, then turn the flan over onto a plate. The golden, caramelized sugar will spill down over the edges of the flan. Forget about the leftover hardened sugar that stays inside the ramekin. Let the dishwasher deal with it.

- MAKES 6 SERVINGS.

• • • •

3½"

300° WILL DO IT

COVER WITH PARCHMENT BEFORE BAKING

VANILLA CUSTARD

CUSTARD DARKENS HERE

CARAMELIZED SUGAR & CINNAMON

6-OUNCE RAMEKIN

DON'T USE

SUGAR

EGGS

WHOLE MILK

CUSTARD

SUGAR SYRUP FLOWS ONTO PLATE

PLATE

SERVING SUGGESTION

TW

PROJECT:	CHEVYS FLAN	
CATEGORY:	DESSERT	JOB NO. C406669009-F

CHILI'S
SALSA

This super simple salsa can be made in a pinch with a can of diced tomatoes, some canned jalapenos, fresh lime juice, onion, spices and a food processor (or blender). Plus you can easily double the recipe by sending in a larger 28-ounce can of diced tomatoes, and simply doubling up on all the other ingredients. Use this versatile salsa as a dip for tortilla chips or plop it down onto any dish that needs flavor assistance—from eggs to taco salads to wraps to fish—for that extra special restaurant-style zing. You can adjust the heat level to suit your taste by tweaking the amount of canned jalapenos in the mix.

one 14.5-ounce can diced
   tomatoes
3 tablespoons canned diced
   jalapenos

1 tablespoon lime juice
1 teaspoon salt
¼ teaspoon ground cumin
½ cup diced Spanish onion

1. Combine diced tomatoes, jalapenos, lime juice and spices in a food processor. Run food processor on high speed for just a few moments until the tomatoes have been nearly pureed, yet still chunky. The jalapenos should be chopped into visible minced bits. Be careful not to over-process.

2. Pour the mixture into a bowl and add the sliced onion. Stir well, cover and store overnight for the flavors to properly develop.

• MAKES 2 CUPS.

· · · ·

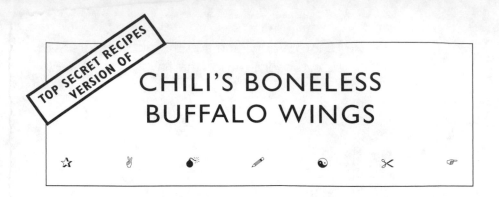

CHILI'S BONELESS BUFFALO WINGS

MENU DESCRIPTION: *"Breaded chicken breast tossed in spicy wing sauce. Served with cool bleu cheese dressing."*

This clone gives us the zesty flavor of traditional Buffalo chicken wings, but the bones and skin are left back in Buffalo. That's because these "wings" are actually nuggets sliced from chicken breast fillets, then breaded and fried, and smothered with the same type of spicy wing sauce used on traditional wings. If you like the flavor of Buffalo wings, but wish you could use a fork, your spicy dreams have come true. Serve up these puppies with some celery sticks and bleu cheese dressing on the side for dipping.

1 cup all-purpose flour
2 teaspoons salt
½ teaspoon ground black pepper
¼ teaspoon cayenne pepper
¼ teaspoon paprika
1 egg
1 cup milk

2 skinless chicken breast fillets
6 to 10 cups vegetable or canola oil (amount required by your fryer)
¼ cup Frank's or Crystal hot sauce
1 tablespoon margarine

ON THE SIDE
bleu cheese dressing (for dipping)
celery sticks

LOUISIANA HOT SAUCE

EAT WITH FINGERS OR A FORK

CRISPY BREADING

SPICY SAUCE

BREADING AND SPICY SAUCE

MOIST WHITE MEAT CHICKEN

$\frac{3}{4}$"

CROSS SECTION

$1\frac{3}{4}$"

3"

BONELESS WINGS

375° OIL

FRYING "WINGS"

A SHARP KNIFE WORKS BEST

SLICE EACH FILLET

BONELESS CHICKEN BREAST

TW

PROJECT:	CHILI'S BONELESS BUFFALO WINGS	
CATEGORY:	APPETIZER	JOB NO. C369324094-BBW

1. Combine flour, salt, peppers and paprika in a medium bowl.
2. In another small bowl, whisk together egg and milk.
3. Slice each chicken breast into 6 pieces. Preheat 6 to 10 cups of vegetable oil in a deep fryer to 375 degrees.
4. One or two at a time, dip each piece of chicken into the egg mixture, then into the breading blend; then repeat the process so that each piece of chicken is double-coated.
5. When all chicken pieces have been breaded, arrange them on a plate and chill for 15 minutes.
6. When the chicken is done resting, drop each piece into the hot oil and fry for 5 to 6 minutes or until breading is golden brown.
7. As chicken fries, combine the hot sauce and margarine in a small bowl. Microwave sauce for 20 to 30 seconds or just until the margarine is melted, then stir to combine. You can also use a small saucepan for this step. Just combine the hot sauce and margarine in the saucepan over low heat and stir until margarine is melted and ingredients are blended.
8. When chicken pieces are done frying, remove them to a plate lined with a couple paper towels.
9. Place the chicken pieces into a covered container such as a Tupperware bowl or large jar with a lid. Pour the sauce over the chicken in the container, cover, and then shake gently until each piece of chicken is coated with sauce. Pour the chicken onto a plate and serve the dish with bleu cheese dressing and celery sticks on the side.

- SERVES 2 TO 4 AS AN APPETIZER.

• • • •

CHILI'S BONELESS SHANGHAI WINGS

MENU DESCRIPTION: *"Crispy breaded chicken breast topped with sweet and spicy ginger-citrus sauce. Served with spicy-cool wasabi-ranch dressing for dipping."*

So you're into boneless wings but you need a break from the traditional cayenne flavor of the Buffalo style. If fresh ginger-laced sweet-and-sour sauce sounds seducing, here is a variation worth snacking on. Along with the secret sauce recipe is an easy way to fabricate a carbon copy of Chili's great wasabi-ranch dressing simply by adding a few ingredients to Hidden Valley Ranch dressing. I've even suggested a drop of green food coloring to give the dressing the exact same green tint of the original. The wasabi powder won't really add much color, so this is the trick. By the way, you can find the dry, powdered form of wasabi horseradish in the supermarket aisle with the other Asian foods.

GINGER-CITRUS SAUCE

1 ¼ cups water	1 teaspoon minced garlic
1 tablespoon cornstarch	2 tablespoons lime juice
¾ cup dark brown sugar	1 tablespoon lemon juice
¼ cup soy sauce	¼ teaspoon crushed red pepper
2 tablespoons minced fresh ginger	flakes

WASABI-RANCH DRESSING

½ cup Hidden Valley Ranch
    bottled salad dressing
2 tablespoons buttermilk (or
    whole milk)
1 teaspoon prepared horseradish
½ teaspoon powdered wasabi
1 drop green food coloring

1 cup all-purpose flour
2 teaspoons salt
½ teaspoon ground black pepper
¼ teaspoon cayenne pepper
¼ teaspoon paprika
1 egg
1 cup milk
2 skinless chicken breast fillets
6 to 10 cups vegetable or canola
    oil (amount required by your
    fryer)

1. Combine flour, salt, peppers and paprika in a medium bowl.
2. In another small bowl, whisk together egg and milk.
3. Slice each chicken breast into 6 pieces. Preheat 6 to 10 cups of canola oil in a deep fryer to 375 degrees.
4. One or two at a time, dip each piece of chicken into the egg mixture, then into the breading blend; then repeat the process so that each piece of chicken is double-coated.
5. When all chicken pieces have been breaded, arrange them on a plate and chill for 15 minutes.
6. As the chicken is resting, make the ginger-citrus sauce by dissolving the cornstarch in the water. Pour the mixture into a medium saucepan along with the rest of the sauce ingredients and bring the mixture to a boil over medium heat. When the sauce begins to bubble, reduce heat and simmer for 10 to 15 minutes or until thick. Remove the sauce from the heat and let it cool a bit.
7. Make the wasabi-ranch dressing while your ginger-citrus sauce is simmering. Simply whisk together the ranch dressing, buttermilk, prepared horseradish, powdered wasabi, and green food coloring in a small bowl. Cover and chill this until the wings are done.
8. When the chicken has rested and you're ready to cook,

lower the boneless wings into the oil and fry for 5 to 6 minutes or until each piece is browned. Depending on the size
of your fryer, you may want to fry the chicken in batches so
that the chicken isn't too crowded in there.

9. When chicken pieces are done frying, remove them to a
draining rack or a plate lined with a couple paper towels.

10. When all the chicken is fried, place the pieces into a covered
container such as a large jar with a lid. Pour the ginger-citrus
sauce over the chicken in the container, cover it up, and then
gently shake everything around until each piece of chicken is
coated with sauce. Pour the chicken onto a plate and serve
the dish with wasabi-ranch dressing on the side.

• SERVES 2 TO 4 AS AN APPETIZER.

•   •   •   •

CHILI'S
CHILI QUESO

MENU DESCRIPTION: *"Our appetizing cheese dip with seasoned beef. Served with warm tostada chips."*

Take your chips for a dip in this top secret take on Chili's Queso Dip that comes to your table in a small cast iron skillet along with a big bowl of tortilla chips. A popular recipe that's been circulating calls for combining Velveeta with Hormel No-Beans chili. Sure, it's a good start, but there's more to Chili's spicy cheese dip than that. Toss a few other ingredients into the saucepan and after about 20 minutes you'll have a great dip for picnic, party, or game time.

1 16-ounce box Velveeta Cheese
1 15-ounce can Hormel Chili
    (No Beans)
1 cup milk
4 teaspoons chili powder

2 teaspoons paprika
1 tablespoon lime juice
½ teaspoon ground cayenne
    pepper
½ teaspoon ground cumin

1. Cut the Velveeta into cubes. Combine the cheese with the remaining ingredients in a medium saucepan over medium heat. Stir frequently until cheese melts, then reduce heat and simmer for 20 minutes. Serve hot with tortilla chips for dipping.

• • • •

CHILI'S
LETTUCE WRAPS

MENU DESCRIPTION: *"Grilled Asian-spiced chicken w/carrots, water chestnuts, green onions & almonds. Served with crisp Bibb lettuce and sesame-ginger & peanut sauces for dipping."*

Chili's take on the appetizer made popular at P. F. Chang's Asian Bistro got diners across the country wrapping lettuce around chopped chicken. Now you can bring Chili's version of the Asian tacos home along with the mega-addictive sesame-ginger and peanut dipping sauces. After you make the sauces and prepare the chicken, assemble the wraps by arranging some of sliced chicken into the center of a leaf of butter lettuce, sprinkle on some shredded carrot, perhaps a few crunchy bean threads, add a little dipping sauce and open wide.

STIR FRY SAUCE

¼ cup water
1 teaspoon arrowroot
⅓ cup soy sauce
¼ cup granulated sugar
¼ cup white vinegar
1 tablespoon dried chives

1 tablespoon vegetable oil
2 teaspoons sesame seeds
1 teaspoon red pepper flakes
1 teaspoon chili oil
1 teaspoon peanut butter
½ teaspoon finely minced ginger

SESAME-GINGER DIPPING SAUCE

¼ cup water

¾ teaspoon arrowroot

⅓ cup granulated sugar

⅓ cup white vinegar

¼ cup soy sauce

1 teaspoon finely minced ginger

1 teaspoon vegetable oil

½ teaspoon sesame seeds

¼ teaspoon garlic powder

dash red pepper flakes

dash parsley

PEANUT DIPPING SAUCE

½ cup peanut butter

⅓ cup water

2 tablespoons white vinegar

½ teaspoon finely minced ginger

⅛ teaspoon crushed red pepper

¼ cup granulated sugar

¼ teaspoon garlic powder

½ teaspoon chili oil

½ teaspoon vegetable oil

1 tablespoon brown sugar

1 tablespoon vegetable oil

4 skinless chicken breast fillets

4 green onions

¼ cup minced water chestnuts

¼ cup sliced almonds

1 head butter lettuce

GARNISH

fried bean threads (see Tidbits)

shredded carrots

1. To prepare the stir-fry sauce, combine the water and arrow-root in a small bowl and stir until arrowroot is dissolve. Add this solution to the other stir-fry sauce ingredients in a small saucepan over medium heat. Bring to a boil, and then reduce heat to low and simmer for 5 to 6 minutes, or until thick.
2. To make the sesame-ginger dipping sauce combine the water and arrowroot in a small bowl and mix until arrowroot is dissolved. Combine this solution with the other dipping sauce ingredients in small saucepan over medium heat. Bring to a boil, and then reduce heat to low and simmer for 2 minutes.

3. Combine all ingredients for the peanut dipping sauce in a small saucepan over medium/low heat. Heat while whisking until sauce becomes smooth. Remove from heat when done.
4. To prepare the chicken heat 1 tablespoon of vegetable oil in a large skillet over medium heat. Cook the chicken breasts until done—3 to 5 minutes per side—turning every couple of minutes. You can tell when the chicken is done by pressing down on the middle of each chicken breast. It should be firm.
5. Remove the cooked chicken breast to a cutting board and slice it into strips with a sharp knife. Keep the pan hot. Load the chicken back into the same pan over medium/high heat, and add the water chestnuts. Heat for 1 minute.
6. Add 5 tablespoons of the stir-fry sauce to the chicken and heat for 2 minutes, stirring often. The sauce should be bubbling.
7. Add the sliced green onions and stir. The chicken is done.
8. Prepare each serving plate with a bed of bean threads. Spoon one-fourth of the chicken onto the bean threads. Sprinkle the chicken with about a tablespoon of sliced almonds. Add three leaves of butter lettuce to the plate, along with a garnish of shredded carrots. Repeat for the remaining servings. Serve with the sesame-ginger dipping sauce and peanut dipping sauce on the side.

• MAKES 4 SERVINGS.

TIDBITS

Bean threads can be found in the Asian food section of your supermarket. Before using as a garnish the threads must be flash-fried in a skillet in 2 inches of hot vegetable oil. When the threads float to the top remove them to a towel to drain.

• • • •

CHILI'S SOUTHWESTERN EGGROLLS

MENU DESCRIPTION: *"Smoked chicken, black beans, corn, jalapeno Jack cheese, red peppers and spinach wrapped inside a crispy flour tortilla. We serve it with our avocado-ranch dipping sauce."*

Chili's was the first chain to popularize the Southwestern-style eggroll, but as with any successful menu item, clones have been popping up on other major chains' appetizer menus over the past several years. Even though it's more like a small chimichanga than an eggroll, this appetizer is a fabulous creation with monster flavor. A flour tortilla is stuffed with a spicy blend of corn, green onions, black beans, spinach, jalapeno peppers, Monterey Jack cheese and spices; then it's deep-fried. Slice the rolls diagonally, dunk the wedges into a creamy avocado ranch sauce, and you've done your taste buds a solid. Make these several hours before you plan to serve them so that they can freeze before frying (it's a great dish to make a day ahead of a party or event). This freezing step will help the outside fry to a golden brown, but the eggrolls will stay folded, and oil won't seep in. Assembling the eggrolls takes a little time, so if you like these, I suggest making a double batch. Since you'll be freezing them, you'll have extra on hand in the freezer ready to cook with just a little additional effort.

1 skinless chicken breast fillet
1 tablespoon vegetable oil
2 tablespoons minced red bell
    pepper
2 tablespoons minced green onion
⅓ cup frozen corn
¼ cup canned black beans, rinsed
    and drained
2 tablespoons thawed and
    drained frozen spinach
2 tablespoons diced, canned
    jalapeno peppers
½ tablespoon minced fresh
    parsley
½ teaspoon ground cumin
½ teaspoon chili powder
¼ teaspoon salt
dash cayenne pepper
¾ cup shredded Monterey Jack
    cheese
five 7-inch flour tortillas
6 to 10 cups vegetable or
    canola oil

AVOCADO-RANCH DIPPING SAUCE
¼ cup smashed, fresh avocado
    (about half of an avocado)
¼ cup mayonnaise
¼ cup sour cream
1 tablespoon buttermilk
1 ½ teaspoons white vinegar
⅛ teaspoon salt
⅛ teaspoon dried parsley
⅛ teaspoon onion powder
dash dried dill weed
dash garlic powder
dash pepper

GARNISH
2 tablespoons chopped tomato
1 tablespoon chopped onion

1. Preheat barbecue grill to high heat.
2. Rub the chicken breast with some vegetable oil then grill it on the barbecue for 4 to 5 minutes per side or until done. Lightly salt and pepper each side of the chicken while it cooks. Set chicken aside until it cools down enough to handle.
3. Preheat 1 tablespoon of vegetable oil in a medium-size skillet over medium-high heat.
4. Add the red pepper and onion to the pan and sauté for a couple minutes until tender.

5. Dice the cooked chicken into small cubes and add it to the pan. Add the corn, black beans, spinach, jalapeno peppers, parsley, cumin, chili powder, salt, and cayenne pepper to the pan. Cook for another 4 minutes. Stir well so that the spinach separates and is incorporated into the mixture.
6. Remove the pan from the heat and add the cheese. Stir until the cheese is melted.
7. Wrap the tortillas in a moist cloth and microwave on high for 1½ minutes or until hot.
8. Spoon approximately one-fifth of the mixture into the center of a tortilla. Fold in the ends and then roll the tortilla over the mixture. Roll the tortilla very tight, then pierce it with a toothpick to hold it together. Repeat with the remaining ingredients until you have five eggrolls. Arrange the eggrolls on a plate, cover the plate with plastic wrap and freeze for at least 4 hours. Overnight is best.
9. While the eggrolls freeze prepare the avocado-ranch dipping sauce by combining all of the ingredients in a small bowl.
10. Preheat 6 to 10 cups oil (use the amount required by your fryer) to 375 degrees.
11. Deep fry the eggrolls in the hot oil for 12 to 15 minutes and remove to paper towels or a rack to drain for about 2 minutes.
12. Slice each eggroll diagonally lengthwise and arrange on a plate around a small bowl of the dipping sauce. Garnish the dipping sauce with the chopped tomato and onion.

- SERVES 3 TO 4 AS AN APPETIZER.

• • • •

SPINACH PARSLEY GREEN ONION

CORN

RED BELL
PEPPER

JALAPENO

BLACK BEAN

CHICKEN

CROSS SECTION

SLICE
HERE

CRISPY
FRIED
TORTILLA

2"

4"

7"

FLOUR
TORTILLA

①

②

ZESTY
FILLING

③

FOLDING TECHNIQUE

TW

PROJECT: *CHILI'S SOUTHWESTERN EGGROLLS*

CATEGORY: *APPETIZER* JOB NO. *C964047550-SE*

CHILI'S CHICKEN ENCHILADA SOUP

It's an item that you won't find on the menu at this national restaurant chain, but ask your server about the soups du jour you'll find this one is available every day of the week. This soup also happens to be one of Chili's most raved-about items, and the subject of many a recipe search on the *TSR* website (www.Top SecretRecipes.com). Part of the secret in crafting your clone is the addition of masa harina—a corn flour that you'll find in your supermarket near the other flours, or where all the Mexican foodstuffs are stashed.

1 tablespoon vegetable oil	3 cups water
1 lb. of skinless chicken breast fillets (approx. 3 fillets)	1 cup enchilada sauce
½ cup diced onion	one 16-ounce box Velveeta, diced
1 clove garlic, pressed	1 teaspoon salt
4 cups chicken broth	1 teaspoon chili powder
1 cup masa harina	½ teaspoon ground cumin

GARNISH
shredded Cheddar cheese
crumbled corn tortilla chips
salsa or pico de gallo

1. Add 1 tablespoon of oil to a large pot over medium heat. Add chicken breasts to pot and brown for 4 to 5 minutes per side. Set chicken aside.
2. Add onions and garlic to pot and sauté over medium heat for about 2 minutes, or until onions begin to become translucent. Add chicken broth.
3. Combine masa harina with 2 cups of water in a medium bowl and whisk until blended. Add masa mixture to pot with onions, garlic and broth.
4. Add remaining water, enchilada sauce, cheese and spices to pot and bring mixture to a boil.
5. Shred the chicken into small, bite-size pieces and add it to the pot. Reduce heat and simmer soup for 30 to 40 minutes or until thick.
6. Serve soup in cups or bowls, and garnish with shredded Cheddar cheese, crumbled corn tortilla chips, and a spoonful of your favorite salsa or pico de gallo.

• MAKES APPROXIMATELY 12 SERVINGS.

•   •   •   •

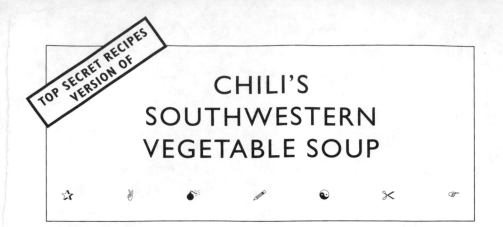

CHILI'S SOUTHWESTERN VEGETABLE SOUP

If you like soup that's packed with veggies, that's low in fat, and has some of that Southwestern za-za-zing to it, this is the soup for you. Just toss all the ingredients in a pot and simmer. Garnish with some shredded cheese and crumbled tortillas, and prepare to take the chill off.

6 cups chicken broth (Swanson is best)
1 14.5-ounce can diced tomatoes, with juice
1 cup water
1 cup canned dark red kidney beans, with liquid
1 cup frozen yellow cut corn
1 cup frozen cut green beans

1 4-ounce can diced green chilies
½ cup diced Spanish onion
½ cup tomato sauce
6 corn tortillas, minced
1½ teaspoons chili powder
dash garlic powder

GARNISH
1 cup grated Cheddar/Jack cheese blend
1 cup crumbled corn tortilla chips

1. Combine all the soup ingredients in a large saucepan or soup pot over high heat. Be sure to mince the corn tortillas into

small pieces with a sharp knife before adding them to the soup.

2. Bring soup to a boil, then reduce the heat and simmer for 45 minutes to 1 hour, or until the soup has thickened and tortilla pieces have mostly dissolved.

3. To serve soup ladle 1½ cups into a bowl. Sprinkle a heaping tablespoon of the grated Cheddar/Jack cheese blend over the top of the soup, and then a heaping tablespoon of crumbled corn tortilla chips over the cheese.

• MAKES 6 SERVINGS.

•   •   •   •

CHILI'S HONEY MUSTARD DRESSING

☆ ✌ 💣 ✏ ☯ ✂ ☞

One of America's favorite casual chains brings us a popular salad dressing that you can't buy in stores. Instead, buy these six simple ingredients at a store and make your own version cheaply and quickly.

⅔ cup mayonnaise
¼ cup honey
2 tablespoons Grey Poupon Dijon
   mustard

1 teaspoon white vinegar
pinch paprika
pinch salt

Combine all ingredients in a medium bowl and whisk until combined.

- MAKES 1 CUP.

TIDBITS

Use low-fat mayo for a lighter version, but you already figured that out, huh?

•   •   •   •

CHILI'S
GRILLED BABY BACK RIBS

MENU DESCRIPTION: *"Full rack of ribs 'double-basted' w/BBQ sauce. Served w/cinnamon apples & homestyle fries."*

One day the suits are sitting around a conference table taking in a pitch for TV ads filled with songs about baby back ribs and barbecue sauce. Soon after that Chili's launches its campaign featuring choreographed cooks in the back kitchen banging on pots and pans and belting out a jazzy ode to the meaty entrée. Silly as it may seem, the tune was catchy, and the baby back ribs racked up big sales. Now you can sing your own tune as you recreate the Chili's baby back experience without leaving the house. The flavor is found in the sauce, and the cooking secret is a slow-braising technique prior to grilling that will keep the meat juicy and tender like the original. And, hopefully, no one will see you dance.

SAUCE

1 ½ cups water
1 cup apple cider vinegar
½ cup tomato paste
1 tablespoon yellow mustard
⅔ cup dark brown sugar, packed
1 teaspoon liquid hickory smoke

1 ½ teaspoons salt
½ teaspoon onion powder
¼ teaspoon garlic powder
¼ teaspoon paprika

4 racks baby back ribs

1. Make the barbecue sauce by combining all of the ingredients for the sauce in a medium saucepan over medium heat. When it comes to a boil, reduce heat and simmer sauce, stirring often, for 45 to 60 minutes or until sauce is thick.
2. When you're ready to make the ribs, preheat the oven to 300 degrees.
3. Brush sauce over the entire surface of each rack of ribs. Wrap each rack tightly in aluminum foil and arrange the packets on a baking sheet with the seam of the foil facing up. Bake for 2 to 2½ hours or until the meat on the ribs has pulled back from the cut ends of the bones by about ½ inch. When the ribs are just about done, preheat your barbecue grill to medium heat.
4. Remove the ribs from the foil (careful not to burn yourself—the liquid inside will be hot!) and grill them on the barbecue for 4 to 8 minutes per side or until the surface of the ribs is beginning to char. Brush sauce on both sides of the ribs a few minutes before you remove them from the grill. Just be sure not to brush on the sauce too soon or it could burn.
5. Serve the ribs with extra sauce on the side and lots of napkins.

• MAKES 4 SERVINGS.

•   •   •   •

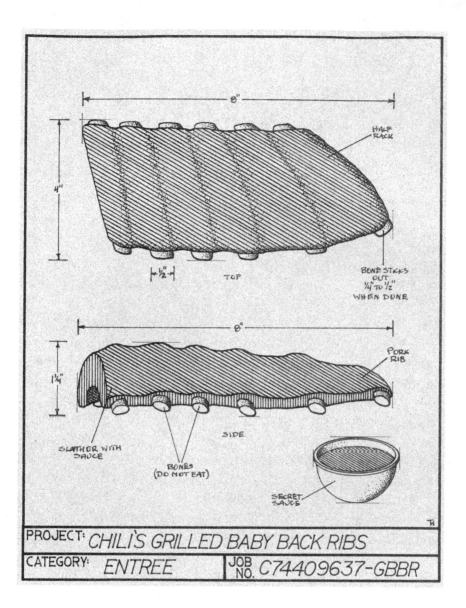

8"

4"

HALF
RACK

BONE STICKS
OUT
1/4" TO 1/2"
WHEN DONE

|←1/2"→| TOP

8"

1 1/4"

PORK
RIB

SLATHER WITH
SAUCE

BONES
(DO NOT EAT)

SIDE

SECRET
SAUCE

TW

PROJECT: *CHILI'S GRILLED BABY BACK RIBS*

CATEGORY: *ENTREE*   JOB NO. *C74409637-GBBR*

CHILI'S CHOCOLATE CHIP PARADISE PIE

MENU DESCRIPTION: *"We start with a warm, chewy bar layered with chocolate chips, walnuts and coconut. Topped with vanilla ice cream and drizzled with hot fudge and caramel."*

One thing that makes this dessert special is the way it comes to your table sizzling in a cast iron skillet—just like fajitas. The chocolate chip cookie and graham cracker crust "pie" sits in a hot skillet on top of bubbling cinnamon butter. It's topped with a scoop of vanilla ice cream, and then finished with walnuts, chocolate and caramel syrup. If you're a cloning perfectionist and want to present this dessert exactly like they do at the restaurant, you'll need a small skillet for each serving. Small cast iron skillets are the best, but any 6 or 8-inch frying pan will do fine. You just have to be sure your pan is good and hot to get that authentic Chili's "sizzle" when you lay in the goodies. If you've got a big crew to feed and don't have enough skillets for each serving, you can add the cinnamon butter to individual serving plates, microwave the plates until the butter melts, then build each serving on the warm plates. It may not have the sizzle of the real thing, but it'll still taste like paradise.

COOKIE LAYER

1 cup all-purpose flour
½ teaspoon baking soda
¼ teaspoon baking powder
½ cup butter, softened (1 stick)
⅓ cup granulated sugar

1 egg
1 tablespoon milk
½ teaspoon vanilla extract
½ cup shredded coconut

CRUST LAYER

6 tablespoons butter (¾ stick)
¼ cup sugar
1 ½ cups graham cracker crumbs

1 ¼ cups semi-sweet chocolate
    chips
½ cup chopped walnuts

CINNAMON BUTTER

½ cup butter, softened (1 stick)
3 tablespoons granulated sugar
1 ½ teaspoons ground cinnamon

chocolate syrup
caramel syrup
6 tablespoons chopped walnuts

9 scoops vanilla ice cream

1. Preheat the oven to 325 degrees.
2. Combine the flour, baking soda and baking powder in a medium bowl.
3. In a separate large bowl, beat together the butter and sugar with an electric mixer. Continue beating for about 30 seconds or until mixture turns lighter in color. Add the egg, milk, and vanilla and beat until smooth.
4. Slowly mix the dry mixture into the wet mixture. Beat until combined and then mix in the coconut flakes. Set this cookie dough aside for now.
5. Melt 6 tablespoons of butter in a medium bowl in the microwave on high for about 30 seconds. Add the sugar and stir well for 30 seconds. Add the graham cracker crumbs and stir. Press this mixture into the bottom of a 9x9-inch baking dish or pan.

6. Sprinkle the cup of chocolate chips evenly over the graham cracker crust.
7. Press the cookie dough into the dish, covering the chocolate chips. Use flour on your fingers to keep the soft dough from sticking.
8. Sprinkle the chopped walnuts over the dough. Use your fingers to press the nuts into the dough.
9. Bake for 40 to 45 minutes or until the edges of the "pie" become light brown.
10. Prepare the cinnamon butter by creaming together the butter, sugar and cinnamon in a small bowl with an electric mixer on high speed.
11. When you are ready to make your dessert, heat up a small skillet over medium heat. When the skillet is hot, remove it from the heat then add about 1 tablespoon of the cinnamon butter to the pan. It should quickly melt and sizzle. Slice the "pie" into 9 pieces and place one into the hot skillet. If the "pie" has cooled, you can reheat each slice by zapping it in the microwave for 30 to 40 seconds.
12. Place a scoop of ice cream on top of the "pie." Drizzle chocolate and caramel syrup over the dessert and then sprinkle about 2 teaspoons of chopped walnuts over the top. Repeat for the remaining ingredients and serve sizzling in the skillet.

• MAKES 9 DESSERTS.

•   •   •   •

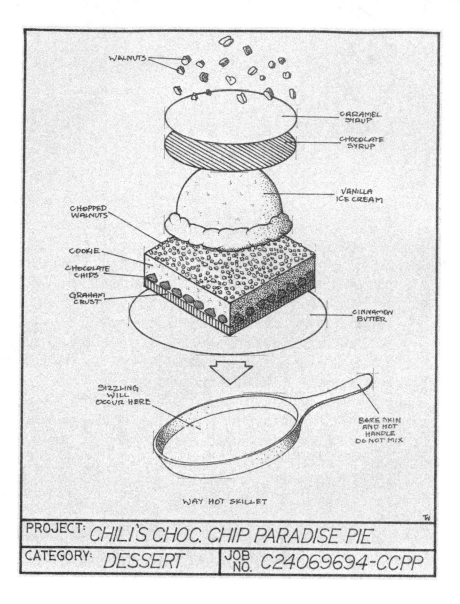

WALNUTS

CARAMEL SYRUP

CHOCOLATE SYRUP

VANILLA ICE CREAM

CHOPPED WALNUTS

COOKIE

CHOCOLATE CHIPS

GRAHAM CRUST

CINNAMON BUTTER

SIZZLING WILL OCCUR HERE

BARE SKIN AND HOT HANDLE DO NOT MIX

WAY HOT SKILLET

PROJECT: *CHILI'S CHOC. CHIP PARADISE PIE*

CATEGORY: *DESSERT*   **JOB NO.** *C24069694-CCPP*

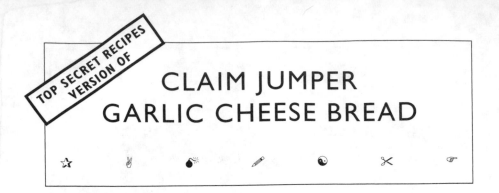

CLAIM JUMPER
GARLIC CHEESE BREAD

Claim Jumper restaurants may only be found in the West, but the chain can claim national recognition for its delicious garlic cheese bread and toast. That's because you can find boxed loaves of the stuff ready for baking in the frozen food section of your well-stocked local supermarket. The recipe is such a simple one though, that it doesn't take much longer to make the cheesy goodness from scratch, and you save a few shekels to boot. Plus, it's nice to use fresh bread—your choice of either Texas toast or your favorite French loaf. (The restaurant serves the Texas toast version, and the supermarket version is a French loaf.) All you have to do for a clone is mix together a few basic ingredients, spread it generously on the bread of your choice, and pop it in the oven.

SPREAD

½ cup butter (1 stick)
¾ cup shredded Cheddar cheese
2 tablespoons grated Parmesan
    cheese
½ teaspoon garlic powder

¼ teaspoon Worcestershire sauce
¼ teaspoon salt
dash ground black pepper
dash paprika

BREAD
*12 slices Texas toast (thick-sliced
    white bread) or 1 large
    French bread loaf, sliced
    through the middle*

1. Preheat oven to 400 degrees.
2. Combine all ingredients for the spread in a small bowl.
3. Smear spread generously on one side of each slice of Texas
    toast or on the face of each half of French bread loaf.
4. Bake for 10 to 12 minutes or until cheese begins to brown
    and bubble. Cut each slice of Texas toast in half before serving,
    as they do in the restaurant. For the French bread, slice it as
    thick as you like.

*   MAKES ABOUT 12 SLICES TOAST OR TWO LARGE HALVES OF FRENCH
    BREAD.

•   •   •   •

CAN USE FRENCH BREAD
LOAF OR TEXAS TOAST

12"

SLICE
BREAD
THROUGH
THE
MIDDLE

SPREAD
GOES
HERE

FRENCH BREAD LOAF

BUTTER, CHEESE,
GARLIC, ETC.

TEXAS TOAST

1"

USE
SPREAD
ON JUST
ONE
SIDE

SLICE
HERE
BEFORE
SERVING

4½"

FRONT

SIDE

TW

PROJECT: *CLAIM JUMPER GARLIC CHEESE BREAD*

CATEGORY: *SIDE DISH* **JOB NO.** *CJ9074I5672-GCB*

CLAIM JUMPER
FIRE-ROASTED ARTICHOKE

MENU DESCRIPTION: *"Marinated Fire-Roasted Split Artichokes Served with Tomato Relish and Garlic Mayo."*

I've been searching for the chain restaurant with the best recipe for roasted artichokes, and I think I've found it. With roasted garlic mayonnaise and a delicious tomato relish on the side, Claim Jumper takes the prize. This recipe is for just one artichoke, but feel free to add another if more than a couple hungry mouths are waiting. Just be sure to double up on the tomato relish.

1 large artichoke	juice of 2 lemons
8 cups water	4 cups ice
3 tablespoons salt	

ROASTED GARLIC MAYONNAISE

⅓ cup mayonnaise	¼ teaspoon lemon juice
1 head garlic	dash salt
1 tablespoon olive oil	

TOMATO RELISH

1 medium tomato, diced (about ½ cup)	1 clove garlic, minced (about 1 teaspoon)

1 teaspoon minced onion
2 basil leaves, minced
½ teaspoon olive oil
½ teaspoon balsamic vinegar

¼ teaspoon salt
dash ground black pepper

1 tablespoon butter, melted

1. Prepare the artichoke by cutting about an inch off the top with a sharp knife. Use scissors to clip the thorny tips off of all the outer leaves so no one gets punctured. Cut the artichoke in half down through the middle. Dissolve 3 tablespoons salt in 8 cups of water in a large bowl. Add juice of 2 lemons and ice, then drop the artichoke halves in the cold brine to marinate for 2 to 3 hours.

2. While artichoke is marinating, roast the head of garlic by preheating your oven to 325 degrees. Cut the top off of a head of garlic and cut the bottom (the root end) so that the garlic will sit flat. Remove most of the papery skin from the garlic, but leave just enough to hold the garlic together. Drizzle 1 tablespoon of olive oil over the garlic, then place it in a small oven-safe casserole dish. Cover it with a lid or aluminum foil and bake for 1 hour or until the garlic begins to brown. When you can handle the garlic, squeeze about 1 tablespoon of roasted garlic from the head and combine it with the mayo, lemon juice and salt. Stir well.

3. While the garlic is roasting prepare the tomato relish by combining all of the ingredients in a small bowl. Stir well, then cover and refrigerate until needed.

4. When you are ready to cook the artichoke, bring some water to a boil in a large saucepan with a steamer basket. You don't want the water to touch the artichoke if you can help it. If you don't have a steamer basket, fill the pan with just an inch or so of water. When the water is simmering, add the artichoke halves, cover, and steam for 40 to 50 minutes or until the artichoke is tender. While artichoke halves are steaming, preheat your barbecue grill to high heat.

5. When the steamed artichokes are cool enough to handle,

use a spoon to scrape out the fuzzy choke inside each half. Brush melted butter over the entire surface of each steamed artichoke half and place each half, flat side-down on the pre-heated grill. Grill for 4 to 6 minutes or until dark charring marks appear on the face of each half. Serve grilled-side-up with tomato relish (strain the liquid from the relish before serving) and roasted garlic mayonnaise on the side.

• SERVES 2 AS AN APPETIZER.

•   •   •   •

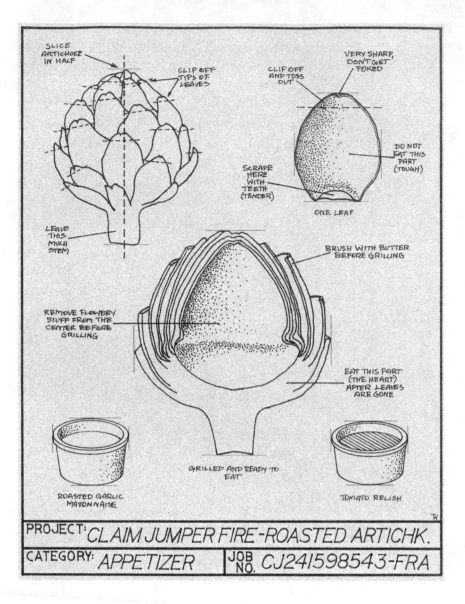

SLICE ARTICHOKE IN HALF

CLIP OFF TIPS OF LEAVES

VERY SHARP, DON'T GET POKED

CLIP OFF AND TOSS OUT

DO NOT EAT THIS PART (TOUGH)

SCRAPE HERE WITH TEETH (TENDER)

ONE LEAF

LEAVE THIS MUCH STEM

BRUSH WITH BUTTER BEFORE GRILLING

REMOVE FLOWERY STUFF FROM THE CENTER BEFORE GRILLING

EAT THIS PART (THE HEART) AFTER LEAVES ARE GONE

ROASTED GARLIC MAYONNAISE

GRILLED AND READY TO EAT

TOMATO RELISH

| PROJECT: | *CLAIM JUMPER FIRE-ROASTED ARTICHK.* | |
| CATEGORY: *APPETIZER* | JOB NO. | *CJ241598543-FRA* |

CLAIM JUMPER
CHEESE POTATOCAKES

MENU DESCRIPTION: *"(Our most popular appetizer.) Parmesan, Cheddar & Monterey Jack cheeses, cilantro, onion, fresh dill & mashed potato lightly breaded and fried crispy topped with fresh cut chives. Served with herbed ranch salsa."*

This top-seller is a versatile side dish alternative to mashed potatoes, but also stands well on it's own as an appetizer. With cilantro, green onion, and three different cheeses in there, the flavor is the bomb. When you add a crispy breading and some herbed ranch salsa drizzled over the top, it's clear why this is the most popular appetizer on the huge Claim Jumper menu. Try dropping a pinch or two of cayenne pepper into the herbed ranch salsa for an extra spicy boost.

HERBED RANCH SALSA

½ cup sour cream
¼ cup seeded and diced tomato
   (about ½ tomato)
2 tablespoons minced onion
1 tablespoon white vinegar

1 teaspoon fresh minced cilantro
½ teaspoon salt
¼ teaspoon ground black pepper
pinch dried dill weed

POTATOCAKES

4 medium red potatoes, with skin
   (about 1 pound)
¼ cup shredded Cheddar cheese
¼ cup shredded Monterey Jack
   cheese
2 tablespoons shredded Parmesan
   cheese

1 green onion, chopped
½ teaspoon minced fresh cilantro
½ teaspoon salt
¼ teaspoon ground black pepper
¼ teaspoon garlic powder

BREADING

⅔ cup unseasoned breadcrumbs
   (Progresso is good)
⅓ cup all-purpose flour
½ teaspoon dried dill weed

1 egg, beaten
1 cup milk

2 to 3 cups vegetable shortening

GARNISH

fresh cut chives

1. Boil potatoes for 25 to 30 minutes or until mostly soft, but still slightly firm. Be careful not to overcook those boys. Your potatocakes will hold together best when the potatoes aren't too mushy.
2. As the potatoes boil make your herbed ranch salsa by combining all of the ingredients in a small bowl. Cover and chill this sauce until you need it.
3. Drain the potatoes and mash them with the skin on in a medium bowl. You don't need a completely smooth consistency for the potatoes. There should be some small chunks of potato in there. Add the remaining ingredients for the potatocakes and mix well.
4. Combine breadcrumbs with flour and ½ teaspoon dill in a large bowl. Combine beaten egg and milk in another large bowl. Measure about ⅓ cup of the potato mixture into your

hands and shape it into a patty about the size of a hamburger patty. Drop the potato mixture into the breading mixture, then into the egg and milk, then back into the breading, being sure to cover the entire surface of the potatocake with the breading. Arrange the potatocake on a plate and repeat the process with the remaining potato mixture. Cover and chill the potatocakes for about 1 hour, so that they'll be sure to stick together when fried.

5. Heat up the shortening in a skillet over medium/low heat. You should have about 1 inch of shortening in the pan. Fry the potatocakes for 2 to 4 minutes or until golden brown, then drain on a rack or paper towels.

6. Serve potatocakes with a bit of ranch salsa poured over the top and sprinkle with fresh cut chives.

• MAKES 6 POTATOCAKES.

•   •   •   •

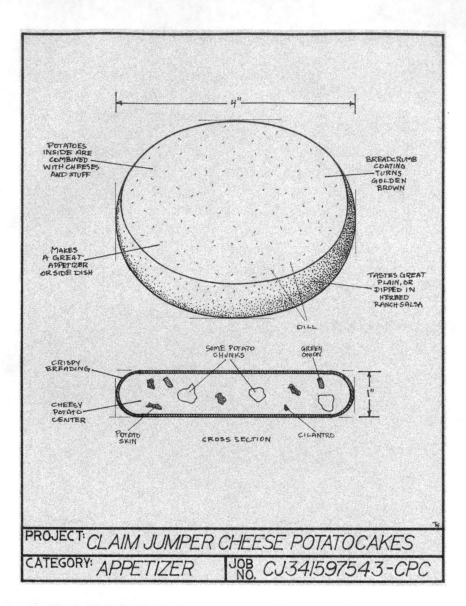

4"

POTATOES
INSIDE ARE
COMBINED
WITH CHEESES
AND STUFF

BREADCRUMB
COATING
TURNS
GOLDEN
BROWN

MAKES
A GREAT
APPETIZER
OR SIDE DISH

TASTES GREAT
PLAIN, OR
DIPPED IN
HERBED
RANCH SALSA

DILL

SOME POTATO
CHUNKS

GREEN
ONION

CRISPY
BREADING

1"

CHEESY
POTATO
CENTER

POTATO
SKIN

CROSS SECTION

CILANTRO

TW

PROJECT: CLAIM JUMPER CHEESE POTATOCAKES

CATEGORY: APPETIZER   JOB NO. CJ341597543-CPC

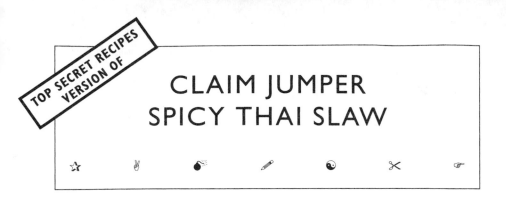

CLAIM JUMPER
SPICY THAI SLAW

MENU DESCRIPTION: *"Mixed greens, carrots, zucchini, green onions, peanuts and crunchy cappellini. Tossed in a sweet and spicy dressing."*

If you dig the sweet, sour, and spicy flavor combinations of Thai food, you'll love this tasty twist on cole slaw. Just find yourself a medium-size head of napa cabbage and a few other special ingredients and you're on your way to a perfect side dish for grilled grub, sandwiches, or as a quick solo snack. The menu mentions cappellini but we'll substitute with soba noodles that can be found in the supermarket aisle with other Asian foods (the rice vinegar and chili paste will be over there too). If you can't find soba noodles, the thicker chow mein noodles will also work. The mixed baby greens can often be found in ready-to-serve-plastic bags in the produce section. But the real secret ingredient for great tasting slaw is patience. The flavors of cole slaw improve after several hours in the cool box, and letting it sit overnight is even better.

DRESSING

⅓ cup rice vinegar
½ cup granulated sugar
1 tablespoon chili paste
    (sambal)

4 teaspoons fresh lime juice
2 teaspoons canola oil
½ teaspoon salt

2 ounces soba noodles, cooked
   (1 ½ cups)
10 cups thinly sliced napa
   cabbage (approx. 1 head)
2 cups mixed baby greens
1 ½ cups julienned carrot (approx.
   1 carrot)

1 cup julienned zucchini, (approx.
   ½ zucchini)
1 cup chopped fresh cilantro
1 cup dry roasted unsalted
   peanuts
½ cup sliced almonds

1. Prepare the dressing first by combining the ingredients in a small bowl or glass measuring cup. Heat up this mixture in the microwave on high for 30 to 60 seconds or until dressing is hot, but not boiling. This will help to dissolve the sugar and salt. Stir the dressing well and set it aside to cool.

2. Cook 2 ounces of soba noodles following the directions on the package (the directions will say something like: "Cook noodles for 5 minutes in rapidly boiling water"). Drain the soba noodles, run cold water over them and let them sit to cool while you prepare the other ingredients.

3. Use a large sharp knife to thinly slice a medium head of napa cabbage. You can also use a mandoline to slice the cabbage into thin, uniform strips so that you have 10 cups of sliced cabbage. You can use a mandoline with a julienne attach-ment for slicing the carrots and zucchini as well. Make sure to chop the julienne slices into bite-size strips.

4. Chop the soba noodles into bite-size pieces, then combine them with the cabbage, baby greens, carrot, zucchini, cilantro, and nuts in a large bowl. Toss everything around real well while adding the dressing, then cover and chill the bowl for at least 4 hours. If you have the patience, wait overnight for it, because the cole slaw will taste even better. Your slaw should last for up to a week covered in the fridge.

• MAKES APPROXIMATELY 10 CUPS.

• • • •

CLAIM JUMPER
MEATLOAF

MENU DESCRIPTION: *"Our own special recipe made with fresh ground chuck, pork, mild onions, green peppers and more. Served with mashed potatoes, brown gravy and garlic toast."*

Here's a great meatloaf recipe to add to your mealtime repertoire. This luscious loaf combines ground chuck with ground pork along with breadcrumbs, green onion, garlic, carrots and green pepper for one of the best flavor experiences you'll get from a good old-fashioned American loaf of meat. Use a perforated nesting meatloaf pan if you've got one so that the fat drains out into the pan below. If you don't have one of those a regular loaf pan will still work fine. But use a large one. This recipe makes a pretty big beefy slab of goodness.

2 teaspoons vegetable oil
1 green onion, minced
2 cloves garlic, minced
2 tablespoons minced green bell
   pepper
2 tablespoons grated carrot
2 eggs, beaten
1 cup milk
2 teaspoons salt
½ teaspoon ground black pepper

½ teaspoon garlic powder
½ teaspoon onion powder
1 ½ pounds ground chuck
¾ pound ground pork
1 cup breadcrumbs (such as
   Progresso)
½ cup all-purpose flour
¼ cup ketchup plus an additional
   ¼ cup ketchup (for top)

1. Preheat oven to 350 degrees.
2. Sauté green onion, garlic, green pepper, and carrot in vegetable oil over medium heat for a couple minutes.
3. Combine beaten eggs with milk, salt, black pepper, garlic powder, and onion powder in a medium bowl.
4. In a large bowl, mix breadcrumbs and flour into ground chuck and ground pork with your hands. Add egg and milk mixture, sautéed veggies, ¼ cup ketchup and mix it up using your hands. Get in there and squish it all around for a while. Enjoy yourself.
5. Press the mixture into a meat loaf pan (the kind of pan with drainage holes in the bottom) or a large loaf pan. Bake for 30 minutes, then spread ¼ cup of ketchup over the top of the meatloaf and bake it for another hour. Let it sit for a bit after you remove it from the oven before you slice it to serve.

• SERVES 8.

• • • •

DENNY'S FABULOUS FRENCH TOAST

MENU DESCRIPTION: *"Three thick slices grilled golden brown and sprinkled with powdered sugar."*

This popular breakfast choice at America's number one diner chain takes center stage on the cover of the menu. Three slices of thick bread are dipped in a slightly sweet egg batter, browned to perfection and served up with a dusting of powdered sugar, some soft butter and thick maple syrup on the side. Find the thick-sliced Texas toast bread in your bakery, or use any white bread that's sliced around ¾-inch thick. This recipe will make enough for two servings of three slices each, and it's the perfect recipe for waking up a special someone with breakfast in bed. (Many points will be earned.)

4 eggs
⅔ cup whole milk
⅓ cup all-purpose flour
⅓ cup granulated sugar
½ teaspoon vanilla extract

¼ teaspoon salt
⅛ teaspoon ground cinnamon
6 slices thick bread (such as Texas toast)
3 tablespoons butter

GARNISH
powdered sugar
butter

ON THE SIDE
maple syrup

1. Whisk together eggs, milk, flour, sugar, vanilla, salt, and cinnamon in a large bowl.
2. Heat a large cast iron or non-stick skillet over medium/low heat. When the pan is hot, add 1 tablespoon of butter. If butter smokes, your pan is too hot, turn down the heat.
3. Drop each bread slice into the batter for about 30 seconds per side. Let some of the batter drip off then drop the bread into the buttered pan. Cook each battered bread slice for 1½ to 2 minutes per side or until golden brown. Add more butter to the pan as needed to cook all the French toast.
4. Serve three slices of French toast per plate. Dust each serving with a little powdered sugar (tap it through a strainer), and include some maple syrup on the side.

- MAKES 2 SERVINGS.

• • • •

BATTER COATED BREAD

THICK SLICED BREAD

CRUST

4"

4"

FRONT

¾"

SIDE

MAPLE SYRUP

THREE FABULOUS SLICES

SERVING SUGGESTION

PROJECT: *DENNY'S FABULOUS FRENCH TOAST*

CATEGORY: *BREAKFAST*   JOB NO. *D37969240-FFT*

DENNY'S
BBQ CHICKEN SANDWICH

MENU DESCRIPTION: *"A seasoned, grilled chicken breast topped with Cheddar cheese and a stack of thin crisp onion rings on a sesame seed bun with lettuce, tomato and a sweet hickory spread. Served with a side of BBQ sauce."*

With 1527 restaurants across the country, Denny's is on top as America's largest full-service family restaurant chain. Sure, the chain's famous for its Grand Slam Breakfasts, but Denny's menu is filled with tasty choices for grub way past breakfast time. One such item is this chicken sandwich built with grilled chicken breast, lettuce, tomato, cheddar cheese, crispy onion rings, and a secret sweet hickory spread. That hickory spread is one of the ingredients that makes this sandwich special so the clone is here, and it requires an ingredient called hickory salt. You can find this blend of salt and hickory flavoring in the spice section from Spice Islands under the name "Old Hickory Smoked Salt." If you can't find that stuff, just substitute with ⅛ teaspoon salt and ⅛ teaspoon liquid hickory smoke. For even more flavor, Denny's serves the sandwich with a small dish of barbecue sauce that tastes remarkably similar to Bull's-Eye Original, so that's what we'll use. While homemade crunchy onion rings are the way to go for a true clone, you can certainly shortcut this step by using the canned French's French Fried Onions found in practically every supermarket.

SWEET HICKORY SPREAD

3 tablespoons butter
1 cup minced onion
2 teaspoons all-purpose flour
¼ cup molasses

¼ cup water
2 tablespoon white vinegar
⅛ teaspoon hickory salt

CRUNCHY ONION RINGS (SEE TIDBITS)

1 cup thinly sliced onion,
    separated into rings
1 cup milk
1 cup all-purpose flour

1 teaspoon salt
½ teaspoon ground black pepper
2 cups canola oil

2 skinless chicken breast fillets
vegetable oil
salt
ground black pepper
2 sesame seed hamburger buns

2 tablespoons melted butter
2 leaves green leaf lettuce
4 tomato slices
2 slices Cheddar cheese

ON THE SIDE

Bull's-Eye Original Barbecue Sauce

1. Prepare sweet hickory spread by melting 3 tablespoons butter over medium/low heat. Add 1 cup minced onion and sauté for 7 to 10 minutes or until the onions start to brown. Add 2 teaspoons flour and stir until the flour is mixed in. Let this cook for a minute or two, then add molasses, water, vinegar, and hickory salt. Simmer sauce for 3 to 4 minutes or until thick. Remove from heat and cover.

2. Make the crunchy onion rings by pouring milk into a large bowl. Combine flour, salt, and black pepper in another bowl. Dip onions in flour mixture first, then into milk and back into flour. Arrange all of the coated rings to a plate to rest while you heat up 2 cups canola oil in a large saucepan over

medium/low heat (you can also use a deep fryer for this step, just use the amount of oil required by the fryer manufacturer and set the temperature to 375 degrees). Test the oil by dropping in a pinch of flour. It should bubble. When the oil is hot, fry a handful of onion rings at a time in the oil until golden brown (3 to 5 minutes). Drain them on paper towels. (See Tidbits.)

3. To cook the chicken, preheat a skillet or griddle pan over medium heat. Pound your chicken with a kitchen mallet so that it has a uniform thickness of about ½ inch (it will plump a bit as you cook it), then trim any excess meat away that would hang off the sandwich. Rub each chicken breast with some canola oil, then sprinkle each breast with salt and a pinch of pepper. Grill chicken breast fillets for 4 to 6 minutes per side until done.

4. As your chicken cooks, spread a little melted butter on the faces of your two hamburger buns and toast the faces of the buns on another skillet or griddle set to medium heat until light brown.

5. Build each sandwich by first spreading some of the sweet hickory spread on the face of the bottom bun.

6. Tear a leaf of green leaf lettuce to fit on the bottom bun.

7. Arrange two tomato slices on the lettuce on each sandwich.

8. Stack the grilled chicken breast on the tomato slices.

9. Place a slice of Cheddar on the chicken breast on each sandwich.

10. Stack a handful of crunchy onion rings on the sandwich, then top the sandwich off with the crown bun. Serve with a small bowl of barbecue sauce on the side.

• MAKES 2 SANDWICHES.

TIDBITS

You can skip step #2 by using the canned French's French Fried Onions. A small can will be plenty.

TOP

4¼"

BBQ SAUCE ON THE SIDE

TOP SESAME SEED BUN

CRUNCHY ONION RINGS

SLICED CHEDDAR CHEESE

CHICKEN BREAST FILLET

SLICED TOMATO

GREEN LEAF LETTUCE

SWEET HICKORY SPREAD

BOTTOM BUN

PROJECT: *DENNY'S BBQ CHICKEN SANDWICH*

CATEGORY: *SANDWICH*   **JOB NO.** *D77540935-BBQCS*

DENNY'S
CLUB SANDWICH

MENU DESCRIPTION: *"Thinly sliced turkey, crisp bacon, lettuce and tomato on toasted white bread."*

Get out your toothpicks, because you'll have a hard time keeping the slices of this triple-decker sandwich from falling apart when slicing the only way you slice a true club sandwich: From corner to corner. This trusty, old-fashioned club sandwich recipe seems like it's been around forever, and yet this sandwich is still one of the top choices from Denny's for lunch. One day you'll find yourself with some white bread, sliced turkey, bacon, lettuce, tomato and mayo, and you'll realize you're just a *Top Secret Recipe* away from the secret stacking order to making the perfect club sandwich.

3 slices toasted white bread
4½ teaspoons mayonnaise
3 ounces sliced turkey breast
 (deli-sliced)

2 iceberg lettuce leaves
2 to 3 slices cooked bacon
2 tomato slices

1. Spread about 1½ teaspoons mayonnaise on one side of each toasted white bread slice.
2. Arrange the turkey breast on one slice of toast.
3. Tear or fold one iceberg lettuce leaf to fit on the sliced turkey.
4. Stack on another slice of toast with the mayo side facing up.

5. Break 2 or 3 slices of cooked bacon to fit on top of the second slice of toast.
6. Tear or fold the second lettuce leaf to fit on top of bacon.
7. Arrange the two tomato slices to fit on the lettuce.
8. Top off the sandwich with the last piece of toast turned with the mayo-coated side facing down.
9. Pierce the sandwich with four toothpicks between the corners, so that when the sandwich is sliced twice from corner to corner with a serrated knife, the toothpicks wind up in the center of each of the four slices.

• MAKES 1 SANDWICH.

•   •   •   •

SLICE

TOP

TOOTHPICK

ONE
SLICE

PLATED

TOASTED
WHITE
BREAD

MAYONNAISE

LETTUCE

SLICED
TOMATO

BACON

MAYONNAISE

TOASTED
WHITE
BREAD

LETTUCE

3 OUNCES
SLICED
TURKEY

MAYONNAISE

TOASTED
WHITE
BREAD

PROJECT: *DENNY'S CLUB SANDWICH*

CATEGORY: *SANDWICH*   JOB NO. *DI44095377-CS*

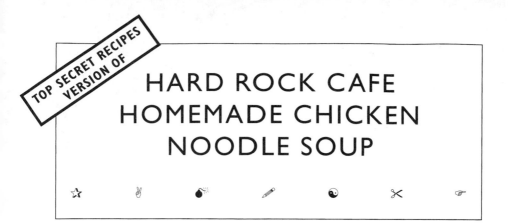

HARD ROCK CAFE HOMEMADE CHICKEN NOODLE SOUP

Give this simple soup clone a shot and I guarantee you'll never again want to eat chicken soup from a can. The recipe is a breeze since you use pre-cut chicken fillets—rather than cutting up a whole chicken—and you don't have to create a stock from scratch. Swanson sells a 32-ounce carton of chicken broth that's the perfect amount (4 cups) for this recipe.

1 pound skinless chicken breast
    fillets
1 pound skinless chicken thigh
    fillets
2 tablespoons vegetable oil
1 tablespoon butter
1 cup diced onion (about ½ of a
    medium onion)
1 cup diced carrot (about
    2 medium carrots, peeled)

½ cup diced celery (about
    1 stalk)
4 cups chicken broth
4 cups water
1 teaspoon salt
1 teaspoon freshly ground black
    pepper
1 teaspoon minced fresh parsley
3 cups wide egg noodles (dry)

GARNISH
minced fresh parsley

1. Heat 2 tablespoons vegetable oil in a large skillet over medium heat. Sauté chicken breasts and thighs for 10 to 15 minutes or until lightly browned on both sides and cooked through. Remove chicken from the skillet to a cutting board to cool a bit.
2. Reduce heat to medium/low, add butter to skillet then toss in onion, carrot and celery. Slowly cook the veggies (sweat them) for 10 minutes, stirring often, or until carrots are beginning to soften.
3. Chop the chicken, then dump all of it, plus the veggies, chicken broth, water, salt, pepper and 1 teaspoon parsley into a large soup pot. Bring soup to a boil then reduce heat and simmer for 10 minutes. Add noodles and simmer for an additional 15 minutes or until noodles are soft. Serve with a pinch of minced fresh parsley sprinkled on top.

• MAKES 8 SERVINGS.

•   •   •   •

HARD ROCK CAFE BAR-B-QUE BEANS

If you like baked beans you'll go nuts over this clone recipe from the world's first theme restaurant chain. It's real easy to make too, since you just stir the ingredients into a covered casserole dish, and bake for an hour and a half. This makes the dish handy if transporting to another location for a party or potluck, since you can fill the dish, cover it, then pop it into the oven once you arrive. The only element that may give you pause is the pulled pork from the recipe that follows (on page 143) for Hard Rock Cafe Pig Sandwich. It's an effortless addition if you've got some of that pork on hand. If not, just leave that ingredient out. Or you could add a couple tablespoons crumbled cooked bacon. Either way the beans will still come out great as a nosh-worthy side dish or solo snack.

2 15-ounce cans pinto beans
   (with liquid)
2 tablespoons water
2 teaspoons cornstarch
½ cup ketchup
⅓ cup white vinegar
¼ cup brown sugar
2 tablespoons diced onion

1 teaspoon prepared mustard
½ teaspoon chili powder
¼ teaspoon salt
¼ teaspoon coarse ground black
   pepper
½ cup shredded pork (from recipe
   on page 143)

1. Preheat oven to 350 degrees.
2. Pour entire contents of the can of pinto beans into a casserole dish (with a lid).
3. Dissolve the cornstarch in a small bowl with the 2 tablespoons of water. Add this solution to the beans and stir.
4. Add the remaining ingredients to the dish, stir well and cover.
5. Bake for 90 minutes or until the sauce thickens. Stir every 30 minutes. After removing the beans from the oven, let the beans cool for 5 to 10 minutes before serving.

• SERVES 6 TO 8 AS A SIDE DISH.

•   •   •   •

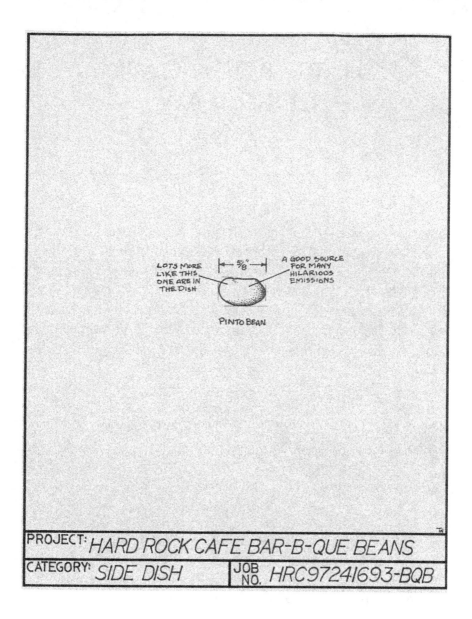

LOTS MORE LIKE THIS ONE ARE IN THE DISH

5/8"

A GOOD SOURCE FOR MANY HILARIOUS EMISSIONS

PINTO BEAN

PROJECT: *HARD ROCK CAFE BAR-B-QUE BEANS*

CATEGORY: *SIDE DISH*　　JOB NO. *HRC9724I693-BQB*

HARD ROCK CAFE
COLE SLAW

Smashing a guitar and hanging it on the wall will not give you the true Hard Rock Café experience unless you then eat a sandwich with this cole slaw served on the side. You have to be patient though since it's not something you can enjoy right away. Good cole slaw needs a little time to chill in the cool box—24 hours at least. The cabbage needs a chance to get it together with the other ingredients before rocking out at the gig inside your mouth.

1 ⅓ cups mayonnaise
3 tablespoons white vinegar
2 tablespoons plus 2 teaspoons
    granulated sugar
2 tablespoons milk

dash salt
8 cups chopped cabbage
    (1 head)
½ cup shredded carrot

1. Combine all ingredients except the cabbage and carrots in a large bowl and blend until smooth with an electric mixer.
2. Add cabbage and carrots and toss well.
3. Cover and chill overnight in the refrigerator. The flavors fully develop after 24 to 48 hours.

• SERVES 6 TO 8 AS A SIDE DISH.

• • • •

HARD ROCK CAFE PIG SANDWICH

MENU DESCRIPTION: *"Select pork, hickory-smoked then hand-pulled, so it's tender and juicy. 'An old Southern delicacy' with our famous vinegar-based bar-b-que sauce. Served with fries, ranch beans and homemade coleslaw."*

Take a big honkin' bite out of one of these and you'll soon know why it's the Hard Rock Cafe's most popular sandwich. The pork is hickory smoked for 10 hours, but since we're impatient hungry people here, we'll cut that cooking time down to under 4 hours using a covered grill and carefully arranged charcoal. Just sprinkle wet hickory chips over the hot charcoal arranged around the inside edge of a grill (such as a round Weber), and let the smoking begin. You can certainly use an actual smoker if you've got one, and go the full 10 hours with this puppy. But while you're still waiting for your sandwiches, the rest of us will have already dragged our full, round bellies over to the couch for a nap. By the way, you should try to make your marinated cabbage a day ahead of time so it has time to soak up the flavors.

MARINATED CABBAGE

2 tablespoons white vinegar
1 tablespoon granulated sugar
4 cups thinly-sliced cabbage

4 cups hickory smoking chips

RUB

2 tablespoons kosher salt
2 teaspoons cracked black pepper
1 teaspoon paprika
½ teaspoon onion powder
½ teaspoon ground sage
½ teaspoon dried thyme

¼ teaspoon cayenne pepper

1 boneless pork loin roast (3 to 4
    pounds)
vegetable oil

SAUCE

2 15-ounce cans tomato puree
1 cup apple cider vinegar
¾ cup brown sugar
2 tablespoons vegetable oil
½ teaspoon onion powder
½ teaspoon liquid hickory smoke

1 clove garlic, minced
¼ teaspoon salt
¼ teaspoon coarse ground black
    pepper

8 kaiser rolls

1. Make the marinated cabbage at least one day prior to building your sandwiches. Like cole slaw, this garnish needs some time to develop in the fridge. Combine the vinegar and sugar in a medium bowl. Add the cabbage, stir, cover the bowl and store it in the refrigerator until you are ready to make the sandwiches.

2. Put the wood chips in a bowl and cover with water. Let the wood soak for at least 1 hour. Light the charcoal after it has been arranged around the inside edge of your grill. You don't want coals directly under your pork. When the coals are hot, drain the water from the wood chips and sprinkle the chips over the top of the coals. You should now have smoke.

3. Combine the ingredients for the rub in a small bowl and mix well.

4. Rub some vegetable oil over the surface of the pork roast. Sprinkle the rub over the entire surface of the roast.

5. Place the roast in the center of your grill and put the lid on. Let the pork cook for 3 to 4 hours or until the internal temperature of the roast reaches 170 degrees.

6. As the pork cooks, make the sauce by combining the ingredi-

ents in a medium saucepan over medium/low heat. Let the sauce simmer for 15 to 20 minutes, then cover and remove from heat. Set this aside until your pork is ready.

7. When the pork is done, remove it from the grill and let it sit to cool for 15 to 20 minutes or until you can handle it. Now you want to tear the meat along the grain, making bite-size strips of shredded pork.

8. Put the shredded pork into a large saucepan over medium heat. Add 2 cups of the sauce to the pan and stir. Keep the rest of the sauce for later to serve on the side. Cook the pork for 15 minutes or until it is heated through.

9. Grill the faces of the rolls and stack about 1 cup of pork onto the bottom half of each roll. Add a rounded tablespoon of marinated cabbage on top of the pork, add a tablespoon or so of extra sauce on top of that, then cap off each sandwich with the top half of the roll. Serve with clones for the Hard Rock's cole slaw (page 142) and baked beans (page 139) on the side, if desired.

- MAKES 8 SANDWICHES.

• • • •

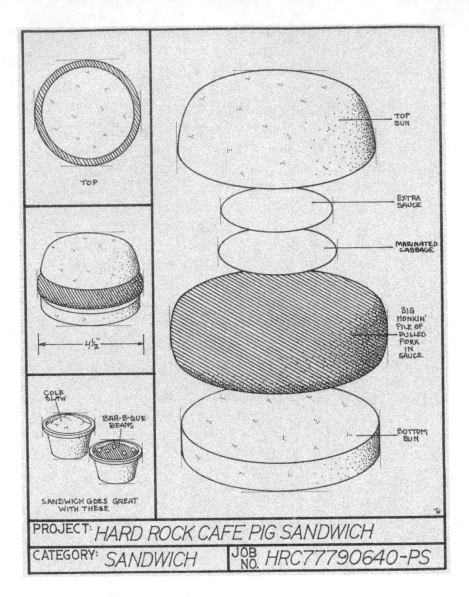

TOP

4½"

COLE SLAW

BAR-B-QUE BEANS

SANDWICH GOES GREAT WITH THESE

TOP BUN

EXTRA SAUCE

MARINATED CABBAGE

BIG HONKIN' PILE OF PULLED PORK IN SAUCE.

BOTTOM BUN

PROJECT: *HARD ROCK CAFE PIG SANDWICH*

CATEGORY: *SANDWICH*   **JOB NO.** *HRC77790640-PS*

HOUSTON'S CHICAGO-STYLE SPINACH DIP

These days just about every casual dining chain has its version of this appetizer: Spinach and artichoke hearts mixed with cheese and spices, served up hot with chips or crackers for dipping. Making the rounds over the years, I've tried many of them, and most formulas are nearly identical. That is, except for this one. Houston's makes their spinach dip special by using a blend of sour cream, Monterey Jack cheese and Parmigiano-Reggiano—the ultimate Parmesan cheese. Parmigiano-Reggiano is born in Italy and is usually aged nearly twice as long as other, more common Parmesan cheeses. That ingredient makes the big difference in this dip. So hunt down some of this special Parm at your well-stocked market or gourmet store, and you'll find out why Houston's spinach dip has been one of the most requested recipe clones at *TSR* Central.

One 12-ounce box frozen
    chopped spinach, thawed
½ cup chopped canned artichoke
    hearts (not marinated)
1 tablespoon chopped white onion
¼ cup heavy cream

¼ cup sour cream
1 ¼ cups shredded Monterey Jack
    cheese
⅓ cup grated Parmigiano-
    Reggiano cheese
¼ teaspoon garlic salt

ON THE SIDE
Corn tortilla chips

1. Mix together the spinach, chopped artichoke hearts, and onion in a microwave-safe glass or ceramic bowl. Cover bowl with plastic wrap, then cut a small slit in the center of the wrap so that the steam can sneak out. Microwave on high for 4 minutes. Keep spinach covered while you prepare the cream sauce.
2. Combine cream, sour cream, Jack cheese, grated Parmigiano-Reggiano cheese, and garlic salt in a medium saucepan over medium/low heat. Heat this up slowly for about 10 minutes or until the sauce reaches a simmer and thickens. Just don't let the mixture boil.
3. Add the spinach mixture to the sauce and continue to heat over medium/low. Cook for about 10 more minutes or until mixture reaches a thick dip-like consistency. Pour into a bowl and serve with tortilla chips for dipping (or crackers, bread, whatever you want).

- MAKES 2 CUPS.

•   •   •   •

HOUSTON'S
HONEY-LIME VINAIGRETTE

This 38-unit casual dining chain may be small compared to many of the other chains whose food I've cloned, but Houston's has a huge following of loyal customers throughout the country. I know this because for many years the restaurant sat at the top of my "most requested clones" list. I was finally ready to take on the challenge, but since there are no Houston's where I live in Las Vegas, it required a road trip—this time to Orange County, California. A couple plane rides, a bit of driving, some walking and a stumble or two later, I had a cooler full of Houston's goodies secured safely back at the underground lab. After a few hours of chopping and mixing this simple sweet-and-sour salad slather from Houston's was cracked.

⅓ cup vegetable oil
¼ cup rice vinegar
¼ cup honey
2 tablespoons Grey Poupon Dijon
    mustard
1 tablespoon chopped fresh
    cilantro
2½ teaspoons fresh lime juice

1 teaspoon sesame oil
1½ teaspoons minced red bell
    pepper
1 teaspoon minced onion
¼ teaspoon freshly ground black
    pepper
pinch salt

1. Combine all ingredients in a small glass or ceramic bowl. Stir well.
2. Heat dressing in the microwave on high for 1 to 1½ minutes or until mixture begins to bubble. Remove dressing from microwave and whisk for 1 minute. This will emulsify the dressing and it should begin to thicken as it cools.
3. Cover and chill for 2 hours before serving.

- MAKES 1 CUP.

• • • •

HOUSTON'S
COLE SLAW

It's not your typical cole slaw. The sweet pickle relish and green onion is a nice touch, and all that parsley really sets this dish apart from any other cole slaw I've tried. If you like cole slaw and you've never had this version at the restaurant, I encourage you to give this one a go.

¾ cup mayonnaise
3 tablespoons white vinegar
2 tablespoons granulated sugar
⅛ teaspoon salt
8 cups chopped green cabbage
   (1 head)

½ cup chopped fresh parsley
½ cup chopped green onion
   (green part only)
2 tablespoons sweet pickle relish
½ teaspoon celery seed

1. Whisk together mayonnaise, vinegar, sugar, and salt in a medium bowl.
2. Combine cabbage, parsley, green onion, and relish in a large bowl.
3. Pour the dressing over the cabbage and mix well. Add celery seed and mix, then cover the bowl and chill for at least 4 hours before munching out. Chilling the slaw overnight is even better.

• MAKES 8 SERVINGS.

• • • •

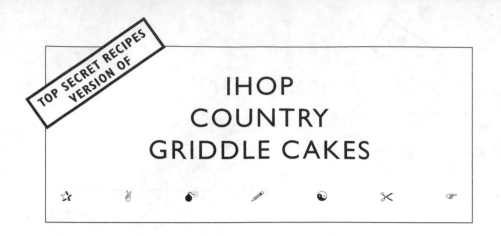

IHOP
COUNTRY
GRIDDLE CAKES

MENU DESCRIPTION: *"Delicious blend of buttermilk and real Cream of Wheat."*

This nationwide chain, which is known for it's big bargain breakfasts, serves an impressive number of non-breakfast items as well. In 1997, IHOP dished out over 6 million pounds of french fries and over half a million gallons of soft drinks. But it's the Country Griddle Cakes on the breakfast menu that inspired this *Top Secret Recipe*. The unique flavor and texture of this clone comes from the Cream of Wheat in the batter. Now you can have your pancakes, and eat your cereal too.

nonstick spray
1 ¼ cups all-purpose flour
1 ½ cups buttermilk
⅓ cup instant
    Cream of Wheat (dry)
1 egg

⅓ cup granulated sugar
1 teaspoon baking powder
1 teaspoon baking soda
¼ cup vegetable oil
½ teaspoon salt

1. Preheat a skillet over medium heat. Apply nonstick spray.
2. Combine all ingredients in a large bowl with a mixer set on medium speed. Mix until smooth, but don't over mix.
3. Pour the batter by ⅓-cup portions into the hot pan and

cook pancakes for 1 to 3 minutes per side or until brown. Repeat with remaining batter.

• MAKES 8 TO 10 PANCAKES.

• • • •

IHOP
COUNTRY OMELETTE

Sure, IHOP is famous for pancakes, but the joint makes a pretty killer omelette when put to the task. What makes this three-egg creation so cool is the top secret folding method. For all of IHOP's omelettes, the beaten eggs are mixed with the appropriate chunky ingredients, and the whole thing is poured out thin on a giant griddle. When the eggs have firmed up, two sides are folded over, the filling is positioned, and the omelette is rolled over once, twice, three times so it ends up looking like a burrito, sort of. Now we can execute the same egg origami at home with a 12-inch electric skillet, or a 12-inch stovetop griddle pan. You can find easy-to-cook hash brown potatoes in bags in the freezer section.

3 eggs
⅛ teaspoon salt
2 tablespoons diced cooked ham
2 tablespoons diced white onion

½ tablespoon butter
3 tablespoons cooked shredded
   hash brown potatoes
¼ cup shredded Cheddar cheese

GARNISH
2 tablespoons sour cream

1. Heat a 12-inch electric skillet to 275 degrees (or heat a 12-inch griddle pan over medium low heat). Preheat oven to 300 degrees.

2. Add salt to eggs and beat for about 30 seconds. Stir in diced cooked ham and white onion.
3. Melt ½ tablespoon of butter in hot griddle or pan. When butter melts pour eggs into the pan and swirl the pan around to coat the bottom evenly. Use a spatula to evenly distribute ham and onion.
4. Cook eggs for 4 to 6 minutes or until top of omelette is mostly firm. Fold over 1-inch of top and bottom of the omelette. Sprinkle 2 tablespoons shredded cheddar cheese down omelette at about one-third of the way from the left side of the omelette. Arrange about 3 tablespoons of cooked hash brown potatoes on top of the cheese. Starting at the left end, use a spatula to roll the eggs over the filling ingredients. Continue rolling the omelette two more times. Use a spatula to lift the omelette onto an oven safe plate. Sprinkle 2 tablespoons of shredded Cheddar over the top of the omelette and place the plate in the 300 degree oven for 1 to 2 minutes or until the cheese has melted. If you're making more than one omelette, set your oven to 200 degrees to keep ready-to-eat omelettes on hold.
5. Just before serving, spoon 2 tablespoons of sour cream onto the middle of the omelette.

• MAKES 1 SERVING.

•   •   •   •

3 EGGS

BEAT EGGS

ONION

HAM

ADD THESE TO THE EGGS

12"

MINCED ONION AND HAM

① ②

FOLD TOP & BOTTOM

FOLD EGGS OVER FILLING

③

FILL AND BEGIN THE ROLL

ELECTRIC SKILLET

④

NOW KEEP ROLLING

MELTED CHEDDAR CHEESE

SOUR CREAM

PLATE

HOT

SERVING SUGGESTION

PROJECT:	*I.H.O.P. COUNTRY OMELETTE*	
CATEGORY: *BREAKFAST*	JOB NO.	*IHOP4076959-CO*

IHOP
HARVEST GRAIN 'N NUT
PANCAKES

MENU DESCRIPTION: *"Hearty grains, wholesome oats, almonds and English walnuts."*

Wholesome grains and nuts get it on in this clone for the signature pancakes from the country's largest pancake chain. The whole wheat flour and oats add more flavor, while the nuts pitch in for a crunch in every bite. Take a break from gummy, bland traditional pancakes. Make a breakfast that pacifies your pancake urge, and leaves you feeling peppy.

¾ cup Quaker oats
¾ cup whole wheat flour
⅓ cup all-purpose flour

2 teaspoons baking soda	2 eggs
1 teaspoon baking powder	¼ cup granulated sugar
½ teaspoon salt	3 tablespoons finely chopped
1 ¼ cups buttermilk	blanched almonds
⅓ cup whole milk	3 tablespoons finely chopped
¼ cup vegetable oil	walnuts

1. Lightly oil a skillet or griddle and preheat it to medium heat.
2. Grind the oats in a blender or food processor until fine, like flour.

3. Combine oat flour, whole wheat flour, all-purpose flour, baking soda, baking powder and salt in a medium bowl.
4. In another bowl combine buttermilk, milk, oil, eggs and granulated sugar with an electric mixer until smooth. Combine dry ingredients with wet ingredients, add nuts and mix well by hand.
5. Ladle ⅓ cup of the batter onto the hot skillet and cook the pancakes for 1 to 3 minutes per side or until brown.

• MAKES 12 PANCAKES.

TIDBITS

You can cover and freeze these after they cool. To reheat, just put a stack in the microwave on high for 1 to 2 minutes.

•　•　•　•

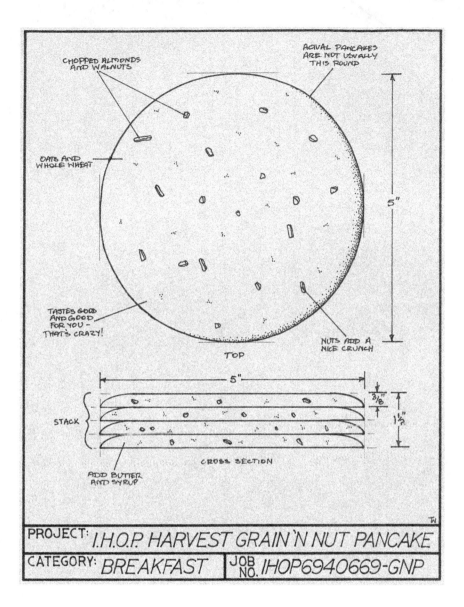

CHOPPED ALMONDS AND WALNUTS

ACTUAL PANCAKES ARE NOT USUALLY THIS ROUND

OATS AND WHOLE WHEAT

5"

TASTES GOOD AND GOOD FOR YOU — THAT'S CRAZY!

NUTS ADD A NICE CRUNCH

TOP

5"

STACK

3/8"

1½"

CROSS SECTION

ADD BUTTER AND SYRUP

PROJECT:	*I.H.O.P. HARVEST GRAIN 'N NUT PANCAKE*
CATEGORY: *BREAKFAST*	JOB NO. *IHOP6940669-GNP*

IHOP
PUMPKIN PANCAKES

During the holiday season this particular pancake flavor sells like . . . well, you know. It's one of 16 varieties of pancakes served at this national casual diner chain. You can make your own version of these delicious flapjacks with a little canned pumpkin, some spices and traditional buttermilk pancake ingredients. Get out the mixer, fire up the stove, track down the syrup.

nonstick spray
2 eggs
1 ¼ cups buttermilk
4 tablespoons butter, melted
3 tablespoons canned pumpkin
¼ cup granulated sugar

¼ teaspoon salt
1 ¼ cups all-purpose flour
½ teaspoon baking powder
½ teaspoon baking soda
¼ teaspoon ground cinnamon
¼ teaspoon ground allspice

1. Preheat a skillet over medium heat. Coat pan with oil cooking spray.
2. Combine eggs, buttermilk, butter, pumpkin, sugar, and salt in a large bowl. Use an electric mixer to blend ingredients.
3. Combine remaining ingredients in a small bowl. Add dry ingredients to wet ingredients and blend with mixer on medium speed until smooth.
4. Pour the batter in ⅓ cup portions into the hot pan.
5. When the batter stops bubbling and edges begin to harden,

flip the pancakes. They should be dark brown. This will take from 1 to 3 minutes.
6. Flip the pancakes and cook other side for the same amount of time, until brown.

• MAKES 8 TO 10 PANCAKES.

•   •   •   •

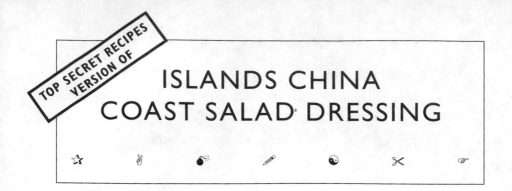

ISLANDS CHINA
COAST SALAD DRESSING

This 30-store Hawaiian-themed chain of restaurants is known for it's hand-made burger buns, specialty sandwiches and taco platters with names like Shorebird, Pelican, Sandpiper, Baja, and Northshore. Some people, though, go to the Islands just for the China Coast salad. It's a huge bowl filled with sliced chicken breast, lettuce, red cabbage, julienned carrots, fried noodles, sesame seeds, mandarin orange wedges and chives, and then tossed with this top secret dressing. Many diners think the dressing's so good they ask for extra and discreetly smuggle it home. No more smuggling required. Now, with this simple formula, you can make your own clone at home and use it on any of your favorite bowls of green.

½ cup mayonnaise
5 tablespoons rice vinegar
2 tablespoons granulated sugar

2 tablespoons sesame oil
1 tablespoon soy sauce
¼ teaspoon garlic powder

Combine all ingredients in a medium bowl and mix with an electric mixer until blended and sugar is dissolved. Chill.

- MAKES 1 CUP.

• • • •

ISLANDS
ISLAND FRIES

MENU DESCRIPTION: *"Our famous fries are fresh cut daily from whole potatoes with the skins left on."*

Not only can I show you the best way to make french fries at home in this clone of Islands top-selling version, but I'm also supplying you with a super simple way to make the same type of salt blend that Islands uses to make those fries so dang addicting. As with any good french fry recipe, you'll need to slice your potatoes into strips that are all equal thickness. That means you need a mandoline, or similar slicing device, that makes ¼-inch slices. Once you've got your potatoes cut, you must rinse and soak them in water to expel the excess starch. The frying comes in two stages: A quick blanching stage, and the final frying to put a crispy coating on the suckers. Islands uses a combination of peanut and vegetable oils in their fryers, so you simply combine the two in your home fryer. The whole process is not that tough once you get going, and certainly worth the effort if hungry mouths are waiting for the perfect homemade french fries. However, if you want to simplify the process because your hungry mouths aren't of the patient sort, you could certainly buy frozen french fries, cook 'em up following the instructions on the bag, and then sprinkle on this garlic/onion salt blend for a quick-and-easy kitchen clone.

GARLIC/ONION SALT

1 tablespoon garlic salt
1 teaspoon onion salt

¼ teaspoon ground black pepper

FRIES

2 medium russet potatoes
3 to 5 cups vegetable oil (fryer
    filled halfway)

3 to 5 cups peanut oil (fryer filled
    rest of the way)

1. Combine garlic salt, onion salt, and pepper in a small bowl.
2. Slice potatoes with a slicer or mandoline set to ¼-inch thick slices. Hold potato at a slight angle when slicing to produce fries that are about 2 to 3 inches in length.
3. Drop sliced potatoes into a bowl of water to rinse away starch. Pour out water, then fill bowl again. Pour out that water, then fill bowl again with water and add some ice. Let potatoes sit for 1 hour in the ice water.
4. Heat oils in fryer to 350 degrees.
5. When the potatoes are done soaking, drain them, then pour them out onto a clean dish towel. Blot fries dry.
6. When fries are dry drop about half into the hot oil and blanch for 2 to 3 minutes (fries should be soft in the center). Remove the fries onto a towel to cool. When all the fries are blanched, let them sit to cool for about 30 minutes. When fries are cool, fry them for the second time for 5 to 7 minutes or until fries are golden and crispy.
7. Pour fries onto a rack or towels to drain. Toss fries with several pinches of the garlic/onion salt and serve hot.

• SERVES 4.

•   •   •   •

ISLANDS
YAKI SOFT TACOS

MENU DESCRIPTION: *"Three flour tortillas stuffed w/marinated chicken, teriyaki sauce, Jack cheese, pineapple, lettuce, tomatoes & scallions."*

If you love the sweet taste of teriyaki-marinated chicken, you'll dig the Yaki Soft Tacos at this Hawaiian-themed burger chain. Sure, Islands is famous for its burgers, but many also go for the several choices of soft tacos—and the one I've cloned here is the top-seller. After testing all popular brands of teriyaki sauce on the market, I found that none have the heavy ginger notes of the chain's version, so you'll want to make the sauce from scratch. Which is really no big deal, since it's an easy process and you'll end up with a teriyaki sauce/marinade that's better than any store version, and you can use it in all sorts of recipes. When you buy the canned pineapple, go for the 20-ounce can or get two 8-ounces cans. You'll need that much since you'll use the pineapple chunks in both the sauce and on the tacos (and you'll even use some of the juice from the can in your teriyaki sauce). When chopping the chunks, take the time to slice each chunk into quarters (lengthwise, with the grain) so you get thin pineapple pieces that are the exact size of the stuff they use in the restaurant. Or you can find smaller pineapple chunks in some stores (see Tidbits).

TERIYAKI SAUCE

1¾ cups water
1 tablespoon cornstarch
¾ cup light brown sugar
½ cup soy sauce
½ cup canned pineapple chunks
(chunks sliced into quarters)

¼ cup juice from can of pineapple
chunks
½ teaspoon garlic powder
¼ teaspoon onion powder
2 teaspoons minced fresh ginger

12 chicken tenderloins
12 7-inch flour tortillas
2 cups shredded Monterey Jack
cheese
4 cups iceberg lettuce, chopped
very thin or shredded
1½ cups canned pineapple
chunks, (chunks sliced into
quarters)

1½ cups diced tomatoes (about
2 medium tomatoes)
½ cup chopped green onion
(green part only)

1. Make the teriyaki sauce by whisking cornstarch into the water in a medium saucepan. Add remaining ingredients, then bring mixture to a boil. Reduce heat and simmer for 7 to 10 minutes or until thicker. Let sauce cool before you use it for marinating.
2. When the sauce is cool, measure out 1 cup of sauce and set it aside. Use the remaining sauce to pour over chicken tenders in a medium bowl. Cover chicken and let it marinate for at least 6 hours. Overnight is even better.
3. When chicken has marinated, preheat a large skillet over medium/low heat. Wipe the pan with a little oil. Remove the chicken from the marinade (and toss out the marinade) and sauté chicken in the pan for 8 to 10 or until chicken is cooked through and browned on both sides. Slice each chicken filet into 3 or 4 pieces and spoon all the chicken into a medium bowl. Microwave the leftover 1 cup of teriyaki

sauce in the oven for 30 to 60 seconds or until it's hot. Pour the sauce over the sliced chicken in the bowl.

4. When you're ready to build the tacos, preheat another skillet over medium heat. Toss a tortilla into the pan for a minute, then flip it over and add 2 to 3 tablespoons of shredded cheese across the center of the tortilla. Let the tortilla sit in the pan for about a minute or so (until the cheese starts melting) then remove the tortilla and immediately spoon the equivalent of one chicken tender into the tortilla (3 or 4 chunks of chicken). Spoon about 1½ tablespoons teriyaki sauce from the cooked chicken bowl over the chicken in each taco.

5. Arrange about ⅓ cup shredded lettuce over the chicken in each taco. Follow that up with 1 to 2 tablespoons of pineapple chunks, 1 to 2 tablespoons diced tomato, and a couple pinches of chopped green onion. Repeat process for remaining tacos. The restaurant serves 3 tacos with each order.

•   MAKES 12 TACOS (4 SERVINGS).

TIDBITS

If you can find them, Del Monte offers canned pineapple that's pre-cut into the perfect size for this recipe. And I love the name: They're called "Tidbits."

•   •   •   •

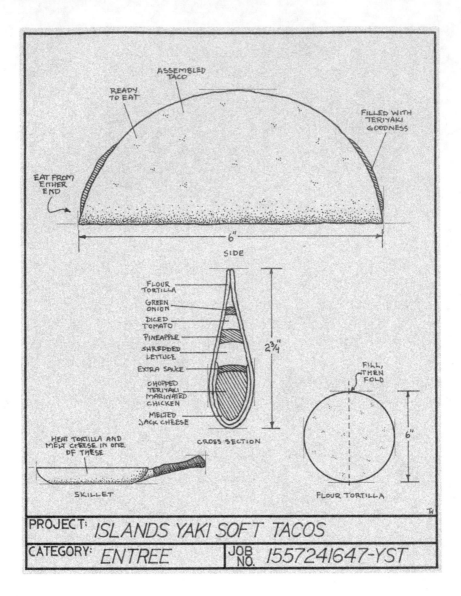

READY
TO EAT

ASSEMBLED
TACO

FILLED WITH
TERIYAKI
GOODNESS

EAT FROM
EITHER
END

6"

SIDE

FLOUR
TORTILLA

GREEN
ONION

DICED
TOMATO

PINEAPPLE

SHREDDED
LETTUCE

EXTRA SAUCE

CHOPPED
TERIYAKI
MARINATED
CHICKEN

MELTED
JACK CHEESE

2¾"

CROSS SECTION

FILL,
THEN
FOLD

6"

FLOUR TORTILLA

HEAT TORTILLA AND
MELT CHEESE IN ONE
OF THESE

SKILLET

PROJECT: *ISLANDS YAKI SOFT TACOS*

CATEGORY: *ENTREE*

JOB NO. *155724/647-YST*

JOE'S CRAB SHACK
BLUE CRAB DIP

The number one appetizer on Joe's menu is called Blue Crab Dip but you don't need blue crab to clone it. You don't even need to use fresh crab. I used some delicious lump crabmeat from Phillips Seafood that comes in 16-ounce cans (you'll find it at Costco, Sam's Club, Wal-Mart, and Von's) and the dip came out amazing. You could also use crabmeat that comes in 6-ounce cans found at practically every supermarket—you'll need two of them. Just be sure to get the kind that includes leg meat, and don't forget to drain off the liquid before you toss it in.

one 8-ounce pkg. cream cheese,
    softened
2 cups crabmeat (canned is fine)
¼ cup diced green onion
1 tablespoon minced mild red chili
    pepper

1 tablespoon mild green chili
    pepper (Anaheim)
¼ teaspoon salt
¼ teaspoon ground white pepper
2 tablespoons shredded Parmesan
    cheese

GARNISH
paprika

1 teaspoon minced fresh parsley

1. Preheat oven to broil.
2. Combine cream cheese with crab, green onion, chili peppers, salt and white pepper in a medium bowl. Stir well to combine.

3. Spread mixture into the bottom of an oven-safe dish. Use a wide dish for this so that the dip is only about an inch deep in the bottom.
4. Sprinkle Parmesan cheese over the surface of the dip.
5. Broil for 3 to 4 minutes or until cheese on top begins to brown.
6. Sprinkle paprika over the dip, followed by fresh minced parsley. Serve with tortilla chips or crackers for dipping.

• MAKES APPROX. 2 CUPS (SERVES 4 TO 6 AS AN APPETIZER).

JOE'S CRAB SHACK
GARLIC KING CRAB LEGS

These legs from the king of crabs come already cooked at your supermarket (usually previously frozen), so we won't have to boil them long to finish them off. But we do want to give them a long enough bath to get the flavor of garlic into the meat. To aid in this process we need to poke several holes in the shell along each leg so that the garlic water can seep in. Use the handle end of a nut-cracker (the kind that is often served with crab to help crack the shells), or the back end of a wooden spoon to make those holes. This step also makes removing the shells easier when eating the crab. And you don't have to worry about peeling the garlic cloves. Just pound 'em flat with a mallet or foil-wrapped brick and toss 'em into the water.

1 cup vegetable oil

2 large heads garlic

1 tablespoon dried parsley flakes

2 pounds king crab legs

ON THE SIDE
melted butter

1. Fill a large pot halfway with water. Add oil and bring to a boil. Crush all of the unpeeled garlic cloves with a mallet. When the water and oil comes to a boil add the garlic and parsley flakes and boil for 15 minutes.

2. Cut the crab legs in half so that they will fit into the pot. Use the handle end of a thin wooden spoon or nutcracker to poke several holes in the shell of each crab leg. This will allow the flavor of the garlic to seep into the crab. Lower the crab into the pot and boil for 5 to 6 minutes.
3. Remove crab legs and drain. Arrange one pound of crab on each plate. Serve with melted butter on the side.

- SERVES 2.

• • • •

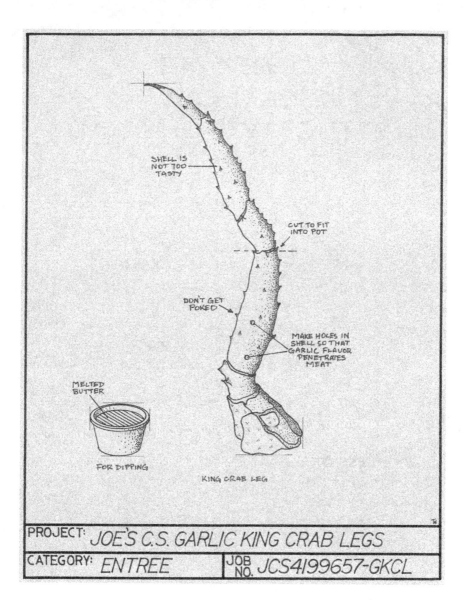

SHELL IS NOT TOO TASTY

CUT TO FIT INTO POT

DON'T GET POKED

MAKE HOLES IN SHELL SO THAT GARLIC FLAVOR PENETRATES MEAT

MELTED BUTTER

FOR DIPPING

KING CRAB LEG

PROJECT: *JOE'S C.S. GARLIC KING CRAB LEGS*

CATEGORY: *ENTREE*

JOB NO. *JCS4199657-GKCL*

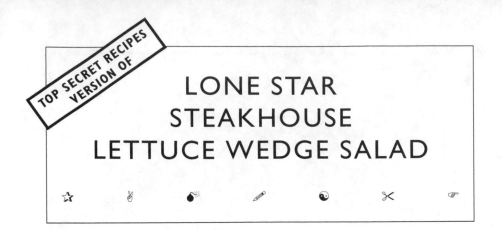

LONE STAR
STEAKHOUSE
LETTUCE WEDGE SALAD

Why waste time chopping up the lettuce when you can just hack a head into four chunks, dress it up and serve? This unique presentation is not only easy to make, but is also a deliciously different way to serve your next salad. The creamy bleu cheese dressing is a breeze to craft from scratch and tastes much better than anything you'll buy in a store. Add a bit of extra crumbled bleu over the top, some freshly diced tomatoes, and you're well on your way to a fancy-pants side salad that'll surely impress.

BLEU CHEESE DRESSING

¾ cup mayonnaise
½ cup buttermilk
¼ cup crumbled bleu cheese
½ teaspoon granulated sugar

¼ teaspoon ground black pepper
¼ teaspoon garlic powder
⅛ teaspoon onion powder
⅛ teaspoon salt

1 head iceberg lettuce
1 cup crumbled bleu cheese

1 cup diced tomato (1 large tomato)

1. Use an electric mixer to combine all ingredients for bleu cheese dressing in a medium bowl.
2. Slice a head of iceberg lettuce into quarters through the

stem end. Cut the stem off of the wedges and arrange each one on a plate.

3. Spoon about ¼ cup of bleu cheese dressing over each lettuce wedge.
4. Sprinkle ¼ cup of crumbled bleu cheese over the dressing.
5. Sprinkle ¼ cup of diced tomato over the top and serve.

- MAKES 4 SERVINGS.

• • • •

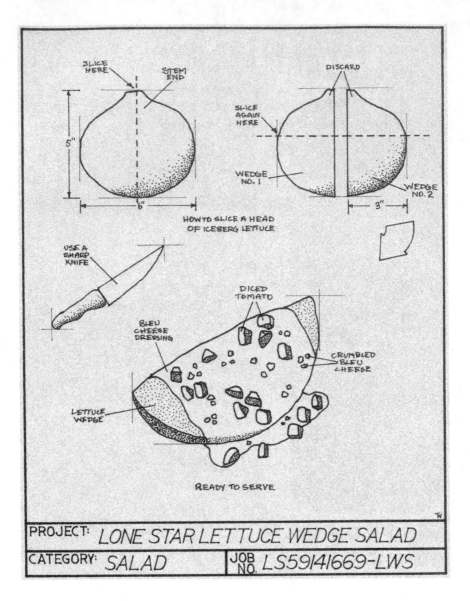

SLICE HERE
STEM END
5"
6"
HOW TO SLICE A HEAD OF ICEBERG LETTUCE

DISCARD
SLICE AGAIN HERE
WEDGE NO. 1
WEDGE NO. 2
3"

USE A SHARP KNIFE

DICED TOMATO
BLEU CHEESE DRESSING
CRUMBLED BLEU CHEESE
LETTUCE WEDGE

READY TO SERVE

PROJECT: *LONE STAR LETTUCE WEDGE SALAD*

CATEGORY: *SALAD*   JOB NO. *LS59141669-LWS*

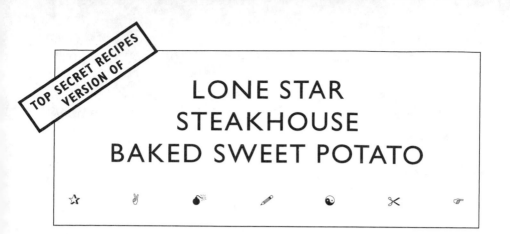

LONE STAR
STEAKHOUSE
BAKED SWEET POTATO

Sweet potatoes are not related to the more common russet potatoes and are often confused with yams in the grocery store and on menus (the yam is actually starchier and less flavorful). Just be sure you're buying sweet potatoes when you get to the produce section—even the produce stockers get mixed up! Although these puppies are not really potatoes, the baking times are the same. And when you spoon on some butter and sprinkle cinnamon/sugar over the top, you've got a treat that tastes more like dessert than a versatile side dish.

4 sweet potatoes
vegetable oil
3 tablespoons granulated sugar

1 ½ teaspoons ground cinnamon
½ cup whipped butter

1. Preheat oven to 350 degrees. Rub a little oil on the skin of the sweet potato and bake it for 45 to 75 minutes (bigger sweet potatoes take longer to cook). When they are done, the outside will have darkened and the inside will be soft. You may see liquid from the sweet potato oozing out when it's close to done.

2. As potatoes bake, combine sugar and cinnamon in a small bowl.
3. To serve, slice a sweet potato down the center. Add two tablespoons of whipped butter, and sprinkle some cinnamon/sugar over the top.

• MAKES 4 SERVINGS.

•   •   •   •

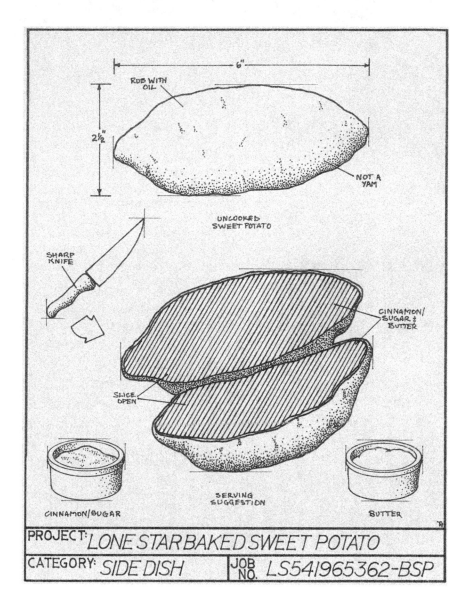

6"

RUB WITH OIL

2½"

NOT A YAM

UNCOOKED
SWEET POTATO

SHARP
KNIFE

CINNAMON/
SUGAR &
BUTTER

SLICE
OPEN

SERVING
SUGGESTION

CINNAMON/SUGAR

BUTTER

PROJECT: *LONE STAR BAKED SWEET POTATO*

CATEGORY: *SIDE DISH*   JOB NO. *LS541965362-BSP*

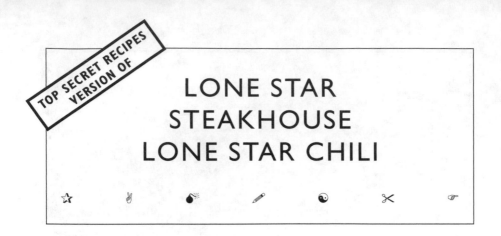

LONE STAR STEAKHOUSE LONE STAR CHILI

MENU DESCRIPTION: *"Meaty and spicy, served piping-hot with chopped onions, shredded cheddar, and a whole jalapeno."*

This chain makes a tasty chili that warms the bones on a nippy day. This clone recipe is easy-to-make, low in fat, and delicious. And if it's super brisk outside, you might want to add an additional tablespoon of diced jalapeno to the pot to aggressively stoke those internal flames.

1 pound ground beef
1 diced onion
1 tablespoon diced fresh jalapeno pepper
1 15-ounce can kidney beans with liquid
1 14.5-ounce can peeled diced tomatoes

1 8-ounce can tomato sauce
1 cup water
1 tablespoon apple cider vinegar
1 teaspoon salt
1 teaspoon chili powder
¼ teaspoon garlic powder
1 bay leaf

GARNISH

grated Cheddar cheese
diced onion

canned whole jalapeno chili peppers

1. Brown ground beef in a large saucepan over medium heat. Drain fat.
2. Add onion and pepper and sauté for about two minutes.
3. Add remaining ingredients and simmer for 1 hour, stirring occasionally. Serve one cup in a bowl with the optional cheese, diced onion and whole jalapeno garnish on top.

- MAKES 4 SERVINGS.

•   •   •   •

MARGARITAVILLE CRAB, SHRIMP AND MUSHROOM DIP

MENU DESCRIPTION: *"Our signature appetizer . . . jumbo lump blue crab meat, gulf shrimp and mushrooms, simmered in a Cajun cream sauce and served with toasted garlic bread. We make it here so you know it's good!"*

This dips rocks, and I'm not the only one who thinks so. According to the Margaritaville menu, it's the theme chain's signature appetizer. And what's not to like: Delicious blue crab, little bay shrimp and sliced mushrooms are all swimming in a Cajun-style cream sauce, topped with melted cheddar and Jack cheeses, and broiled until the cheese melts . . . oh, hold me back. Serve up your clone with slices of freshly toasted buttery garlic bread and you've got a great party snack. The restaurant version is a tiny little serving that's barely enough for two, so I've supersized this clone recipe to make enough dip to satisfy the Brady Bunch; if Alice sits out.

DIP

2 tablespoons butter
¼ cup minced celery
¼ cup minced onion
1 teaspoon crushed red pepper
   flakes

2 cups heavy cream
1½ cups sliced white mushrooms
1 cup blue crab
1 cup bay shrimp, cooked
   (smallest shrimp)

¼ teaspoon salt

1 cup shredded Cheddar
   cheese

1 cup shredded Monterey Jack
   cheese

2 green onions, sliced

BREAD

2 loaves Italian bread

½ cup butter, melted (1 stick)

½ teaspoon dried parsley flakes

¼ teaspoon garlic powder

1. Melt 2 tablespoons of butter over low heat in a large sauce-pan. Add celery, onions and red pepper flakes and simmer slowly (sweat) the ingredients over low heat for 20 minutes. You don't want the ingredients to turn brown, rather you want them to cook slowly until the celery softens and the onions begin to turn translucent.

2. Add cream, mushrooms, crab, shrimp and salt to the pan. Turn the heat up a bit until the liquid begins to bubble, then bring the heat back down and let the mixture simmer for 20 minutes or until it reduces to about ½ the volume and be-comes thick. Watch the saucepan carefully to make sure the mixture doesn't bubble over. In the meantime, crank your oven up to broil.

3. Prepare the bread by cutting the loaves into ½-inch thick slices. Combine the dried parsley flakes and garlic powder with a stick of melted butter in a small bowl. Brush some of this garlic butter on each side of each bread slice and toast the bread under the hot broiler for 1 to 2 minutes per side or until the bread is toasted to a light brown.

4. When the dip has thickened pour it into an 8x8-inch casse-role dish. Combine the shredded Cheddar and Jack cheese and sprinkle the cheese mixture over the dip. Broil the dip for 3 to 4 minutes or until the cheese is melted. Sprinkle sliced green onions over the top and serve hot with the

garlic toast on the side, and some spoons or forks for spreading the dip onto the toast.

- MAKES 6 TO 8 SERVINGS.

• • • •

MARGARITAVILLE JAMAICA MISTAICA WINGS

MENU DESCRIPTION: *"Come back to Jamaica! Our wings tossed in habanero-honey wing sauce with cucumber sticks and house-made mango ranch dipping sauce."*

Oh, wings. You gotta love those flavorful little non-functioning chicken parts. When they're good, they're real good. And these little guys from Jimmy Buffett's chain of island-themed restaurants rock my tiny inflatable boat. The preparation is no big secret: Fry the wings, add the sauce. But it's that habanero honey sauce recipe that makes these suckers so addicting. Add to that an easy-to-make mango ranch dipping sauce and you're off on a non-stop cruise to chicken wing paradise. The restaurant serving size is for 10 wings, but these *Top Secret* sauces will be enough for 30 wings, and you'll need it! If I have one word of caution it's to be very careful mincing that habanero. You may even want to use rubber gloves to handle it. This is the hottest pepper in the world folks, so if you touch the minced pieces with your bare fingers, and then proceed to touch a crucial and sensitive body part, you'll discover one big "mistaica" real fast.

HABANERO HONEY SAUCE

1 cup water
1 6-ounce can tomato paste
½ cup Worcestershire sauce
¼ cup honey
¼ cup molasses

1 teaspoon minced habanero pepper (1 pepper)
1 teaspoon crushed red pepper flakes
1 teaspoon ground black pepper

½ teaspoon onion powder

½ teaspoon chili powder

½ teaspoon dried minced onion

½ teaspoon dried parsley

¼ teaspoon garlic powder

⅛ teaspoon liquid hickory smoke

⅓ cup white vinegar

MANGO RANCH DIPPING SAUCE

1 8-ounce bottle Hidden Valley
   Ranch dressing

¼ cup mango juice (Kern's is
   good)

½ jalapeno, minced

6 to 10 cups vegetable oil (as
   required by fryer)

10 chicken wings

salt

pepper

ON THE SIDE

cucumber sticks

1. Prepare habanero honey sauce by combining all ingredients except the vinegar in a large saucepan. Bring mixture to a boil, then reduce heat and simmer sauce for 1 hour uncovered, or until sauce reduces to about half of its original volume and thickens. Remove sauce from heat, mix in ⅓ cup white vinegar and cover.
2. Make the mango ranch dipping sauce by combining the ingredients in a small bowl. Cover and chill sauce until needed.
3. In your deep fryer, bring 6 to 10 cups of vegetable oil (or whatever is required by your fryer) to 375 degrees.
4. Drop in the wings and fry for 8 to 12 minutes or until the wings become golden brown. Drain wings for a few minutes on paper towels. Sprinkle with salt and pepper.
5. Put wings in a large metal or glass bowl, add ½ cup of the habanero honey sauce and toss the wings until they are all

coated. Serve with dipping sauce on the side and cucumber sticks, if desired.

- MAKES 10 WINGS (PLUS SAUCE FOR 20 MORE).

• • • •

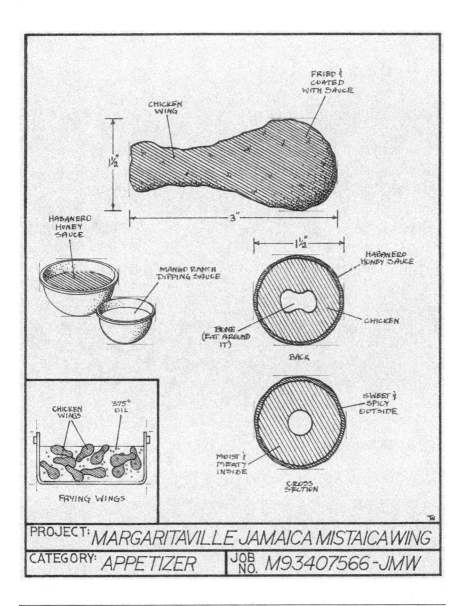

FRIED &
COATED
WITH SAUCE

CHICKEN
WING

1½"

3"

HABANERO
HONEY
SAUCE

1½"

HABANERO
HONEY SAUCE

MANGO RANCH
DIPPING SAUCE

CHICKEN

BONE
(FAT AROUND
IT)

BACK

CHICKEN
WINGS

375°
OIL

SWEET &
SPICY
OUTSIDE

MOIST &
MEATY
INSIDE

CROSS
SECTION

FRYING WINGS

PROJECT: MARGARITAVILLE JAMAICA MISTAICA WING

CATEGORY: APPETIZER   JOB NO. M93407566-JMW

MARGARITAVILLE KEY LIME PIE

MENU DESCRIPTION: *"A true taste of the tropics. National award winning recipe."*

Many of the key lime pie recipes circulating, including the recipe found on bottles of key lime juice, have a glaring error: They don't make enough filling to fit properly into a standard 9-inch graham crust pie shell. That's probably because those recipes are designed around one 14-ounce can of sweetened condensed milk. But come on, if we're going to make a beautifully thick key lime pie like the one served at Jimmy Buffett's Margaritaville restaurants we need to use something like 1½ cans of sweetened condensed milk, or more accurately, two cups of the stuff. The clone recipe for the pie is a simple one that's for sure, with only four ingredients including the pie shell. But don't stop there. I'm also including a special way to make mango sauce by simply reducing a couple cans of Kern's mango juice. And there's a raspberry sauce recipe here that's made easily with frozen raspberries. These two sauces are used to jazz up the plate at the restaurant and are certainly optional for your clone version, even though I've made them as easy as, um, you know.

2 cups sweetened condensed milk   ⅔ cup key lime juice
6 egg yolks   1 graham cracker pie shell

MANGO SAUCE

2 11.5-ounce cans Kern's
   mango juice

RASPBERRY SAUCE

1 ½ cups water   ½ cup granulated sugar
2 cups frozen raspberries

GARNISH

canned whipped cream
4 thin lime slices, halved

1. Pre-heat oven to 325 degrees.
2. Use an electric mixer on medium speed to combine sweetened condensed milk, egg yolks, and lime juice. Mix just until
   ingredients are combined.
3. Pour filling into graham pie shell and bake on middle rack for
   20 minutes or until filling jiggles only slightly when shaken.
   Cool. Cover pie and chill in refrigerator for a couple hours
   before serving.
4. Make mango sauce by bringing two cans of Kern's mango
   juice to a boil in a medium saucepan over medium heat. Reduce heat and simmer for 30 minutes or until sauce thickens.
   Cover and chill.
5. Make raspberry sauce by combining water and raspberries in
   a medium saucepan over medium heat. Bring to a boil then
   reduce heat and simmer raspberries for 10 minutes. Use a
   potato masher or a large spoon to crush the raspberries as
   they boil. Strain raspberry seeds from water, then put the
   liquid back into the saucepan and add the sugar. Bring mixture back to a boil, reduce heat and simmer for 15 to 20
   minutes or until the sauce thickens. Cover and cool sauce
   until you are ready to serve the pie.

6. Prepare dessert by dribbling some mango sauce and some raspberry sauce onto a small plate (you can use spoons or squirt bottles for this). Place a slice of pie onto the sauce, add a dollop of whipped cream to the top of the pie slice with one half of a thin lime slice on top of the whipped cream.

• MAKES 8 SERVINGS.

• • • •

9"

8"

SLICE HERE

KEY LIME FILLING

ONLY THREE INGREDIENTS IN HERE!

FILLING IS EVEN WITH TOP OF CRUST

6½"

WHOLE PIE

MANGO SAUCE

RASPBERRY SAUCE

9-INCH GRAHAM CRACKER PIE CRUST

WHIPPED CREAM

SLICED LIME

2⅝"

1½"

FILLING

GRAHAM CRUST

3¼"

4½"

ONE SLICE

PROJECT:	*MARGARITAVILLE KEY LIME PIE*	
CATEGORY: *DESSERT*	JOB NO.	*M33407968-KLP*

MARIE CALLENDER'S
LEMON CREAM CHEESE PIE

MENU DESCRIPTION: *"Our melt-in-your-mouth cream cheese pie with a tangy lemon topping."*

Here's a great double-layered pie with lemon topping covering a creamy cheesecake filling. It's two great pies in one dessert. This creation has been huge seller for Marie Callender's, and I've had nothing but raves from anyone who's tried it—including a couple high fives and one affectionate rabbit punch. Make the crust from scratch like the pros using the recipe here, or take the easy route with a pre-made graham cracker crust found in the baking aisle. Either way it's pie heaven.

CRUST

1 cup graham cracker crumbs
¼ cup butter, melted (½ stick)

2 tablespoons granulated sugar

CREAM CHEESE FILLING

one 8-ounce pkg. cream cheese,
    softened
¼ cup granulated sugar

½ teaspoon vanilla extract
1 egg

LEMON FILLING

½ cup granulated sugar
2 tablespoons cornstarch
dash salt
1 cup water

2 egg yolks
2 tablespoons fresh lemon juice
1 tablespoon butter

1. Preheat oven to 350 degrees.
2. Make the crust by combining the graham cracker crumbs with melted butter and sugar in a small bowl. Press the crust mixture into an 8-inch pie pan.
3. Prepare the cream cheese filling by mixing cream cheese with ¼ cup sugar, vanilla and an egg using an electric mixer. Mix well until smooth. Pour cream cheese filling into graham cracker crust and bake for 30 to 35 minutes or until center is cooked. A knife stuck in the middle of the filling should come out mostly clean.
4. As the pie cools, make the lemon filling by combining ½ cup sugar with cornstarch, salt and water in a small saucepan. Set mixture over low heat and bring to a simmer, stirring often.
5. Whisk in egg yolks, then add lemon juice and butter. When mixture simmers again immediately remove it from the heat.
6. Pour the lemon filling over the cream cheese filling, and let the pie cool. When cool, chill pie in the refrigerator for several hours before serving. Slice into 6 pieces to serve restaurant-size portions.

• MAKES 6 SERVINGS.

•　•　•　•

9"

8"

SLICE HERE

THE DIET REALLY STARTS NEXT WEEK

CREAM CHEESE & LEMON FILLING

GRAHAM CRACKER CRUST MADE FROM SCRATCH

THIS IS EVEN EASIER

6¼"

WHOLE PIE

PRE-MADE CRUST

9-INCH PIE PAN

3½"

LEMON FILLING

CREAM CHEESE FILLING

1½"

4"

4½"

ONE SLICE

TW

PROJECT: *M.C.'s LEMON CREAM CHEESE PIE*

CATEGORY *DESSERT*   JOB NO. *MC6696940-LCCP*

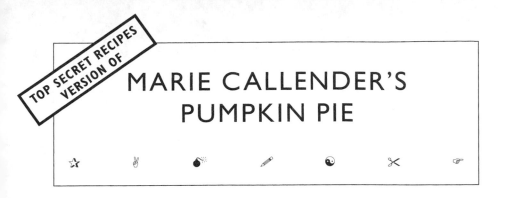

MARIE CALLENDER'S PUMPKIN PIE

MENU DESCRIPTION: *"Our famous pumpkin pie has just the right amount of spice."*

The vittles from Marie Callender's have made an impression beyond the chain's West Coast roots with home-style packaged entrees and side dishes available in frozen food sections of supermarkets across the country. But pie making is where the chain excels. A fresh slice of a Marie Callender's pie is as close as you'll get to homemade heaven this side of grandma's porch window. This clone is an obvious selection, since the restaurant sells more pumpkin pies than any other, even in non-holiday months. This clone is a perfect opportunity to improve on icky pumpkin pie recipes (like those found on cans of canned pumpkin, for example) in many ways. For one thing, there's no need to use canned evaporated milk when fresh whole milk and cream is so much better. Also, I've added a little brown sugar in there to contribute hints of molasses that go so well with the pumpkin and spices. And three eggs, versus two found in many recipes, will add to the richness and firmness of the cooked filling. After mixing the filling we'll let it sit for a bit while waiting for the oven to preheat. This way it can come closer to room temperature, and the pie filling will bake more evenly. And then, of course, you've got the crust. Marie Callender's pie crust is a treat, and the clone recipe included here—which uses a chilled combination of butter and shortening—results in the perfect mix of flavor and flakiness.

¼ cup butter, softened (½ stick)
¼ cup vegetable shortening
1 ¼ cups all-purpose flour
1 tablespoon granulated sugar

¼ teaspoon salt
1 egg yolk
2 tablespoons ice water

FILLING

3 eggs
1 15-ounce can pumpkin
½ cup granulated sugar
¼ cup packed dark brown sugar
1 teaspoon ground cinnamon
½ teaspoon salt

½ teaspoon ground ginger
¼ teaspoon ground cloves
¼ teaspoon ground nutmeg
¾ cup whole milk
¼ cup heavy cream

1. Prepare the crust by beating together the butter and short-ening until smooth and creamy. Chill until firm.
2. Sift together the flour, sugar and salt in a medium bowl.
3. Using a pastry knife or fork, cut the chilled butter and short-ening into the dry ingredients until the flour is mixed in and it has a crumbly texture. Mix egg yolk and ice water into the dough with a spoon then form it into a ball with your hands. Don't work the dough too much or your crust will lose its flakiness. Flakey crust is good crust. Cover dough ball with plastic wrap to sit until the filling is ready.
4. Prepare filling by beating eggs. Add pumpkin and stir well to combine.
5. Combine sugars, cinnamon, salt, ginger, cloves, and nutmeg in a small bowl. Stir spice mixture into the pumpkin. Mix in milk and cream.
6. Preheat oven to 425 degrees. While oven preheats let filling sit so that it can come closer to room temperature.
7. Unwrap pie dough, then roll it flat on a floured surface and line a 9-inch pie dish.
8. When oven is hot pour filling into pie shell, and bake for 15 minutes. Reduce heat to 350 degrees and bake for another

50 to 60 minutes or until a knife stuck in the middle comes out clean.

9. Cool pie, then chill. Slice chilled pie into 6 pieces to serve restaurant-size portions. Whipped cream on top is optional, but highly recommended.

- MAKES 6 SERVINGS.

•   •   •   •

9"

8"

SLICE HERE

TENDER, FLAKEY PIE CRUST

WHOLE PIE

6½"

TURN THE DOUGH NOT THE PIN

ROLLING DOUGH

9-INCH PIE PAN

3½"

1½"

SECRET BLEND OF PUMPKIN AND SPICES

4"

4½"

ONE SLICE

TW

PROJECT: MARIE CALLENDER'S PUMPKIN PIE

CATEGORY: DESSERT

JOB NO. MC040695655-PP

MIMI'S CAFÉ
CARROT RAISIN BREAD

It's dark, moist and delicious, and it comes in a breadbasket to your table at this French-themed West Coast casual restaurant chain. Now the tastiest carrot bread ever can be yours to create at home with a couple of grated carrots, molasses, raisins and chopped walnuts. You'll be baking this one in the oven for at least an hour. That should be enough time to warm up the house and send amazing smells wafting through every room. Line the carpet with newspaper to catch the family drool.

1 ½ cups all-purpose flour
1 teaspoon cinnamon
1 teaspoon baking powder
1 teaspoon baking soda
1 teaspoon salt
1 cup vegetable oil
1 cup plus 2 tablespoons
    granulated sugar

3 eggs
¼ cup molasses
½ teaspoon vanilla extract
1 cup shredded carrot
1 cup raisins
¾ cup chopped walnuts

1. Preheat oven to 350 degrees.
2. Combine flour, cinnamon, baking powder, baking soda, and salt in a large mixing bowl.
3. In another bowl, combine oil, sugar, eggs, molasses, and vanilla with an electric mixer. Add shredded carrot and mix. Add raisins and walnuts and mix well by hand.

4. Pour flour mixture into the other ingredients and stir until combined.
5. Pour batter into two ungreased 8-inch loaf pans. Bake for 60 minutes, or until done.

- MAKES 2 LOAVES.

. . . .

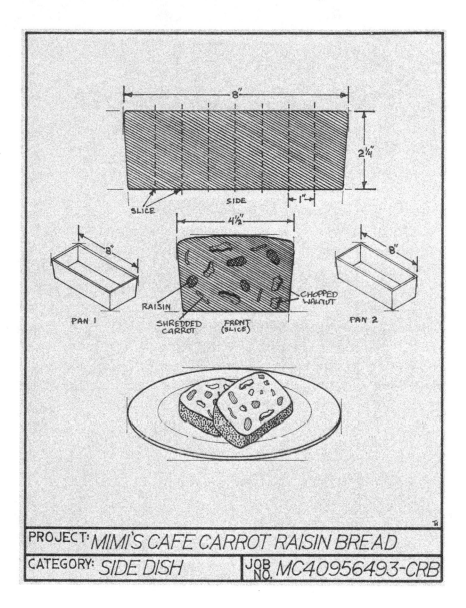

8"

2¼"

SLICE   SIDE |← 1" →|

4½"

PAN 1

RAISIN

SHREDDED   FRONT
CARROT   (SLICE)

CHOPPED
WALNUT

8"

PAN 2

PROJECT: *MIMI'S CAFE CARROT RAISIN BREAD*

CATEGORY: *SIDE DISH*   JOB NO. *MC40956493-CRB*

MIMI'S CAFÉ
CAFÉ CORN CHOWDER

Arthur Simms was in the restaurant business for many years before he opened the first Mimi's Café with his son, Tom, in Anaheim, California in 1978. Back in the Golden Age of Hollywood Arthur was the guy running things in the MGM Studios commissary where, on any given day, Jean Harlow, Clark Gable and Judy Garland might stop in for a grazing. Arthur named his New Orleans-influenced, bistro-style restaurant after a woman he met and fell in love with in Paris during the war. Today it's Tom who runs the show at this growing 93-unit chain where regulars return for the staple favorites including the French Market Onion Soup (on page 204), Carrot Raisin Bread (on page 199) and the delicious Café Corn Chowder, cloned here.

2 tablespoons butter
2 large celery stalks, chopped
   (about 1½ cups)
½ cup diced white onion
4 cups water
1 russet potato, peeled and cut
   into ½-inch cubes (about
   2 cups)
1 bay leaf

1 15-ounce can cream-style corn
   (with liquid)
1 15-ounce can whole kernel corn
   (with liquid)
2 teaspoons granulated sugar
½ teaspoon salt
⅛ teaspoon ground white pepper
½ cup all-purpose flour
1½ cups half-and-half

1. Sauté celery and onion in the butter for 5 minutes in a large saucepan or stock pot. Don't brown.
2. Add 4 cups of water, chopped potato, and bay leaf. Bring to a boil, then reduce heat and simmer for 15 minutes, stirring occasionally.
3. Add creamed corn (with liquid), canned whole corn (with liquid), sugar, salt, and white pepper and simmer for 20 minutes, stirring occasionally.
4. Combine flour with half-and-half and stir until smooth. Add this mixture to the soup and simmer for an additional 10 to 15 minutes, until thick.
5. Serve by spooning a 1-cup portion into a small bowl and sprinkle a little minced fresh parsley on top.

• MAKES 2 QUARTS (EIGHT 1-CUP SERVINGS).

MIMI'S CAFÉ FRENCH MARKET ONION SOUP

You might not think that a tough World War II flying ace would open a restaurant called "Mimi's," but that's exactly what happened in the 70's. Arthur J. Simms flew spy missions over France during the war and helped liberate a small French town near Versailles. After the war Arthur ran the commissary at MGM studios in Hollywood, stuffing the bellies of big-time celebs like Judy Garland, Clark Gable and Mickey Rooney. He later joined his son Tom in several restaurant ventures including one called "French Quarter" in West Hollywood. This was the prototype for the French-themed Mimi's Café. In 1978, the first Mimi's opened in Anaheim, California. Today there are over 90 Mimi's in the chain with a new one opening every other week; all of them serving this amazing French onion soup that's topped with not one, not two . . . *three* different cheeses. Oui!

¼ cup butter
3 medium white onions, sliced
3 14-ounce cans beef broth
   (Swanson is best)
1 teaspoon salt
¼ teaspoon garlic powder
3 tablespoons Kraft grated
   Parmesan cheese

6 to 12 slices French bread
   (baguette)
6 slices Swiss cheese
6 slices mozzarella cheese
6 tablespoons shredded Parmesan
   cheese

1. Sauté onions in melted butter in a large soup pot or saucepan for 15 to 20 minutes or until onions begin to brown and turn transparent.
2. Add beef broth, salt and garlic powder to onions. Bring mixture to a boil, then reduce heat and simmer uncovered for 1 hour. Add the grated Parmesan cheese in the last 10 minutes of cooking the soup.
3. When soup is done, preheat oven to 350 degrees and toast the French bread slices for about 10 to 12 minutes or until they begin to brown. When bread is done, set oven to broil.
4. Build each serving of soup by spooning about 1 cup of soup into an oven-safe bowl. Float a toasted slice or two of bread on top of the soup, then add a slice of Swiss cheese on top of that. Place a slice of mozzarella on next and sprinkle 1 tablespoon of shredded Parmesan cheese over the top of the other cheeses.
5. Place the soup bowl on a baking sheet and broil for 5 to 6 minutes or until the cheese begins to brown.

- MAKES 6 SERVINGS.

• • • •

OLIVE GARDEN BRUSCHETTA

MENU DESCRIPTION: *"A traditional topping of roma tomatoes, fresh basil and extra-virgin olive oil. Served with freshly toasted ciabatta bread."*

Olive Garden's recently redesigned bruschetta recipe improves on the Italian chain's previous version. The tomato salad includes a little sun-dried tomato and balsamic vinegar, and it is now served in a separate dish rather than on the bread. Now the bread doesn't get soggy. The tomatoes are finely diced before mixing with the other ingredients, and the ciabatta bread is sprinkled with a little grated Parmesan cheese before it's toasted. Try to find a nice, chewy loaf of Italian bread for this dish—get the best bread in the store. The better your bread, the better your bruschetta.

3 firm roma tomatoes, finely diced (about 1½ cups)
1 tablespoon minced fresh basil
2 teaspoons minced garlic
2 teaspoons diced marinated sun-dried tomatoes
2 teaspoons extra virgin olive oil
1 teaspoon balsamic vinegar

¼ teaspoon salt

9 to 10 slices ciabatta bread (or Italian bread)
1 tablespoon grated Parmesan cheese
pinch dried parsley flakes

1. Toss diced tomatoes with basil, garlic, sun-dried tomatoes, olive oil, vinegar, and salt in a medium bowl. Cover and chill 1 hour.
2. When you are ready to serve the dish, preheat oven to 450 degrees.
3. Combine Parmesan cheese with dried parsley in a small bowl. Arrange the bread slices on a baking sheet. Sprinkle a couple pinches of the Parmesan cheese mixture over each bread slice. Bake for 5 minutes or until the bread starts to crisp.
4. Pour tomato mixture into a serving dish (strain off the liquid), and serve it up alongside the toasted bread slices.

• SERVES 4.

• • • •

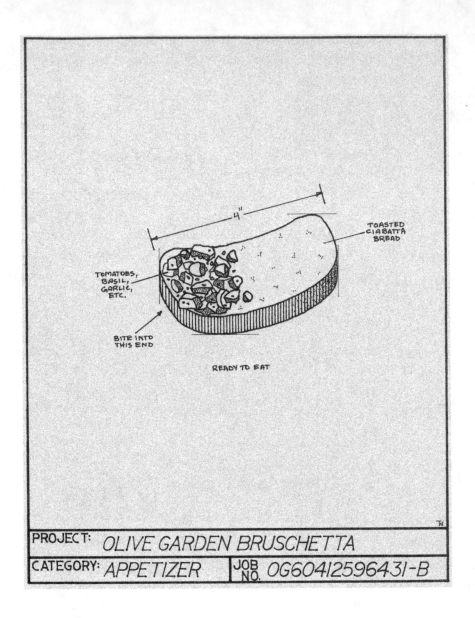

4"

TOASTED
CIABATTA
BREAD

TOMATOES,
BASIL,
GARLIC,
ETC.

BITE INTO
THIS END

READY TO EAT

TW

PROJECT:	OLIVE GARDEN BRUSCHETTA	
CATEGORY: APPETIZER	JOB NO.	OG604I2596431-B

OLIVE GARDEN
SICILIAN SCAMPI

MENU DESCRIPTION: *"Large shrimp sautéed in extra-virgin olive oil with white wine, garlic and lemon."*

Once you have the onion, garlic and parsley all chopped up, this clone of a top appetizer pick at the Garden takes only a few minutes to assemble. Cooks at Olive Garden speed up the process by using what they call "scampi butter"—chilled blocks of butter with all the spices, garlic, and onions already in it—so that each serving is prepared quickly and consistently without any tedious measuring. When the shrimp is done, each one is placed on the inside end of five toasted Italian bread slices which have been arranged on the plate in a spoke-like fashion (you can also use a French baguette with the slices cut at an extreme angle). One shrimp is also placed in the middle of the plate, and the delicious sauce is poured over the top. I've included diced roma tomato here as an optional garnish, since one Olive Garden used it, but another location on the other side of town did not. As for the shrimp, use medium-size (they're called 31/40) that are already peeled, but with the tails left on. Then all you have to do to butterfly them is make a deep cut (don't go all the way through) on the outside of the shrimp where the vein was. As the shrimp cooks, they will curl and spread open.

2 tablespoons butter
1 tablespoon olive oil
1 teaspoon minced white onion
1 teaspoon minced garlic
1 tablespoon Chablis wine
6 fresh medium shrimp, butterfly
   cut with tails on
1 teaspoon lemon juice
½ teaspoon minced fresh parsley

pinch salt
pinch ground black pepper
pinch crushed red pepper flakes
1 tablespoon heavy cream
1 tablespoon sliced canned black
   olives

5 slices Italian bread, toasted

OPTIONAL GARNISH

½ diced roma tomato
freshly grated Parmesan cheese

1. Toast the sliced Italian bread on a sheet pan in your oven set to broil, or in a toaster oven. The bread should toast for 1 to 2 minutes on each side, or until light brown. Arrange the bread slices in a spoke-like fashion on a serving plate then dance over to the stove to whip up the scampi.
2. Heat a small skillet over medium heat. Add 2 tablespoons butter and 1 tablespoon olive oil to the pan.
3. When the butter has melted add the minced onion and garlic. Make sure your heat isn't up too high or the garlic may burn, and turn brown and bitter. When the onion and garlic have sautéed for just a few seconds, add the wine to the pan.
4. Immediately add the shrimp to the pan.
5. After you add the shrimp, quickly add the lemon juice, parsley, salt, black pepper, and crushed red pepper and cook shrimp for 1 to 2 minutes, tossing occasionally.
6. After a minute or two, when the shrimp is done, add the cream and olives. Cook for 15 seconds or so, then use tongs to place one shrimp on the end of each bread slice (the ends that are in the center of the plate), and place one shrimp in the center of the plate (not on bread). Pour the sauce from the pan over the shrimp and serve the dish with a diced

roma tomato sprinkled over the top and freshly grated Parmesan cheese, if that's your thing.

- MAKES AN APPETIZER FOR TWO.

• • • •

BLACK
OLIVES

PLATE

TOASTED
BREAD

DICED
ROMA
TOMATO

SCAMPI
SAUCE

BUTTERFLY
CUT SHRIMP

TOP VIEW

PROJECT: *OLIVE GARDEN SICILIAN SCAMPI*

CATEGORY: *APPETIZER*   JOB NO. *OG39077644I-SS*

OLIVE GARDEN
STUFFED MUSHROOMS

MENU DESCRIPTION: *"Parmesan, Romano and mozzarella cheese, clams and herb breadcrumbs baked in mushroom caps."*

Breadcrumbs, clams and three types of cheese are baked into white mushroom caps in this clone of a top pick from Olive Garden's appetizer menu. Simply mix all the stuffing ingredients together in a bowl, fill the mushroom caps, sprinkle on some minced red bell pepper, cover the mushrooms with a blanket of mozzarella cheese slices, and bake. After 15 minutes you'll have a great appetizer or hors d'oeuvre for 4 to 6 people—that's twice the serving size of the dish from the restaurant.

⅓ cup Progresso breadcrumbs
   (herb flavor)
¼ cup canned minced clams
   (drain liquid)
1 tablespoon shredded Parmesan
   cheese
1 tablespoon shredded Romano
   cheese
½ teaspoon minced garlic

3 tablespoons chicken broth
12 medium white button
   mushrooms with stems
   removed
3 tablespoons butter, melted
2 tablespoons minced red bell
   pepper
2 to 3 slices mozzarella cheese
½ teaspoon minced fresh parsley

1. Preheat oven to 450 degrees.
2. Combine breadcrumbs, clams, Parmesan cheese, Romano cheese, and garlic in a medium bowl. Use your hands to mix everything together. Add the chicken broth 1 tablespoon at a time and stir after each addition with a spoon. Keep the stuffing fluffy by not over stirring.
3. Fill each of the mushroom caps with 1 to 2 teaspoons of the stuffing (depending on the size of the mushroom). Keep the filling pretty loose but make the top surface flat to support the sliced cheese. Arrange the stuffed mushrooms in a shallow baking dish with the stuffing facing up.
4. Use a brush to dab melted butter over each mushroom. Add enough so that the butter trickles down the sides of each mushroom and rests in the baking dish. Pour any leftover butter into the dish, then scoot the mushrooms next to each other.
5. Sprinkle the minced red bell pepper over the tops of the stuffed mushrooms.
6. Arrange the slices of cheese over the mushrooms. Tear the slices to cover all of the mushrooms leaving no stuffing uncovered.
7. Bake the mushrooms for 12 to 15 minutes or until the cheese is golden brown.
8. When the mushrooms come out of the oven immediately sprinkle them with ½ teaspoon of minced parsley and serve.

- SERVES 4 TO 6 AS AN APPETIZER.

•   •   •   •

STEM

BREADCRUMBS
HERBS, CHEESE,
GARLIC & BROTH

MUSHROOM
CAP

STEM OUT

STUFFING IN

MINCED RED
BELL PEPPER

MOZZARELLA
CHEESE SLICE

OVEN SAFE
BAKING
DISH

STUFFED
MUSHROOM
CAPS

READY FOR BAKING

TW

PROJECT: OLIVE GARDEN STUFFED MUSHROOMS

CATEGORY: APPETIZER   JOB NO. OG40646956-SM

215

OLIVE GARDEN
TOASTED RAVIOLI

Sold as a finger-food appetizer along with marinara dipping sauce, Olive Garden's delicious breaded ravioli can be cloned with ease using one of several varieties of pre-made raviolis carried in just about any supermarket. It's best to use the fresher raviolis found in the refrigerated section, but you can also use frozen raviolis; you just have to let them thaw first before breading them. The Toasted Ravioli at O.G. has a beefy inside, but you can use any ravioli that tickles your fancy including chicken, sausage, vegetarian, or cheese. As for the breading, find Progresso brand Italian style breadcrumbs. Contadina is another popular brand, but their version is much too salty for a good clone.

6 to 10 cups canola oil (as
    required by fryer)
1 egg, beaten
1 cup milk
1 cup Progresso Italian style
    breadcrumbs

12 pre-made beef raviolis (fresh,
    or if frozen, thawed)
1 tablespoon grated Parmesan
    cheese

ON THE SIDE
½ cup marinara sauce, warmed

1. Preheat the oil in your deep fryer to 325 degrees.
2. Combine the beaten egg with the milk in shallow bowl. Pour the breadcrumbs into another shallow bowl.
3. Bread the ravioli by dipping each one in the milk and egg, then into the breadcrumbs. Arrange the breaded ravioli on a plate and let them sit for 5 minutes so that the breading sticks like a champ.
4. When the raviolis have rested, drop a handful into the oil. Depending on the size of your fryer, you may want to fry the raviolis in batches so they aren't too crowded. Fry the breaded raviolis for 1 to 2 minutes or until they're golden brown. Remove them to a draining rack or a paper-towel lined plate.
5. When all the raviolis are cooked, arrange them on a serving plate and sprinkle 1 tablespoon of grated Parmesan cheese over the top. Serve the dish with a small bowl of warmed marinara sauce on the side for dipping.

- SERVES 3 TO 4 AS AN APPETIZER.

• • • •

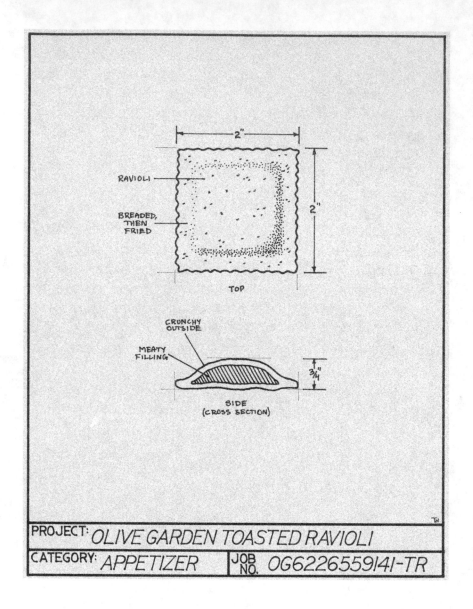

RAVIOLI

BREADED,
THEN
FRIED

2"

2"

TOP

CRUNCHY
OUTSIDE

MEATY
FILLING

3/4"

SIDE
(CROSS SECTION)

PROJECT: OLIVE GARDEN TOASTED RAVIOLI

CATEGORY: APPETIZER

JOB NO. OG6226559141-TR

OLIVE GARDEN
PASTA E FAGIOLI

MENU DESCRIPTION: *"White and red beans, ground beef, tomatoes and pasta in a savory broth."*

It's amazing how many lousy clone recipes for this delicious chili-like soup are floating around the Internet. Cooking message boards, and questionable sites that claim to have "actual restaurant recipes" have for years passed off numerous versions only to have disappointed home chefs waste ingredients. What's puzzling is they leave out major ingredients that you can clearly see in the real thing, like the carrots, or ground beef, or two kinds of beans. Others don't even get the pasta right—it's obviously ditali pasta, which are short little tubes. So, if you want the taste of Olive Garden's famous Pasta e Fagioli at home, this may be the only recipe out there that will live up to a side-by-side taste test. Beware of imitation imitations!

1 pound ground beef
1 small onion, diced (1 cup)
1 large carrot, julienned (1 cup)
3 stalks celery, chopped (1 cup)
2 cloves garlic, minced
2 14.5-ounce cans diced tomatoes
1 15-ounce can red kidney beans (with liquid)
1 15-ounce can Great Northern beans (with liquid)

1 15-ounce can tomato sauce
1 12-ounce can V-8 juice
1 tablespoon white vinegar
1 ½ teaspoons salt
1 teaspoon dried oregano
1 teaspoon dried basil
½ teaspoon ground black pepper
½ teaspoon dried thyme

½ pound (½ pkg.) ditali pasta

1. Brown the ground beef in a large saucepan or pot over medium heat. Drain off most of the fat.
2. Add onion, carrot, celery and garlic and sauté for 10 minutes.
3. Add remaining ingredients, except pasta, and simmer for 1 hour.
4. About 50 minutes into the simmering, cook the pasta in 1½ to 2 quarts of boiling water over high heat. Cook for 10 minutes or just until pasta is *al dente,* or slightly tough. Drain.
5. Add the pasta to the large pot of soup. Simmer for 5 to 10 minutes more and serve.

• SERVES 8.

•   •   •   •

OLIVE GARDEN MINESTRONE SOUP

MENU DESCRIPTION: *"Fresh vegetables, beans and pasta in a light tomato broth—a vegetarian classic."*

This classic Italian soup is jam-packed with beans, zucchini, onion, tomatoes, carrots, pasta, and spices; but O.G.'s secret formula doesn't include chicken broth. Canned vegetable broth found in the soup aisle of most markets works as a base here in this secret formula that bursts with flavor as a purely vegetarian dish.

3 tablespoons olive oil
1 cup minced white onion (about 1 small onion)
½ cup chopped zucchini
½ cup frozen cut Italian green beans
¼ cup minced celery (about ½ stalk)
4 teaspoons minced garlic (about 4 cloves)
4 cups vegetable broth (Swanson is good)
2 15-ounces cans red kidney beans, drained
2 15-ounce cans small white beans or Great

Northern beans, drained
1 14-ounce can diced tomatoes
½ cup julienned or shredded carrot
2 tablespoons minced fresh parsley
1 ½ teaspoons dried oregano
1 ½ teaspoons salt
½ teaspoon ground black pepper
½ teaspoon dried basil
¼ teaspoon dried thyme
2 bay leaves
3 cups hot water
4 cups fresh baby spinach
½ cup small seashell pasta

1. Heat olive oil over medium heat in a large saucepan or stock-pot. Sauté onion, zucchini, green beans, celery and garlic in the oil for 5 minutes or until onions begin to turn translucent.
2. Add broth to pot, plus drained beans, tomatoes, carrot, spices, bay leaves, and hot water. Bring soup to a boil, then reduce heat and simmer for 20 minutes.
3. Add spinach leaves and pasta and cook for an additional 20 minutes or until desired soupy thickness.

- MAKES ABOUT EIGHT 1½-CUP SERVINGS.

• • • •

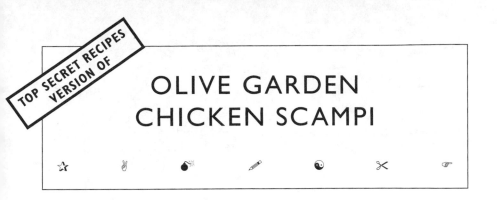

OLIVE GARDEN
CHICKEN SCAMPI

MENU DESCRIPTION: *"Chicken breast tenderloins sautéed with bell peppers, roasted garlic and onions in a garlic cream sauce over angel hair."*

This dish is a big favorite of Olive Garden regulars. Chicken tenderloins are lightly breaded and sautéed along with colorful bell peppers and chopped red onion. Angel hair pasta is tossed into the pan along with a healthy dose of fresh scampi sauce. Then it's time to ring the dinner bell. If you're cooking for two, you can prepare this dish for the table in one large skillet, saving the remaining ingredients for another meal. If you're making all four servings at once, you need two skillets. By the way, if you can't find fresh chicken tenderloins (the tender part of the chicken breast), you can usually find big bags of them in the freezer section. If that's how you buy them, you'll have plenty left over after this recipe, but they're really good to have around.

SCAMPI SAUCE

3 tablespoons butter
2 tablespoons chopped onion
¼ cup minced garlic (8 to 12 cloves)
1½ cups Chablis wine
½ teaspoon salt
½ teaspoon Italian seasoning

½ teaspoon crushed red pepper flakes
¼ teaspoon ground black pepper
2 teaspoons minced fresh parsley
1 cup heavy cream

5 to 6 quarts water
16 ounces angel hair pasta
4 tablespoons olive oil
12 chicken tenderloins
½ cup all-purpose flour
1 green bell pepper, cut into
   bite-size strips

1 red bell pepper, cut into bite-
   size strips
1 yellow bell pepper, cut into bite-
   size strips
1 chopped red onion
2 teaspoons minced fresh parsley

OPTIONAL GARNISH
freshly grated Parmesan cheese

1. Make scampi sauce by melting butter in a preheated pan over medium/low heat. Add 2 tablespoons chopped onions and sauté for 2 to 4 minutes or until the onions begin to brown. If the butter begins to burn, turn down the heat. When the onions are beginning to brown, add the minced garlic and sauté for another 30 seconds. Don't let the garlic burn. After about 30 seconds add the wine, salt, Italian seasoning, red pepper flakes, and black pepper, and bring mixture to a simmer. Simmer for approximately 15 to 18 minutes or until the sauce has reduced by half. Add parsley and heavy cream and simmer uncovered for about 10 minutes. Do not let mixture reach a boil.
2. Bring 4 quarts of water to a boil in a large pot. Add the angel hair pasta and cook for about 4 minutes or until pasta is al dente, or mostly tender with just a slight toughness. Drain the pasta in a colander or sieve when done, then hit it with some cold water to prevent sticking and to keep it from cooking further.
3. If preparing all four servings, preheat the oil in 2 large skillets over medium heat (if making just 2 servings, you'll need only one skillet and half of the total ingredients—save the rest for another meal). Lightly salt and pepper the chicken tenderloins, then coat each one in the flour that has been measured into a large bowl. Arrange all of the coated tenderloins

on a plate before sautéing 6 tenderloins in each pan. Cook the tenderloins for 3 to 5 minutes on one side or until golden brown.

4. When the chicken is brown on one side, flip each of the pieces, and move them to the side of the pans, then add an even amount of the sliced peppers and chopped onions to the center of each skillet. Continue cooking the chicken and vegetables for 4 to 6 minutes or until the chicken is browned and the veggies are beginning to brown on the edges.

5. Divide the scampi sauce in half and pour it over the chicken and other ingredients in each pan. Add 2 portions of pasta to each pan, then toss everything a bit and continue to cook for a couple minutes or until the pasta is heated through. Prepare each dish by serving equal amounts of pasta onto each of four plates. Use a spoon or tongs to add the peppers and onions on top of each pile of pasta. Arrange three chicken tenderloins onto the center of the pasta.

6. Sprinkle each plate with about ½ teaspoon of fresh parsley and serve it up with freshly grated Parmesan cheese if desired.

• MAKES 4 SERVINGS (BUT CAN BE EASILY DIVIDED INTO 2 SEPARATE SERVINGS FOR 2).

• • • •

OLIVE GARDEN
CHOCOLATE LASAGNA

MENU DESCRIPTION: *"Layers of rich chocolate cake and sweet buttercream icing."*

To simplify this clone recipe, we'll start with a box of cake mix,
and tweak it a bit to add a little cherry flavor. The buttercream
frosting spread between the three layers of the "lasagna" is a
breeze to make from scratch. The real secret to this *Top Secret
Recipe* is how we put it all together. You've got to make two slices
through the edge of the baked cake to create the three thin
layers, so grab a long serrated knife. Lay down some wax paper
under the cake to help you turn the cake while you slice. Slide the
whole thing over near the edge of the counter so that you can
keep the knife parallel to the countertop, and you should have no
trouble at all. Another technique is to drag a long piece of dental
floss through the cake twice. The floss will glide right through the
cake with ease, giving you two clean slices. You can use your favorite chocolate cake mix for the recipe, but be sure not to use
one with pudding in it or one that is "extra moist." (Duncan Hines
Moist Deluxe is one such brand.) These mixes make slicing and
layering difficult because the baked cake falls apart so easily.

1 18.25-ounce box dark
   chocolate or chocolate fudge
   cake mix (not too moist)
1 ¼ cups water

⅓ cup vegetable oil
3 eggs
2 teaspoons cherry extract
vegetable shortening

BUTTERCREAM FROSTING

1 ½ cups butter, softened
   (3 sticks)
4 cups powdered sugar
¼ cup milk

½ teaspoon vanilla extract

4 ounces semi-sweet chocolate,
   chilled

1. Make the cake in a 13x9-inch baking pan following instructions on the box of cake mix, but add cherry extract to the mix (Preheat oven to 350 degrees; mix cake mix, water, oil, and eggs together in a large bowl; pour batter into pan greased generously with shortening.). Allow the cake to cool completely.
2. When cake is cool, make buttercream frosting by first whipping the soft butter in a large bowl with an electric mixer on high speed. Add two cups of the powdered sugar, mix well, then add remaining powdered sugar. Add ¼ cup of whole milk and vanilla, then mix on high speed for 2 minutes or until frosting is smooth and creamy.
3. Turn cake out of the pan onto wax paper. Using both hands, carefully flip the cake over, so that it's right side up, onto another strip of wax paper. Now you're going to cut through the cake twice, creating three layers. We'll start at the bottom slice. First slide the cake over to the edge of your kitchen counter. This way you can drop your hand with the knife down below the counter at the edge to get a nice, straight cut through the cake. Using a long bread knife or other long serrated knife, cut through the bottom third of the cake. Spin the cake and wax paper so that you can cut through all sides (your knife probably won't get all the way through to the other side). When the cake is sliced, carefully flip the top section over onto the other sheet of wax paper. Frost the bottom layer of cake with approximately ⅓ of the buttercream frosting. Break the chilled semi-sweet chocolate into little bits that are a tad smaller than chocolate chips. A good way to do this is to put the chilled chocolate into a large zip-top bag, then use the handle of a butter knife to

smash the unsuspecting chocolate into pieces. Sprinkle about ⅓ of the chocolate bits over the frosting on the bottom layer.

4. Turn the top section back over onto the bottom layer. Again, slice through the top section creating the final two layers. Carefully flip the top over onto the wax paper, and frost the new layer as you did with the first layer, adding chocolate bits as well. You may, at this point, wish to slice the top into thirds across the width of the cake. This makes flipping over the top layer much easier. It's also how you're going to slice the cake later, so you'll never see the cuts. Any cracks or breaks are no big deal since you'll just cover up the goofs with frosting.

5. Carefully reassemble the top section on the rest of the cake. If you have a large bulge in the center of the cake, you may wish to slice that off so that the cake is flatter on top. Throw that slice away. Frost the top of the cake with the remaining frosting, then sprinkle on the remaining chocolate bits.

6. The cake is served as triangular slices. So, slice it up by first cutting through the middle of the cake, lengthwise. Next cut across the cake through the middle (widthwise) twice. Now you have six slices that just need to be cut from corner to corner one time each, creating 12 triangular slices. Chill any cake you don't eat that day.

- MAKES 12 SERVINGS.

• • • •

CAN SLICE CAKE INTO LAYERS WITH DENTAL FLOSS

12¾"

8½"

LAYER THE CAKE
(WITH FROSTING BETWEEN THE LAYERS)

SLICE HERE

SPRINKLE SEMI-SWEET CHOCOLATE BITS ON TOP

THREE CHOCOLATEY LAYERS

BUTTER-CREAM FROSTING

FROSTED, READY FOR SLICING

5"

2"

CHOPPED SEMI-SWEET CHOCOLATE

4¼"

4¼"

ONE DELICIOUS SLICE

PROJECT: *OLIVE GARDEN CHOCOLATE LASAGNA*

CATEGORY: *DESSERT*

JOB NO. *OG541465277-CL*

OLIVE GARDEN
TIRAMISU

MENU DESCRIPTION: *"The classic Italian dessert. A layer of creamy custard set atop espresso-soaked ladyfingers."*

In Italian, tiramisu means "pick me up" or "cheer me up." And when you taste the delicious combination of mascarpone cheese (sometimes referred to as Italian cream cheese), cream cheese, ladyfingers, espresso and Kahlua it will be hard not to smile. Olive Garden's tiramisu is very dense, which sets it apart from most tiramisu recipes that require the cheese mixture to be folded into whipped cream. This technique, however, makes a tiramisu that is too fluffy and light to be a decent clone. Besides, the whipped cream hides the cheese flavors, and that's just not a good way to make this tiramisu. So get out your double boiler for the egg yolks (a metal bowl over a saucepan of simmering water will also do) and snag some ladyfingers (ladyfingers are miniature cakes about the size of two fingers side-by-side). You can either make your own espresso, use extra strong coffee as a substitute, or, next time you're at Starbucks, order up a quadruple shot of espresso to go.

4 egg yolks	1 cup heavy cream
2 tablespoons milk	20 to 24 ladyfingers
⅔ cup granulated sugar	½ cup cold espresso
2 cups mascarpone cheese	¼ cup Kahlua coffee liqueur
¼ teaspoon vanilla extract	2 teaspoons cocoa powder

1. Fill a medium saucepan halfway with water and bring it to a boil over medium/high heat, then reduce the heat so that the water is simmering. Whisk egg yolks, milk and sugar together in a medium metal bowl, then place the bowl on top of the saucepan (you can also use a double boiler for this step). Stir the mixture often for 8 to 10 minutes or until the mixtures thickens. Remove the bowl from the heat, and to it add the 2 cups of mascarpone cheese and the vanilla. Get in there and whisk the cheese like the dickens until it smoothes out.
2. In a separate bowl, whip the cream with an electric mixer until thick.
3. Slowly fold the whipped cream into the mascarpone mixture until it's completely incorporated, but don't over mix or that goodness could lose its fluff and flatten out on you.
4. Combine the espresso and Kahlua in a large, shallow bowl. One-by-one, quickly dip each ladyfinger in the espresso. The ladyfinger will soak up the espresso/Kahlua mixture like a sponge, so dip quickly. Arrange half of the dipped ladyfingers side-by-side on the bottom of an 8x8-inch serving dish or baking pan.
5. Spoon about half of the cheese mixture over the ladyfingers, then add another layer of soaked ladyfingers on top of the cheese mixture.
6. Spoon the remaining cheese mixture over the second layer of ladyfingers and spread it evenly.
7. Put two teaspoons of cocoa powder in a tight-mesh strainer and gently tap the side of the strainer to add an even dusting of cocoa powder over the top of the dessert.
8. Cover and chill for several hours. To serve, slice the dessert twice across and down creating 9 even portions. And don't worry about how that first serving looks—it's always the hardest to get out.

• MAKES 9 SERVINGS.

• • • •

SIFTED COCOA POWDER

MASCARPONE CHEESE MIXTURE

SOAKED LADY FINGERS

1¾"

2⅝"

2⅝"

ONE SLICE

CREAMY

CAKEY

1¾"

SIDE

SLICE HERE

8"

2"

CHILL BEFORE SLICING

PROJECT:	OLIVE GARDEN TIRAMISU	
CATEGORY: DESSERT	JOB NO.	OG4166321675-T

232

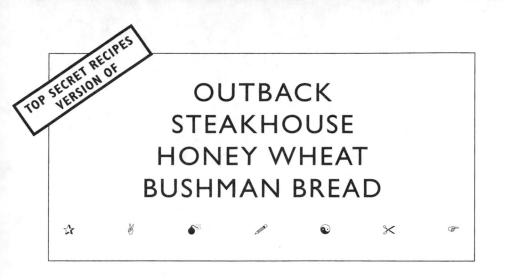

OUTBACK
STEAKHOUSE
HONEY WHEAT
BUSHMAN BREAD

Along with your meal at this huge national steakhouse chain, comes a freshly baked loaf of dark, sweet bread, served on its own cutting board with soft whipped butter. One distinctive feature of the bread is its color. How does the bread get so dark? Even though this recipe includes molasses and cocoa, these ingredients alone will not give the bread its dark chocolate brown color. Usually commercially produced breads that are this dark—such as pumpernickel or dark bran muffins—contain caramel color, an ingredient often used in the industry to darken foods. Since your local supermarket will not likely have this mostly commercial ingredient, we'll create the brown coloring from a mixture of three food colorings—red, yellow and blue. If you decide to leave the color out, just add an additional 1 tablespoon of warm water to the recipe. If you have a bread machine, you can use it for kneading the bread (you'll find the order in which to add the ingredients to your machine in Tidbits). Then, to finish the bread, divide and roll the dough in cornmeal, and bake on a sheet pan in your home oven.

DOUGH

1¼ cups warm water

2 teaspoons granulated sugar

2¼ teaspoons (1 pkg.) yeast

2 cups bread flour

1¾ cups whole wheat flour

1 tablespoon cocoa

1 teaspoon salt

2 tablespoons butter, softened

¼ cup honey

2 tablespoons molasses

COLORING

1¼ teaspoons red food coloring

1 teaspoon yellow food
   coloring

1 teaspoon blue food coloring

cornmeal for dusting

1. Mix sugar with warm water, then dissolve the yeast in the solution. In five minutes the solution will begin to foam as the
   yeast begins its gassy dance party.
2. While the yeast is waking up, mix the flours, cocoa, and
   salt in a large bowl. Mix butter into the dry mixture with
   your hands. Make an impression in the middle of the dry
   mixture. Add the honey and molasses into the well. Mix
   the food coloring with the yeast solution, then pour the
   solution into the well. Stir from the middle bringing the dry
   mixture into the wet stuff, slowly at first, then quickly as
   you incorporate all the ingredients. You will eventually
   have to use your hands to combine everything. Knead the
   dough for 10 minutes on a lightly floured surface, then roll
   the dough into a ball and place it into a covered bowl in a
   warm place for 1 to 1½ hours or until it has doubled in size.
3. When the dough has doubled, separate it into 6 even portions. Roll each dough portion into logs that are 6 inches
   long and 2 inches wide. Pour cornmeal onto your rolling surface. Moisten your hands then rub water onto each dough
   log and roll it in the cornmeal. Arrange the rolled dough on a
   baking sheet and cover it with plastic wrap. Set the dough in
   a warm spot to rise for another hour or so until the loaves
   have doubled in size.

4. Preheat the oven to 350 degrees. Uncover the dough and bake it for 35 to 40 minutes in the hot oven. When the bread is done, take it out of the oven and let it cool for 10 to 15 minutes. Serve the bread with a sharp bread knife and butter on the side. If you want whipped butter, like you get at the restaurant, just use an electric mixer on high speed to whip some butter until it's fluffy.

- MAKES 6 SMALL LOAVES.

TIDBITS

If you'd like to use a bread machine to knead the dough, just add the ingredients in the following order: Mix the food coloring with the water, then add the colored water to the bread pan followed by the flours, sugar, salt, butter, cocoa, honey, molasses, and yeast. Set the machine to knead and walk away. When the dough's done kneading and rising, go to step #3 of this recipe and take it from there.

• • • •

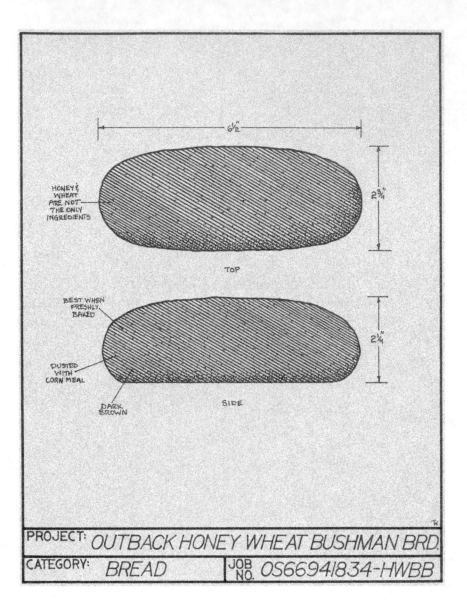

6½"

HONEY &
WHEAT
ARE NOT
THE ONLY
INGREDIENTS

2¾"

TOP

BEST WHEN
FRESHLY
BAKED

2¼"

DUSTED
WITH
CORN MEAL

DARK
BROWN

SIDE

PROJECT: *OUTBACK HONEY WHEAT BUSHMAN BRD.*

CATEGORY: *BREAD*

JOB NO. *OS66941834-HWBB*

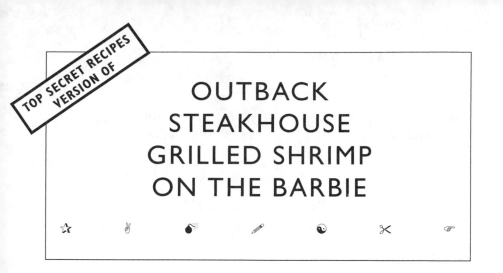

OUTBACK STEAKHOUSE GRILLED SHRIMP ON THE BARBIE

MENU DESCRIPTION: *"Seasoned and served with Outback's own Remoulade sauce."*

This recipe makes the same size appetizer serving that you get in the restaurant. That's only 6 shrimp—enough for me, but what are you guys having? Thank goodness the remoulade sauce and the shrimp seasoning formulas yield enough for more, so you can grill up to a pound of shrimp with this cool clone. You can often find bags of frozen shrimp that have been peeled, but with the tails left on. Those are perfect for this recipe.

REMOULADE SAUCE

¾ cup mayonnaise
5 teaspoons stone ground
    mustard
4 teaspoons milk
2 teaspoons minced celery
2 teaspoons minced green pepper

2 teaspoons minced onion
2 teaspoons sauerkraut
1 teaspoon white vinegar
½ teaspoon paprika
⅛ teaspoon ground black pepper
minced fresh parsley

SHRIMP SEASONING

½ teaspoon salt
¼ teaspoon garlic powder
¼ teaspoon onion powder
¼ teaspoon ground black
    pepper

¼ teaspoon chili powder
¼ teaspoon granulated
    sugar
⅛ teaspoon cayenne pepper
dash ground allspice

6 large shrimp (21 to 25 per
    pound), thawed if frozen
fresh lemon juice

1 tablespoon butter, melted
minced fresh parsley

1. Preheat your grill to high heat.
2. Make the remoulade sauce by mixing the ingredients to-gether in a small bowl. Cover and chill this sauce until you are ready to use it.
3. Prepare the shrimp seasoning by mixing the spices together in a small bowl.
4. Remove the shell from the shrimp. Keep the last segment of the shell and the tail. Remove the black vein that runs down the back of the shrimp. Stick a skewer through the middle of each shrimp. Push them together on the skewer so that they are "spooning" each other.
5. Squeeze some fresh lemon juice over the cuddling shrimp.
6. Brush melted butter generously over the top of the shrimp.
7. Sprinkle a bit of the seasoning on next. Don't use a heavy coating of seasoning
8. Place the shrimp onto your hot grill with the seasoning side down. Brush some more butter over the other side of the shrimp followed by another light sprinkle of seasoning.
9. After 3 minutes or so the face-down side of the shrimp should be browned and showing some light charring. Flip the shrimp over and grill for an additional 2 to 3 minutes or until browned on the other side.
10. Remove the shrimp from the grill and slide them off the

skewer onto a slice of garlic butter coated bread (see Tidbits). Sprinkle with a pinch of fresh parsley.

- MAKES 1 TO 2 SERVINGS.

TIDBITS

It is best to use a clone for the Bushman Bread (on page 233) as a bed for your shrimp. Just slice an inch-thick piece off through the middle of the bread. This will give you a slice that is about 8 inches long and 2 to 3 inches wide. Crush a clove of garlic and mix it with your leftover melted butter. Brush this garlic butter on both sides of the bread and toast it until lightly brown. If you don't feel up to making the bread, you can use any bread you might have around that is in the shape of a hoagie roll. Or you may just wish to serve the shrimp on its own without the bread bed.

•   •   •   •

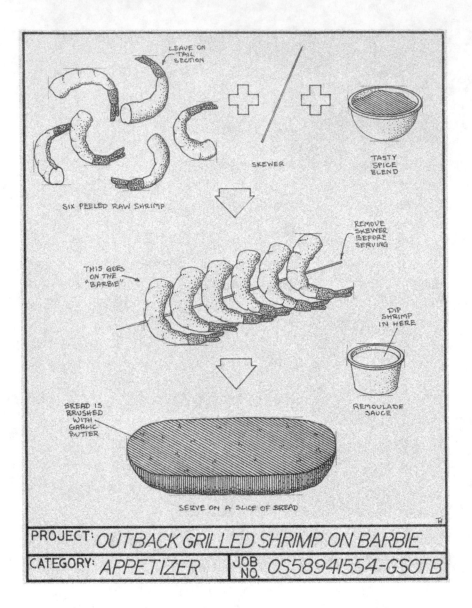

LEAVE ON TAIL SECTION

SIX PEELED RAW SHRIMP

SKEWER

TASTY SPICE BLEND

THIS GOES ON THE "BARBIE"

REMOVE SKEWER BEFORE SERVING

DIP SHRIMP IN HERE

REMOULADE SAUCE

BREAD IS BRUSHED WITH GARLIC BUTTER

SERVE ON A SLICE OF BREAD

PROJECT: *OUTBACK GRILLED SHRIMP ON BARBIE*

CATEGORY: *APPETIZER*   **JOB NO.** *OS58941554-GSOTB*

240

OUTBACK
STEAKHOUSE
KOOKABURRA WINGS

☆　✌　💣　✏　☯　✂　☞

MENU DESCRIPTION: *"Known as Buffalo chicken wings here in the States."*

No, Outback Steakhouse is not the country's largest importer of Australian woodland kingfisher wings. Despite the name, these tasty wings don't come from the wild birds also known as kookaburras. Instead, this appetizer is made the old fashioned way—with good ol' American chickens. And as with the traditional recipe, these wings are coated with Louisiana hot sauce; but it's the breading that makes them unique. This clone recipe uses a secret blend of powdered cheese sprinkles and spices. Kraft powdered cheese can be found near the Kraft Parmesan cheese or near the macaroni and cheese kits in your supermarket. If you can't track it down, use Molly McButter cheese sprinkles. If you can't find that, get a box of macaroni and cheese (it's cheap) and use the cheese from inside there. Keep the leftover macaroni noodles for a pasta recipe later.

10 chicken wing drumettes (see Tidbits)

6 to 10 cups vegetable shortening or oil (amount required by your fryer)

WING COATING

2 tablespoons all-purpose flour

1 tablespoon Kraft Macaroni &
    Cheese cheddar cheese
    topping (or Molly McButter
    cheese sprinkles)

1 ¼ teaspoons salt

1 teaspoon chili powder

¾ teaspoon ground black pepper

½ teaspoon cayenne pepper

¼ teaspoon paprika

¼ teaspoon onion powder

¼ teaspoon garlic powder

⅛ teaspoon ground cumin

dash ground cloves

2 tablespoons Crystal brand
    Louisiana hot sauce

1 teaspoon water

ON THE SIDE

bleu cheese dressing

celery sticks

1. Preheat shortening (you may also use vegetable or canola oil) to 375 degrees.
2. Make the spiced breading for your wings by combining the wing coating ingredients (flour through cloves) in a medium bowl. Stir well.
3. Dip each wing, one at a time into the breading. Give each one a light coating of the stuff. Arrange the breaded wings on a plate and let them sit uncovered in the refrigerator for about 15 minutes.
4. When the shortening or oil is hot, lower the wings into it. Fry for 7 to 10 minutes, or until the wings are brown.
5. While the wings are frying, mix the hot sauce and water together in a small bowl.
6. When the wings are done, drain them for a moment on paper towels or a rack. Drop the hot wings into a large plastic container with a lid. Pour the sauce over the wings. Cover the container and gently shake it to coat the wings with sauce.

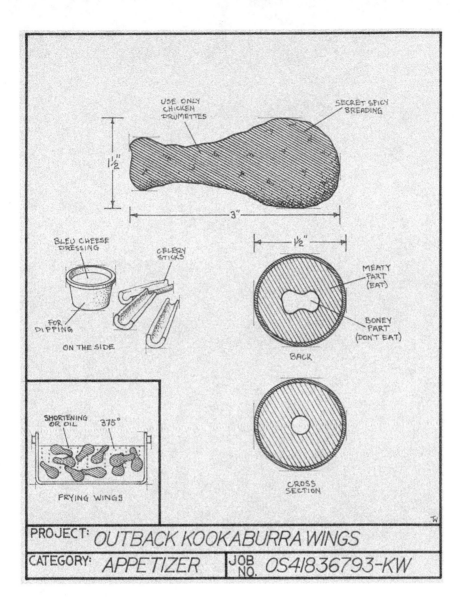

USE ONLY
CHICKEN
DRUMETTES

SECRET SPICY
BREADING

1½"

3"

BLEU CHEESE
DRESSING

CELERY
STICKS

FOR
DIPPING

ON THE SIDE

1½"

MEATY
PART
(EAT)

BONEY
PART
(DON'T EAT)

BACK

SHORTENING
OR OIL

375°

FRYING WINGS

CROSS
SECTION

PROJECT: *OUTBACK KOOKABURRA WINGS*

CATEGORY: *APPETIZER*   **JOB NO.** *OS41836793-KW*

7. Use tongs to remove the wings from the container. Arrange them on a plate with bleu cheese dressing and celery sticks on the side.

- MAKES 2 TO 3 SERVINGS AS AN APPETIZER.

TIDBITS

There are two types of frozen chicken wings out there—the giant party wings that come with a couple dozen pieces per bag, and the smaller wings with nearly twice the number per bag. These smaller wings are what the restaurant uses and what you should use for this recipe. Because of the size of the bigger wings, they just don't fry up as well.

Also, you should know that most restaurants use shortening for frying. That's what I suggest you use if you want your wings closer to the real thing.

• • • •

OUTBACK STEAKHOUSE BLEU CHEESE DRESSING

If you've had the Kookaburra Wings from Outback, then you've tasted the chain's thick and creamy bleu cheese dressing served up on the side. Use this stuff when you need an excellent dipping sauce for your next batch of wings, or just pour it over a salad and dive in.

1 cup mayonnaise
2 tablespoons buttermilk
1 tablespoon crumbled bleu
   cheese
⅛ teaspoon coarse ground black
   pepper
⅛ teaspoon onion powder

⅛ teaspoon garlic powder

1. Mix all ingredients together by hand in a small bowl until smooth.
2. Cover and chill for 30 minutes before serving.

• MAKES 1 CUP.

• • • •

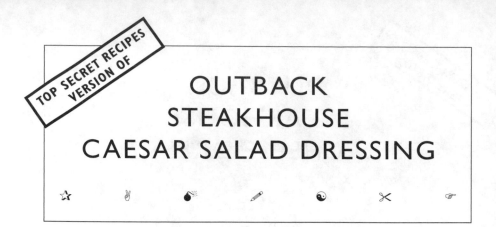

OUTBACK STEAKHOUSE CAESAR SALAD DRESSING

You can't buy it in the stores, but now you can make it from scratch in mere minutes. Best of all, this dressing keeps for a couple weeks in the fridge in a covered container... if it's even around that long.

1 cup mayonnaise
¼ cup egg substitute
¼ cup grated Parmesan cheese
2 tablespoons water
2 tablespoons olive oil
1 ½ tablespoons lemon juice
1 tablespoon anchovy paste

2 cloves garlic, pressed
2 teaspoons granulated sugar
½ teaspoon coarse ground
   pepper
¼ teaspoon salt
¼ teaspoon dried parsley flakes,
   crushed fine

1. Combine all ingredients in a medium bowl. Use an electric mixer to beat ingredients for about 30 seconds.
2. Cover bowl and chill for several hours so that flavors can develop.

• MAKES APPROXIMATELY 2 CUPS.

• • • •

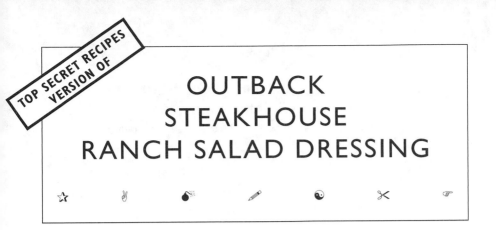

OUTBACK STEAKHOUSE RANCH SALAD DRESSING

This always-popular growing restaurant chain makes a tasty version of creamy ranch dressing for its house and Queensland salads. To get the same unique flavor and creaminess of the original at home, mates, you'll need one teaspoon of Hidden Valley Ranch instant salad dressing mix swimming in there with the mayo and buttermilk and other spices. Since there's three teaspoons of dressing mix per packet, you'll now be able to make three batches of dressing with one envelope of dressing mix.

1 teaspoon Hidden Valley Ranch
    salad dressing mix (Buttermilk
    Recipe)
1 cup mayonnaise
½ cup buttermilk

¼ teaspoon coarse grind black
    pepper
⅛ teaspoon paprika
⅛ teaspoon garlic powder

1. Combine all ingredients in a medium bowl. Mix well.
2. Cover bowl and chill dressing for at least 30 minutes before serving.

• MAKES 1½ CUPS.

TIDBITS

Make sure you are using the Hidden Valley Ranch dressing mix that says "Buttermilk Recipe." It's the one that comes in 0.4 ounce packets. Any other mix won't work as well for this clone.

•　•　•　•

OUTBACK STEAKHOUSE TANGY TOMATO DRESSING

So many folks expressed interest in a knockoff of this dressing, that I couldn't put it off any longer. Suited up in protective gear and tricked out with safety goggles, I set out to tackle the tangy beast. Now, fresh out of the underground laboratory, comes this simple formula for recreating Outback's popular sour/sweet salad topper in your own cozy kitchen. Mix it together, heat it up, cool it down, and store it in the fridge until salad time.

½ cup plus 1 tablespoon ketchup
⅓ cup water
¼ cup granulated sugar
¼ cup white vinegar
2 tablespoons olive oil
¼ teaspoon paprika

¼ teaspoon coarse grind black pepper
¼ teaspoon garlic powder
¼ teaspoon cayenne pepper
⅛ teaspoon onion powder
pinch dried thyme

Combine all ingredients in a small saucepan over medium heat. Bring to a boil, whisking often, then reduce heat and simmer, uncovered, for 5 minutes. Cover the dressing until cool, then pop it in the refrigerator to chill out.

• MAKES 1 CUP.

• • • •

OUTBACK STEAKHOUSE CINNAMON APPLE OBLIVION

MENU DESCRIPTION: *"Vanilla ice cream covered in cinnamon apples and pecans topped with caramel sauce."*

Roll a scoop of creamy vanilla ice cream in homemade candied pecans. Surround the ice cream with warm cinnamon apples and drizzle caramel over the top. Sprinkle fresh cinnamon-butter croutons on the dessert and you've got an irresistible clone that will make your diet cry "uncle!" For the croutons, the restaurant uses leftover Honey Wheat Bushman Bread (clone on page 233). But if you don't have plans to make that one you can use any sweet bread from the store, such as Hawaiian Sweet Bread or Pillsbury Honey White Bread.

CANDIED PECANS

½ cup granulated sugar

2 tablespoons water

½ teaspoon cinnamon

1 teaspoon butter

1 ¼ cups chopped pecans

CINNAMON CROUTONS

2 cups cubed Bushman Bread
 (or any sweet bread)

⅓ cup salted butter (⅔ stick)

2 tablespoons granulated sugar

½ teaspoon ground cinnamon

CINNAMON APPLES

1 20-ounce can apple pie filling
¼ teaspoon ground cinnamon
1 tablespoon brown sugar
1 quart vanilla ice cream

½ cup caramel topping
   (Smucker's is good)
1 ½ cups whipped cream
4 fresh strawberries

1. For candied pecans, combine ½ cup granulated sugar, 2 tablespoons water, 1 teaspoon butter, and ½ teaspoon cinnamon in a small saucepan over medium heat. Heat until mixture boils and all sugar granules are dissolved.

2. Add chopped pecans to mixture and stir for 1 to 2 minutes over heat. Be sure that all pecans are well-coated.

3. Pour mixture onto a large plate and continue to stir until mixture hardens and begins to break up. You should be able to separate all of the nuts.

4. For the croutons, preheat the oven to 300 degrees. Pour the slice bread cubes onto an ungreased cookie sheet and bake for 15 to 20 minutes or until the bread has turned light brown. Stir halfway through cooking time.

5. Melt the butter in a skillet over medium heat. Pour baked croutons into the pan and sauté until the bread is coated with butter. Combine the 2 tablespoons of sugar and ½ teaspoon of cinnamon in a small bowl. Sprinkle this mixture over the croutons while stirring so that the croutons are coated with cinnamon/sugar. Remove croutons from the heat and pour them onto a plate to cool.

6. Prepare apples by carefully mixing them with ¼ teaspoon cinnamon and 1 tablespoon of brown sugar in a large bowl. You want to be sure you don't stir hard enough to break up the apples. Microwave the apples for 1 to 2 minutes or until hot.

7. To assemble the dessert, first roll four cup-size scoops of ice cream in the pecan pieces. You can do this step ahead of time if you like, keeping the pecan-covered scoops in your freezer.

8. Place an ice cream scoop onto a small plate, then pour about

a tablespoon of caramel over the ice cream. Dribble another tablespoon around the base of the ice cream onto the plate.

9. Spread the hot apples around the base of the ice cream being sure to divide them evenly amongst the four servings.

10. Divide the croutons into four portions and sprinkle them on the apples around the base of the ice cream scoop on each plate.

11. Spread a generous portion of whipped cream onto the top of each scoop of ice cream.

12. Top off each dish with a fresh strawberry.

- MAKES 4 SERVINGS.

•   •   •   •

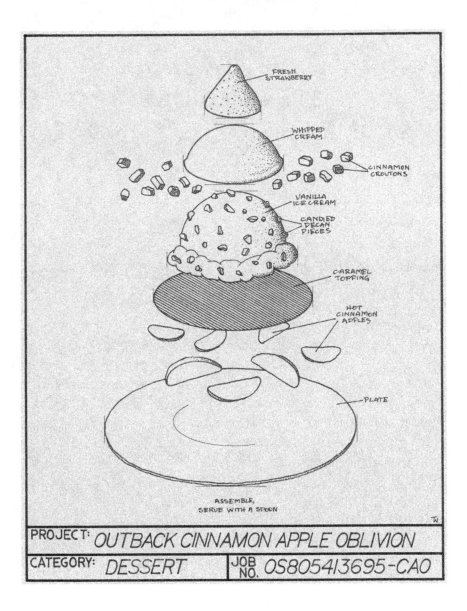

FRESH
STRAWBERRY

WHIPPED
CREAM

CINNAMON
CROUTONS

VANILLA
ICE CREAM

CANDIED
PECAN
PIECES

CARAMEL
TOPPING

HOT
CINNAMON
APPLES

PLATE

ASSEMBLE,
SERVE WITH A SPOON

PROJECT:	OUTBACK CINNAMON APPLE OBLIVION	
CATEGORY: DESSERT	JOB NO.	OS805413695-CAO

OUTBACK STEAKHOUSE SYDNEY'S SINFUL SUNDAE

MENU DESCRIPTION: *"Vanilla ice cream rolled in toasted coconut, covered in chocolate sauce and topped with whipped cream."*

Here's an easy-to-make dessert that will give you a cool way to use the vanilla ice cream that's calling to you from the freezer. The key to this recipe is to plan ahead just a bit by placing your serving plates into the freezer (give 'em at least 30 minutes). While the plates are chilling out, you toast some coconut flakes in the oven. After that, it's all about the presentation. You can top your master-piece with canned whipped cream or make your own from the simple recipe included here.

WHIPPED CREAM

1 cup heavy whipping cream	½ teaspoon vanilla extract
3 tablespoons granulated sugar	pinch salt

1 cup shredded coconut	1 cup fudge topping
4 large scoops vanilla ice cream	8 large, ripe strawberries

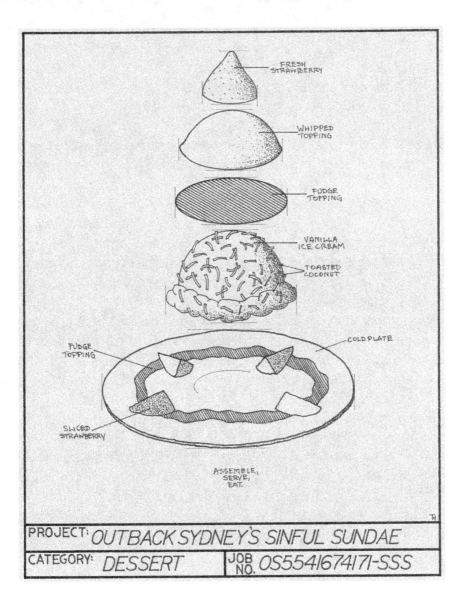

FRESH STRAWBERRY

WHIPPED TOPPING

FUDGE TOPPING

VANILLA ICE CREAM

TOASTED COCONUT

COLD PLATE

FUDGE TOPPING

SLICED STRAWBERRY

ASSEMBLE, SERVE, EAT.

PROJECT: *OUTBACK SYDNEY'S SINFUL SUNDAE*

CATEGORY: *DESSERT*   JOB NO. *OS554I674I7I-SSS*

1. Put four dinner plates into the freezer.
2. Make whipped cream by combining cream with sugar, vanilla and salt with an electric mixer on high speed. It helps if the bowl has been chilled ahead of time. When cream makes stiff peaks, cover and chill until you need it.
3. Preheat the oven to 300 degrees.
4. Spread the coconut over the bottom of the inside of a large oven pan. Shake the pan a little to spread the coconut evenly.
5. Bake the coconut for 25 to 30 minutes or until the coconut is a light, golden brown. You may have to stir or shake the coconut in the last 10 minutes to help it brown evenly. Allow the coconut to cool on a plate or in a large bowl.
6. Heat up the fudge topping for 15 to 20 seconds in the microwave. Get the plates out of the freezer and make a circle of fudge on each of the plates.
7. Roll each scoop of ice cream in the coconut until it is well coated. Press down on the ice cream to help the coconut stick. Place a coconut-covered scoop of ice cream onto the center of the plate, then spoon about 2 tablespoons of fudge over the top of the ice cream.
8. Use an ice cream scoop to scoop a large portion of whipped cream and stack it on each of the scoops of ice cream.
9. Cut the stems from the strawberries. Cut four of the strawberries lengthwise into quarters. Position the sliced strawberries around the base of each scoop of ice cream on the ring of fudge. Place a whole strawberry onto the whipped cream on the top of each dessert. Serve with a spoon and a smile.

- MAKES 4 SERVINGS.

• • • •

P. F. CHANG'S MAI TAI

MENU DESCRIPTION: *"It's our signature recipe."*

Bring the tropical spirit of this drink to your house with a clone of this potent cocktail from the growing Chinese bistro chain. Mai tai is Tahitian for "out of this world," and P. F. Chang's recipe is one of the best and most authentic. The secret to a true mai tai is found in the original recipe developed by Trader Vic in 1944: It's almond-flavored syrup, called "orgeat." You can find the sweet stuff in stores that sell coffee flavorings (Torani is one very popular brand), or from bar supply outlets. Not only can you use the *orgeat* for making the best cocktails on the planet, but you can also use the syrup to wake up your next cup of java. If you can't find orgeat, there's a clone recipe included in tidbits.

1 ½ ounces Bacardi light rum
¾ ounce triple sec
¾ ounce orgeat syrup
3 ounces orange juice

3 ounces pineapple juice
splash Bacardi 151 rum
splash dark rum

GARNISH
pineapple wedge
maraschino cherry

1. Fill a 16-ounce glass with ice.
2. Add the light rum, triple sec, orgeat, orange juice, and pineapple juice; then give the drink a quick stir.
3. Splash the 151 and dark rum on top. Do not stir.
4. Make a small cut in the pineapple wedge, then stick a toothpick into the pineapple wedge on the opposite edge. Pierce a maraschino cherry onto the toothpick. Slip the pineapple slice onto the rim of the glass (into the cut that you made). Add a straw, and serve.

• MAKES 1 DRINK.

TIDBITS

You can maker a pretty close version of orgeat syrup from scratch by dissolving ½ cup granulated sugar in ½ cup boiling water. Add ½ teaspoon of almond extract and ¼ teaspoon coconut extract. Cool before using, then measure as you would the real thing.

• • • •

P. F. CHANG'S
CHANG'S SPARE RIBS

MENU DESCRIPTION: *"Wok-seared with Chang's barbecue sauce."*

One of the most popular eats on P. F. Chang's kickin' appetizer menu are the spare ribs that arrive slathered with Asian-style barbecue sauce. The Asian flavor comes from the addition of sweet hoisin sauce to a fairly rudimentary barbecue sauce formula. Chang's menu says these ribs are spare ribs although they appear to be much smaller, more like baby backs. You can certainly use either for this recipe, just be sure to trim the ribs first, since the restaurant version is lean, clean ribs with no extra meat or fat hanging off. There are several ways to cook pork ribs—P. F. Chang's likes to boil theirs first then move on to a quick deep fry. After that, the ribs are tossed with the sauce in wok and served piping hot. A serving of these ribs at the restaurant is 6 individual ribs, but since a full rack is as many as 12 ribs, this recipe will make twice what you get in a serving at the bustling bistro.

SAUCE

1 cup ketchup	1 tablespoon rice vinegar
1 cup light corn syrup	
½ cup hoisin sauce	1 rack pork spare ribs
½ cup water	4 cups vegetable oil
⅓ cup light brown sugar, packed	1 teaspoon sesame seeds
2 tablespoons minced onion	1 tablespoon diced green onion

1. Make the sauce by combining ingredients in a medium saucepan over medium heat. Bring mixture to a boil, then reduce heat and simmer for 5 minutes, until thick. Cool.
2. To cook the ribs the P. F. Chang's way, you will need to first boil them in water. Heat up 12 to 16 cups of water in a large saucepan or Dutch oven. Add a couple teaspoons of salt to the water. As water boils, trim the excess fat and meat off the ribs. Slice between the bones of each rib to separate the ribs. When the water is boiling, toss the ribs in, bring the water back to a boil and boil the ribs for 12 to 14 minutes. No pink will show when they are done. Remove ribs to a plate to cool.
3. When the ribs have cooled you can either store them in an airtight bag in the refrigerator until you are ready for the final cooking step, or you can move on to that step now by heating up 4 cups of vegetable oil in a large saucepan over medium heat. The oil should be about 375 degrees. You can also use a deep fryer for this step, but your fryer will likely require more oil.
4. When the oil is hot, drop 4 to 6 ribs at a time into the oil. Fry for 2 to 4 minutes or until the meat browns. Drain off the ribs on a rack or paper towels. Fry all the ribs before moving on to the next step.
5. Heat a wok or large skillet over medium heat. When the pan is hot, toss in all the ribs and coat with the sauce. Simmer the ribs in the sauce for about a minute while stirring and dump the ribs onto a serving plate when they are all coated with sauce.
6. Sprinkle the ribs with sesame seeds and about a tablespoon of diced green onion, and serve with a pile of napkins.

- SERVES 2 TO 4 AS AN APPETIZER.

• • • •

4"

1"

PORK
SPARE RIB

BONE
(DO NOT EAT)

TOP

MEAT
(EAT)

COOK IT,
THEN SAUCE IT

SIDE

HOISIN BARBECUE
SAUCE

TW

PROJECT: *P.F. CHANG'S CHANG'S SPARE RIBS*

CATEGORY: *APPETIZER*   **JOB NO.** *PFC411368945-CSR*

P. F. CHANG'S CHICKEN IN SOOTHING LETTUCE WRAPS

MENU DESCRIPTION: *"Quickly-cooked spiced chicken served with cool lettuce cups."*

Throw in a few initials with a little twist on the last part, and you have the name of Paul Fleming and Philip Chiang's Chinese bistro creation, P. F. Chang's. Since the first location opened in Scottsdale, Arizona in 1993, over 124 new ones have sprouted up across the country—in more than 33 states. No matter the location, it's this dish that gets first raves. Like the very-dead McDonald's McD.L.T. hamburger, which disappeared around the time the first P. F. Chang's opened, the contrasting textures of the cool crispy lettuce and the hot meat filling come together in your mouth for a tasty oral dance party. According to waiters, those little dark bits in the chicken filling mix are "black mushrooms," and there's a good chance your local supermarket doesn't stock them. But a great alternative can be found in the Asian food section—canned straw mushrooms. Just remember to chop the chicken, water chestnuts and mushrooms up real good for the final sauté. Slip this filling into a lettuce cup, fold it up like a taco, add a little "special sauce," get down tonight.

SPECIAL SAUCE
¼ cup granulated sugar
½ cup water

2 tablespoons soy sauce
2 tablespoons rice vinegar

2 tablespoons ketchup
1 tablespoon lemon juice
⅛ teaspoon sesame oil
1 tablespoon Chinese hot mustard
    powder (see Tidbits)

2 teaspoons water
1 to 3 teaspoons garlic chili paste

STIR FRY SAUCE

2 tablespoons soy sauce
2 tablespoons dark brown sugar

½ teaspoon rice vinegar

3 tablespoons vegetable oil
2 skinless chicken breast fillets
1 cup diced water chestnuts

⅔ cup diced straw mushrooms
3 tablespoons chopped green onion
1 teaspoon minced garlic (1 clove)

1 cup fried maifun rice sticks (see
    Tidbits)

4 to 5 iceberg lettuce cups

1. Make the special sauce (for spooning over your lettuce wraps) by dissolving the ¼ cup sugar in ½ cup water in a small bowl. Add 2 tablespoons soy sauce, 2 tablespoons rice vinegar, 2 tablespoons ketchup, 1 tablespoon lemon juice and ⅛ teaspoon sesame oil. Mix well and refrigerate this sauce until you're ready to serve the lettuce wraps. Combine the 2 teaspoons water with the Chinese hot mustard and set this aside as well. Eventually you will add your desired measurement of Chinese mustard and garlic chili sauce to the special sauce mixture to pour over your lettuce wraps. In the restaurant chain, waiters prepare the sauce at your table the same way, depending on your desired heat level. We'll talk more about that later.
2. Prepare the stir fry sauce by mixing the soy sauce, brown sugar, and rice vinegar together in a small bowl.
3. To prepare the filling for your lettuce wraps, bring 2 tablespoons of the vegetable oil to high heat in a wok or large frying pan. Sauté the chicken breasts for 4 to 5 minutes per

side or until done. Remove chicken from the pan to cool. Keep the oil in the pan.

4. As the chicken cools be sure your water chestnuts and mushrooms have been diced to about the size of small peas.

5. When you can handle the chicken, hack it up with a sharp knife so that no piece is bigger than a dime. With the wok or pan on high heat, add the remaining tablespoon of vegetable oil. Add the chicken, garlic, water chestnuts and mushrooms to the pan. Add the stir fry sauce to the pan and sauté the mixture for a couple minutes then serve it onto into a dish lined with a bed of fried rice noodles (maifun).

6. Serve chicken with a side of lettuce cups. Make these lettuce cups by slicing the top off of a head of iceberg lettuce right through the middle of the head. Pull your lettuce cups off of the outside of this slice.

7. Make the special sauce at the table by adding your desired number of mustard and chili sauce to the special sauce blend: 1 teaspoon mustard and chili sauce for mild, 2 teaspoons each for medium and 3 teaspoons of each for hot. Stir well.

8. Assemble lettuce wraps by spooning filling into a lettuce cup, adding special sauce over the top, folding the sucker up like a taco, then munching down upon it with reckless abandon.

• SERVES 2 TO 3 AS AN APPETIZER.

TIDBITS

Follow the directions on the package for frying the maifun (rice sticks)—usually by pouring 2 inches of vegetable oil into a pan and heating to around 400 degrees. Add maifun, a little at a time, and when it floats to the top remove it to a paper towel. The rapid noodle expansion is actually quite exciting.

Rather than powdered Chinese hot mustard, you can instead use the kind that comes already prepared in the bottle so that you don't have to add water. Your choice.

• • • •

P. F. CHANG'S
SHRIMP DUMPLINGS

MENU DESCRIPTION: *"Served with a ginger chili pepper soy sauce. (Pan-fried or steamed.)"*

Shrimp Dumplings from P. F. Chang's are scrumptious mounds of shrimp and other yummy ingredients wrapped in wonton wrappers and steamed. You can also order them pan-fried, which makes the bottom of each little package a nice crispy brown. The dumplings are served with a soy-based dipping sauce that can be cloned by combining six ingredients in a saucepan. Recreating that part was easy. But those dumplings—oh, man! I must have gone through a couple boatloads of shrimp trying to figure out the best way to get my filling to hold together like the real thing. I tried adding egg and cornstarch and potato starch and flour to pureed cooked shrimp, but all I got was a shrimp mush that made the dumplings starchy and less flavorful than the real deal. It was only when I remembered hearing about how years ago shrimp molds were created into which pureed raw shrimp was poured and then cooked, creating uniform shrimp shapes that still had the taste and texture of unprocessed shrimp. No binders necessary. So get out your food processor and prepare yourself for the not-so-pretty sight of pulverized raw shrimp. At least you don't have to worry about the size of the shrimp you buy for this recipe, since you're going to mash up the little dudes anyway.

SAUCE

½ cup water

¼ cup soy sauce

2 tablespoons granulated sugar

1 tablespoon rice vinegar

1 tablespoon chopped green
  onion (green part only)

½ teaspoon chili oil

FILLING

½ pound raw shrimp (peeled and
  deveined)

1 tablespoon finely minced carrot

1 tablespoon finely minced green
  onion

½ teaspoon minced fresh ginger

½ teaspoon minced fresh garlic

¼ teaspoon salt

¼ teaspoon granulated sugar

8 wonton wrappers

1 egg, beaten

1. Make dipping sauce by simmering ingredients over medium heat for 1 minute. Remove the sauce from the heat and set it aside to cool.

2. Make shrimp filling for the dumplings by pureeing the shrimp in a food processor until it makes a smooth paste. Add carrot, green onion, ginger, garlic, salt, and sugar and pulse the food processor a couple times to mix.

3. Measure a heaping tablespoon of this filling into the center of a wonton wrapper. Brush beaten egg on each of the top four edges. Bring two opposite corners up to meet in the middle and press together over the filling. Bring the other two opposite corners up and pinch all the edges together making a square package with sealed edges. Repeat with the remaining ingredients and let the dumplings sit for about ten minutes in the refrigerator so that the "egg glue" sets up.

4. Prepare a steamer with hot water. When the water is simmering and steaming nicely drop in the dumplings (four at a time if your steamer is small) and steam them for 15 minutes. Serve these immediately if you want steamed dumplings. To clone the pan-fried version heat up some vegetable oil that's about ¼-inch deep in a skillet over medium heat. When the

oil is hot place the steamed dumpling with the flat side down in the oil and sauté for a couple of minutes or until the bottom is golden brown. Serve with the dipping sauce.

- SERVES 2 TO 4 (MAKES 8 DUMPLINGS).

•   •   •   •

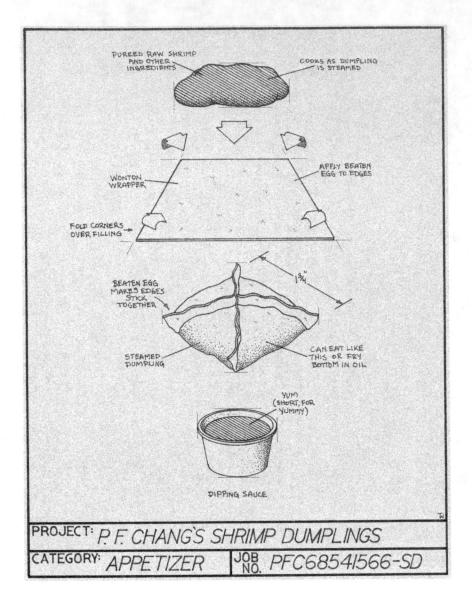

PUREED RAW SHRIMP AND OTHER INGREDIENTS

COOKS AS DUMPLING IS STEAMED

WONTON WRAPPER

APPLY BEATEN EGG TO EDGES

FOLD CORNERS OVER FILLING

BEATEN EGG MAKES EDGES STICK TOGETHER

1 3/4"

STEAMED DUMPLING

CAN EAT LIKE THIS OR FRY BOTTOM IN OIL

YUM (SHORT, FOR YUMMY)

DIPPING SAUCE

PROJECT: *P. F. CHANG'S SHRIMP DUMPLINGS*

CATEGORY: *APPETIZER* | **JOB NO.** *PFC68541566-SD*

P. F. CHANG'S
GARLIC SNAP PEAS

MENU DESCRIPTION: *"Stir-fried with garlic."*

This is a standard side dish at the country's hottest Chinese dinner chain, and it'll take you just a couple minutes to duplicate at home as a good veggie side for any entrée, Chinese or otherwise. It's especially good when you're pressed to slam together a last minute vegetable to go with tonight's dinner. You can certainly stay traditional and use a wok for this, but I always just use a medium-size non-stick skillet. The trick is to sauté the snap peas quickly over pretty high heat, tossing often, until they're hot, yet still crispy and bright green. You get the garlic in right at the end, and then quickly pop it off the heat so the garlic doesn't scorch. You don't want anyone getting "bitter garlic face."

2 cups fresh sugar snap peas   dash ground black pepper
2 teaspoons vegetable oil   2 cloves garlic, minced
⅛ teaspoon salt

1. Prepare snap peas by cutting off the tips on each end of the pods.
2. Preheat oil in a wok or medium skillet over medium/high heat.
3. Sauté snap peas in oil with salt and black pepper for 2½ to 3 minutes, tossing often, until peas are cooked, but still crispy.

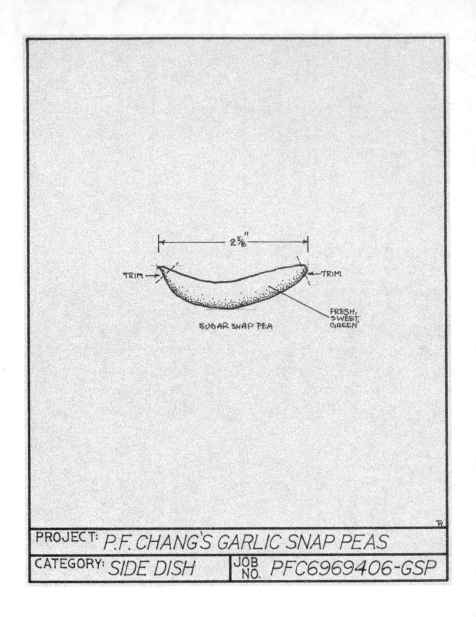

2 5/8"

TRIM →

← TRIM

FRESH,
SWEET,
GREEN

SUGAR SNAP PEA

PROJECT:	P.F. CHANG'S GARLIC SNAP PEAS	
CATEGORY: SIDE DISH	JOB NO.	PFC6969406-GSP

The pods should begin to get a few dark brown scorched spots developing on them when they're done. Add minced garlic, toss a bit more, then immediately pour the snap peas out onto a serving platter. If you keep the garlic in too long it could burn and get bitter on you, so don't leave it in the hot pan for any longer than about 10 seconds.

• SERVES 2 TO 4.

• • • •

P. F. CHANG'S
CHANG'S SPICY CHICKEN

MENU DESCRIPTION: *"Lightly-dusted, stir fried in a sweet Szechwan sauce. (Our version of General Chu's.)"*

The sweet and spicy zing in the secret sauce sets this recipe apart as one of P. F. Chang's top picks. If you're looking for something simple to make with those chicken breasts sitting in the fridge, this is a good choice. Once the sauce is finished all you have to do is sauté your chicken and combine. And you'll probably want to make up a little white or brown rice, like at the restaurant. If you can't find straight chili sauce for this recipe, the more common chili sauce with garlic in it will work just as well.

SAUCE

2 teaspoons vegetable oil
2 tablespoons chopped garlic
   (3 to 4 cloves)
3 tablespoons chopped green
   onions (about 3 onions)
1 cup pineapple juice
2 tablespoons chili sauce
2 tablespoons rice vinegar

4 teaspoons granulated sugar
1 teaspoon soy sauce
2 tablespoons water
½ teaspoon cornstarch

1 cup vegetable oil
2 skinless chicken breast fillets
⅓ cup cornstarch

1. Make the sauce by heating 2 teaspoons vegetable oil in medium saucepan. Sauté the garlic and onion in the oil for just a few seconds, not allowing the ingredients to burn, then quickly add the pineapple juice, followed by chili sauce, vinegar, sugar, and soy sauce.
2. Dissolve cornstarch in 2 tablespoons water and add it to the other ingredients in the saucepan. Bring mixture to a boil and continue to simmer on medium/high heat for 3 to 5 minutes or until thick and syrupy.
3. Heat 1 cup vegetable oil in a wok or a medium saucepan over medium heat.
4. While oil heats up, chop chicken breast fillets into bite-size pieces. In a medium bowl, toss chicken pieces with cornstarch until dusted.
5. Sauté coated chicken in the hot oil, stirring occasionally, until light brown. Remove chicken to a rack or paper towels to drain for a moment. Pour chicken into a medium bowl, add sauce and toss well to coat chicken. Serve immediately with rice on the side.

• SERVES 2.

• • • •

P. F. CHANG'S
LEMON PEPPER SHRIMP

MENU DESCRIPTION: *"Stir-fried with chives and bean sprouts."*

Chefs at P. F. Chang's China Bistro cook most dishes in heavy woks over extremely high heat with sparks flying and flames nipping at their noses. The special stove is designed so that the tall fires work at the back end of the wok, away from the chef. The well-ventilated stove is built with a steady stream of running water nearby to thin sauces and rinse the woks after each dish is prepared. Since we don't have those phat, bad-boy stoves at home, the challenge is to tweak the recipe for standard kitchen equipment. Using a gas stove and a wok will get you the best duplicate, but this recipe can be knocked-off nicely with a large skillet, if that's all you've got. Things are moving fast back in those P. F. Chang's kitchens. The chefs are well-trained, but they eyeball measurements for sauces with a ladle, so each wok-prepared dish is going to come out a little different. Considering this, I figured the best way to get a good clone would be to order the dish several times. I averaged the flavors by combining several batches of sauce (requesting extra on the side) into one large bowl, and then used that mixture to create the recipe. This technique works great for recipes like this one where the sauce is key, and measurements at the restaurant aren't exactly scientific. The shrimp is lightly breaded—they use potato starch, but cornstarch is a good substitute—and flash fried in oil. Strain the shrimp out of the oil, add it back to the pan with the sauce, and you've got yourself a clone.

SAUCE

1 tablespoon vegetable oil
2 tablespoons chopped
  garlic
½ teaspoon minced
  ginger
⅓ cup soy sauce
¾ cup water
2 teaspoons cornstarch
¼ cup dark brown sugar
2 teaspoons lemon juice

2 teaspoons coarse grind black
  pepper

1 pound medium raw shrimp
  (31/40 count), shelled and
  deveined
½ cup cornstarch
1 cup vegetable oil
4 thin lemon slices, each cut into
  quarters

GARNISH

1 teaspoon vegetable oil
2 large green onions

1 cup bean sprouts

1. Make sauce by heating 1 tablespoon oil in a wok or large saucepan over medium heat. Sauté garlic and ginger in the hot oil for about 15 seconds being careful not to burn the garlic. Add the soy sauce, then dissolve cornstarch in the water and add the mixture to the pan. Add brown sugar, lemon juice and black pepper and bring mixture to a boil. Simmer for two minutes then remove it from the heat.

2. Coat all the shrimp generously with cornstarch. Let the shrimp sit for about five minutes so that the cornstarch will adhere better.

3. Heat a cup of oil in a wok or large skillet over medium heat. Add the shrimp to the pan and sauté for 3 to 4 minutes or until the shrimp start to turn light brown. Strain the shrimp out of the oil with a slotted spoon or spider and dump oil. Replace shrimp back in the wok along with the lemon slices, sauté for a minute, then add the sauce to the pan. Toss everything around to coat the shrimp thoroughly. Cook for another minute or so until the sauce thickens on the shrimp.

4. As the shrimp cooks, heat up 1 teaspoon of oil in a separate

medium saucepan. Cut the green part of the green onions into 3-inch lengths. Add those green onion slices and bean sprouts to hot oil along with a dash of salt and pepper. Sauté for a couple minutes until green onions begin to soften.

5. Build the dish by pouring the green onions and sprouts onto a serving plate. Dump the shrimp over the veggies and serve.

• Serves 2.

•   •   •   •

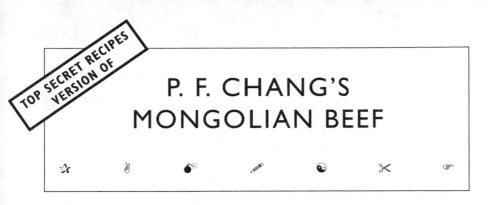

P. F. CHANG'S
MONGOLIAN BEEF

MENU DESCRIPTION: *"Quickly-cooked steak with scallions and garlic."*

Beef lovers go crazy over this one at the restaurant. Flank steak is cut into bite-sized chunks against the grain, then it's lightly dusted with potato starch (in our case we'll use cornstarch), flash-fried in oil, and doused with an amazing sweet soy garlic sauce. The beef comes out tender as can be, and the simple sauce sings to your taste buds. I designed this recipe to use a wok, but if you don't have one a skillet will suffice (you may need to add more oil to the pan to cover the beef in the flash-frying step). P. F. Chang's secret sauce is what makes this dish so good, and it's versatile. If you don't dig beef, you can substitute with chicken. Or you can even brush it on grilled salmon.

SAUCE

2 teaspoons vegetable oil
½ teaspoon minced
    ginger
1 tablespoon chopped garlic
½ cup soy sauce
½ cup water

¾ cup dark brown sugar

1 cup vegetable oil
1 pound flank steak
¼ cup cornstarch
2 large green onions

1. Make the sauce by heating 2 teaspoons of vegetable in a medium saucepan over medium/low heat. Don't get the oil too hot or you'll get a major spatter when adding the other liquids. Add ginger and garlic to the pan and quickly add the soy sauce and water before the garlic scorches. Dissolve the brown sugar in the sauce, then raise the heat to about medium and boil the sauce for 2 to 3 minutes or until the sauce thickens. Remove it from the heat.
2. Slice the flank steak against the grain into ¼-inch thick bite-size slices. Tilt the blade of your knife at about a forty-five degree angle to the top of the steak so that you get wider cuts.
3. Dip the steak pieces into the cornstarch to apply a very thin dusting to both sides of each piece of beef. Let the beef sit for about 10 minutes so that the cornstarch sticks.
4. As the beef sits, heat up one cup of oil in a wok (you may also use a skillet for this step as long as the beef will be mostly covered with oil). Heat the oil over medium heat until it's nice and hot, but not smoking. Add the beef to the oil and sauté for just two minutes, or until the beef just begins to darken on the edges. You don't need a thorough cooking here since the beef is going to go back on the heat later. Stir the meat around a little so that it cooks evenly. After a couple minutes, use a large slotted spoon or a spider to take the meat out and onto paper towels, then pour the oil out of the wok or skillet. Put the pan back over the heat, dump the meat back into it and simmer for one minute. Add the sauce, cook for one minute while stirring, then add all the green onions. Cook for one more minute, then remove the beef and onions with tongs or a slotted spoon to a serving plate. Leave the excess sauce behind in the pan.

• SERVES 2.

•   •   •   •

P. F. CHANG'S OOLONG MARINATED SEA BASS

MENU DESCRIPTION: *"Broiled and served with sweet ginger soy, baby corn and spinach."*

Grab a couple half-pound sea bass fillets (not too thick), whip up a simple marinade and you're on your way to cloning one of the most beloved dishes at America's fastest growing Chinese bistro chain. The marinade is made with only six ingredients so you'll have that done in no time. If you can't find oolong tea, you can use green tea. Loose tea is best, but if you can only find bags, that's okay. One teabag contains 1 teaspoon of tea, so you'll just need half of a teabag for this recipe (in fact, the recipe still works even without the tea). You will need to plan ahead for this dish, however, since the fish must marinate for 5 to 7 hours. Once the fish is marinated, fire up the oven to bake it, then finish it off under the broiler. Sauté some spinach, garlic, and tiny corn for an optional bed that makes the dish indistinguishable from the real thing.

MARINADE/SAUCE

2 cups water
⅔ cup soy sauce
¾ cup light brown sugar
2 teaspoons minced fresh
    ginger

1 teaspoon minced fresh garlic
½ teaspoon oolong tea

Two ½-pound sea bass fillets

OPTIONAL GARNISH

1 tablespoon oil
6 handfuls fresh spinach
½ teaspoon minced fresh garlic

1 5.5-ounce can whole baby sweet
corn (6 to 8 baby corns),
drained

1. Make your sauce and marinade by combining the six ingredients in a medium saucepan over medium heat. Bring to a boil then reduce heat and simmer for 5 minutes. Cool uncovered, then strain out the ginger, garlic, and tea.
2. Put your sea bass fillets in a storage bag or a covered container with 2 cups of the marinade. Let the fish have a nice soak in the marinade for 5 to 7 hours in the fridge. If the sauce doesn't completely cover the fish, be sure to turn the fillets a couple hours in so that all sides get marinated.
3. When you are ready to prepare the fish, preheat your oven to 425 degrees.
4. Arrange the fillets on a baking sheet. Bake the fish for 22 minutes or until the edges of the fillets are starting to turn brown. Crank the oven up to a high broil and broil fish for 2 to 3 minutes or until you get some dark patches around the edge of the fillets. Just don't let them burn.
5. As your fish is baking, heat up a wok or large skillet with one tablespoon of vegetable oil over medium heat. Add the spinach, garlic, and baby sweet corn, and a dash of salt and pepper to the pan. Sauté the veggies just until the spinach is wilted, then arrange half of the spinach and corn on each of two plates.
6. When the sea bass is done broiling, use a spatula to carefully lay each fillet on the bed of spinach and baby corn. Split the remaining sauce and pour it over each of the fillets before serving.

- SERVES 2.

•   •   •   •

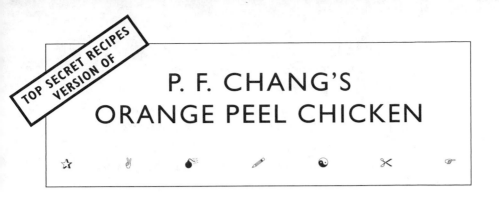

P. F. CHANG'S
ORANGE PEEL CHICKEN

MENU DESCRIPTION: *"Tossed with orange peel and chili peppers for a spicy/citrus combination."*

Several of P. F. Chang's top-selling items are similar in preparation technique: Bite-size pieces of meat are lightly breaded and wok-seared in oil, then doused with a secret sauce mixture. That's the basis for this recipe as well, but I have a special fondness for the citrusy sweet and spicy flavors found in this entrée. The heat comes from chili garlic sauce, which you'll find in the aisle with the Asian foods in your supermarket—the rest of the sauce ingredients are common stuff. The orange peel is julienned into thin strips before adding it to the dish. Since the flavor from the peel is so strong, we won't need to add it until the end. Cook up some white or brown rice to serve alongside this dish and get the chopsticks ready.

SAUCE

1 tablespoon vegetable oil
2 tablespoons minced garlic
4 green onions, sliced
1 cup tomato sauce
½ cup water
¼ cup granulated sugar
2 tablespoons chili garlic sauce

1 tablespoon soy sauce

½ cup vegetable oil
4 skinless chicken breast fillets
½ cup cornstarch
peel from ¼ orange, julienned
    (into ⅛ inch-wide strips)

1. Prepare sauce by heating 1 tablespoon of oil in a medium saucepan over medium heat. Add minced garlic and sliced green onions. Add tomato sauce and water quickly before the garlic burns. Add sugar, chili garlic sauce, and soy sauce and bring to a boil. Simmer 5 to 6 minutes or until sauce thickens, then turn off the heat.
2. Prepare the chicken by heating ½ cup oil in a wok over medium heat. Slice chicken breast fillets into bite-size pieces. Coat each piece of chicken with cornstarch. Arrange coated chicken on a plate until all chicken is coated. When oil in the wok is hot, add about half of the chicken to the oil and cook for a couple minutes or until brown on one side, then flip the chicken over. When chicken is golden brown, remove the pieces to a rack or paper towels to drain. Repeat with the remaining chicken. When all of the chicken is cooked rinse the oil out of the wok with water and place it back on the stove to heat up.
3. When wok is hot again add julienned orange peel and chicken. Heat for 20 to 30 seconds or so, stirring gently. Add sauce to the pan and cook for about 2 minutes. Stir the dish a couple times but do it gently so you don't knock the coating off the chicken. Cook until the sauce thickens then serve with white or brown rice on the side.

- SERVES 3 TO 4.

• • • •

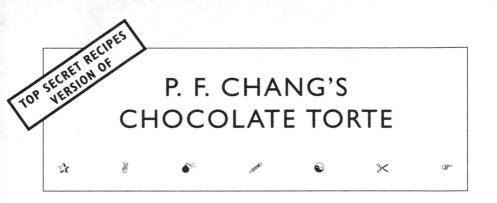

P. F. CHANG'S CHOCOLATE TORTE

MENU DESCRIPTION: *"Served with vanilla bean and raspberry sauce."*

P. F. Chang's contracts with local bakeries to produce these delicious flourless chocolate cakes in each city where the Chinese bistros are based. The restaurants aren't built for baking, and this way the chain can ensure a fresh product every day. Now, if you're a chocolate lover or there's one nearby, this is the recipe for you. The torte is only 5 ingredients, and the versatile sauces create the perfect gourmet touch. Any leftover torte and sauce can be frozen, then thawed at a later date to effortlessly impress.

½ cup butter (1 stick)
3 cups semi-sweet chocolate chips
   (18-ounces)

4 eggs
½ cup granulated sugar
1 teaspoon vanilla extract

VANILLA SAUCE

2 cups cream
½ cup granulated sugar
½ of a vanilla bean (split down
   the middle)

4 egg yolks

RASPBERRY SAUCE

one 12-ounce bag frozen
   raspberries, thawed
3 tablespoons granulated sugar

2 to 4 tablespoons water
2 tablespoons Chambord
   raspberry liqueur

1. Preheat oven to 325 degrees.
2. Melt butter in a medium saucepan over low heat. Add chocolate chips and stir occasionally until chocolate is completely melted. Be very careful not to overcook the chocolate or it may burn and taste funny. Not funny ha-ha—funny bad. Remove chocolate from the heat when it's melted.
3. Beat 4 eggs until fluffy in a large bowl, then add sugar and vanilla and mix well until sugar is dissolved.
4. Temper the egg mixture by stirring in just a few tablespoons of the warm chocolate at first. This will keep the eggs from cooking. Slowly add the rest of the chocolate and mix until well combined.
5. Pour the batter into a 9-inch springform pan that has been lined on the bottom and sides with parchment paper (butter the pan before you add the parchment paper—the butter will make the paper stick). Bake for 40 to 50 minutes or until middle of the cake begins to firm up. Remove, cool, cover and chill the cake until you are ready to serve it.
6. As the torte bakes, prepare vanilla sauce by combining cream with ¼ cup sugar in a medium saucepan over medium/low heat. Use a knife to scrape the seeds from inside the vanilla bean half, then add the seeds and the bean pod to the pan. Heat mixture, stirring often, just until boiling then turn off heat. Watch the cream closely so that it does not boil over.
7. In a medium bowl whisk together remaining ¼ cup of sugar and egg yolks until smooth. Temper the egg yolks by stirring in a few tablespoons of the hot cream mixture. Pour the entire mixture back into the saucepan and heat it up again, stirring often until it begins to boil. Immediately pour the sauce into a medium bowl that has been set in a larger bowl filled with ice. This ice bath will help to quickly cool the sauce so

that it doesn't curdle. Cover and chill the sauce until you are ready for it.

8. Make the raspberry sauce by pureeing the thawed raspberries in a blender. Add 2 to 4 tablespoons of water to thin the pureed berries a bit—if your berries have a lot of juice add 2 tablespoons of water; if they have just a little juice, add 4 tablespoons of water. Strain the seeds from the raspberry puree then pour the puree into a medium saucepan over medium heat. Add 3 tablespoons granulated sugar and 2 tablespoons of raspberry liqueur to the pan. Heat until boiling then remove raspberry sauce from heat. Cover and chill it.

9. When you are ready to serve your torte, first spoon some raspberry sauce and vanilla sauce onto a plate. Carefully place the slice of torte on the sauces, but turn it over so that the top of the torte is on the bottom. This is how a flourless chocolate cake is served—topside down. The restaurant zaps the cake for 30 seconds or so in the microwave before serving, so that it is slightly warm. However, you might prefer yours cold.

• SERVES 8.

•   •   •   •

RED LOBSTER TARTAR SAUCE

Here's a clone for the dollop of sweet, creamy goodness that comes alongside your fish entree at the world's largest seafood chain. This original kitchen replica gives you a quick and tasty sauce that has the look and flavor of the real thing—and it's only five ingredients! Use the sauce to dress up your next home-cooked fish platter or as a spread on fish sandwiches and fish tacos.

½ cup mayonnaise
1 ½ tablespoons finely minced onion
1 tablespoon sweet pickle relish

1 ½ teaspoons shredded and chopped carrot (bits the size of rice)
1 ½ teaspoons sugar

Combine all ingredients in a small bowl. Cover and chill.

• MAKES 4 SERVINGS.

• • • •

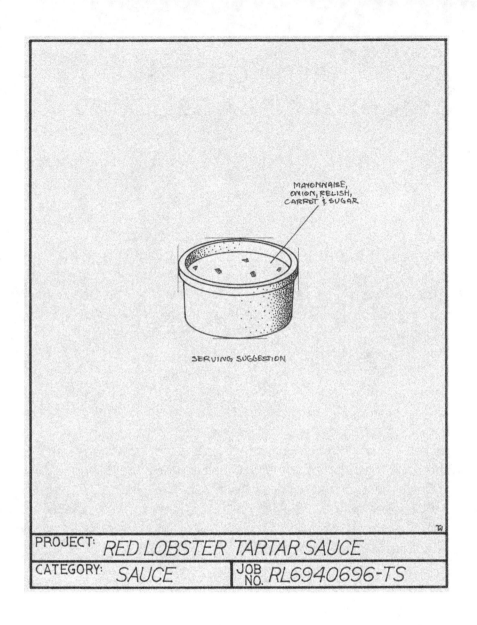

MAYONNAISE,
ONION, RELISH,
CARROT & SUGAR

SERVING SUGGESTION

PROJECT: *RED LOBSTER TARTAR SAUCE*

CATEGORY: *SAUCE*   JOB NO. *RL6940696-TS*

RED LOBSTER
CHEDDAR BAY BISCUITS

Order an entree from America's largest seafood restaurant chain and you'll get a basket of some of the planet's tastiest garlic-cheese biscuits served up on the side. For many years this recipe has been the most-searched-for clone recipe on the Internet, according to Red Lobster. As a result, several versions are floating around, including one that was at one time printed right on the box of Bisquick baking mix.

The problem with making biscuits using Bisquick is that if you follow the directions from the box you don't end up with a very fluffy or flakey finished product, since most of the fat in the recipe comes from the shortening that's included in the mix. On its own, room temperature shortening does a poor job creating the light, airy texture you want from good biscuits, and it contributes little in the way of flavor. So, we'll invite some cold butter along on the trip—with grated Cheddar cheese and a little garlic powder. Now you'll be well on your way to delicious Cheddar Bay. Wherever that is.

2½ cups Bisquick baking mix
4 tablespoons cold butter (½ stick)
1 heaping cup grated Cheddar
    cheese

¾ cup cold whole milk
¼ teaspoon garlic powder

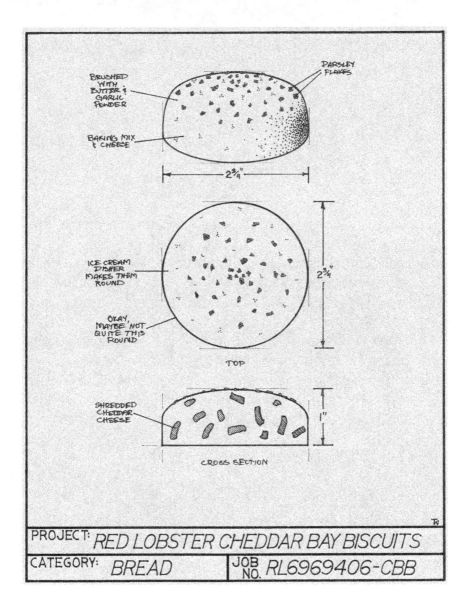

BRUSHED WITH BUTTER & GARLIC POWDER

PARSLEY FLAKES

BAKING MIX & CHEESE

2¾"

ICE CREAM DISHER MAKES THEM ROUND

OKAY, MAYBE NOT QUITE THIS ROUND

2¾"

TOP

SHREDDED CHEDDAR CHEESE

1"

CROSS SECTION

PROJECT: *RED LOBSTER CHEDDAR BAY BISCUITS*

CATEGORY: *BREAD*

JOB NO. *RL6969406-CBB*

BRUSH ON TOP

2 tablespoons butter, melted
½ teaspoon garlic powder

¼ teaspoon dried parsley flakes
pinch salt

1. Preheat your oven to 400 degrees.
2. Combine Bisquick with cold butter in a medium bowl using a pastry cutter or a large fork. You don't want to mix too thoroughly. There should be small chunks of butter in there that are about the size of peas. Add Cheddar cheese, milk, and ¼ teaspoon garlic. Mix by hand until combined, but don't over mix.
3. Drop approximately ¼-cup portions of the dough onto an ungreased cookie sheet using an ice cream scoop. Bake for 15 to 17 minutes or until the tops of the biscuits begin to turn light brown.
4. When you take the biscuits out of the oven, melt 2 tablespoons butter in a small bowl in your microwave. Stir in ½ teaspoon garlic powder and the dried parsley flakes. Use a brush to spread this garlic butter over the tops of all the biscuits. Use up all of the butter.

• MAKES A DOZEN BISCUITS.

• • • •

RED LOBSTER BACON-WRAPPED STUFFED SHRIMP

It's shrimp, it's bacon, it's cheese; what's not to like? It's one of the groovy appetizers on the Red Lobster menu, and now you can create it at your crib. Find some large shrimp, a wooden skewer, and cook the bacon about halfway to done before you begin. Mix up a clone of Red Lobster's top secret seasoning and the cilantro-ranch dipping sauce, and you're minutes away from scarfing down a delectable dish that's meant to be a teaser for what's to come. Looks like you'll need to make the main coarse a real doozy.

SEASONING

¼ teaspoon salt
¼ teaspoon paprika
pinch ground black pepper
pinch garlic powder

pinch onion powder
pinch cayenne pepper
pinch ground allspice

CILANTRO-RANCH DIPPING SAUCE

⅓ cup ranch dressing
1 teaspoon minced fresh cilantro

10 pieces bacon
10 large shrimp

5 fresh jalapeno slices
2 ounces pepper
    Jack cheese

1. Preheat oven to 425 degrees.
2. Make the seasoning blend by combining the ingredients in a small bowl. Set this aside.
3. Make the dipping sauce by combining the ranch dressing with cilantro in another small bowl.
4. Cook the bacon in a frying pan over medium/high heat, but don't cook it all the way to crispy. You want undercooked bacon that, when cool, will easily wrap around the shrimp. Cook the bacon about 3 minutes per side, and don't let it brown. When the bacon is done lay it on paper towels to drain and cool.
5. Shell the shrimp, leaving the last segment of the shell and the tail. Remove the dark vein from the back of the shrimp, and then cut down into the back of the shrimp, without cutting all the way through, so that the shrimp is nearly butterflied open. This will make a pocket for the pepper and cheese.
6. Pour 1 cup of water into a small bowl. Add the shrimp and jalapeno peppers and microwave for 90 seconds or until the shrimp has just cooked through and changed color to white. Immediately pour the water out of the bowl, remove the jalapeno slices and pour cold water over the shrimp. Place the shrimp and jalapeno pepper slices onto paper towels to drain off excess water.
7. Build the appetizer by cutting the jalapeno slices in half and removing the seeds. You should now have 10 jalapeno slices. Place one slice into the slit on the back of a shrimp. Cut an inch-long chunk of cheese (about ¼-inch thick), and place it on the jalapeno slice. Wrap a piece of bacon around the shrimp, starting where the cheese is. Start wrapping with the thinnest end of the bacon. Go 1½ times around the shrimp and then cut off the excess bacon and slide a skewer through the shrimp to hold everything in place. Repeat with the remaining shrimp and slide them onto the skewer with the tails facing the same direction. Make two skewers of 5 shrimp each.
8. Put the skewers onto a baking sheet and sprinkle a light coating of the seasoning blend over the shrimp, then bake for

5 to 7 minutes or until the bacon browns and the cheese begins to ooze. Serve over a bed of rice if desired. Feed the leftover bacon pieces to the dog while you scarf out on the shrimp.

- SERVES 4 AS AN APPETIZER.

• • • •

SHARP KNIFE

PEPPER JACK CHEESE

PEELED RAW SHRIMP

HALF OF A JALAPENO SLICE

MAKE A SLICE IN EACH SHRIMP— BUT DON'T CUT ALL THE WAY THROUGH

LEAVE ON TAIL SECTION

FILL THE GROOVE, MAN

STUFFING THE SHRIMP

SECRET SEASONING BLEND

WRAP BACON AROUND THE STUFFED SHRIMP

SKEWER KEEPS IT ALL TOGETHER

TIGHT AS A ROCKETTES KICK LINE

DIP SHRIMP IN HERE

SHRIMP READY FOR THE BROILER

SKEWER

CILANTRO-RANCH DIPPING SAUCE

PROJECT: R.L. BACON-WRAPPED STUFFED SHRIMP

CATEGORY: APPETIZER   JOB NO. RL794135255-BWSS

RED LOBSTER
CHEDDAR BAY CRAB BAKE

Ahoy. Banking on the popularity of the chain's Cheddar Bay Biscuits, Red Lobster chefs developed this pizza-shaped appetizer with crust made from the cheesy biscuit dough, and crab and Cheddar cheese baked on top. If you like those tender, cheesy garlic biscuits that come with every meal at Red Lobster, then you'll probably like this. If you don't like it, then you're probably not alone. This item is nowhere to be found on Red Lobster's menu these days, and that should tell you something about how well it sold. But hey, even good dishes get discontinued. If you're up for giving this clone a shot, get yourself some fresh crabmeat. If you want to take a shot a little less expensively, find some quality canned stuff. If you don't want to take a shot at all, try the next recipe.

2 cups Bisquick baking mix
1 ¾ cup finely shredded Cheddar
    cheese
⅔ cups milk
2 tablespoons butter, melted

¼ teaspoon garlic powder
½ teaspoon dried parsley flakes
⅓ cup crabmeat (fresh or canned
    lump)

1. Preheat oven to 450 degrees.
2. Combine baking mix, 1 cup of the Cheddar cheese, milk, and half of the melted butter in a medium bowl. Mix by hand until combined.

3. Pat out the dough into circle approximately 8 inches in diameter, with a slight lip around the edge, like a pizza crust.
4. Sprinkle the parsley over the top of the dough. Be sure the dried parsley flakes are crushed fine. You can easily crush the flakes in a small bowl with your thumb and forefinger.
5. Sprinkle the crab over the top of the dough.
6. Sprinkle the remaining cheese over the crab. Don't go all of the way to the edge of the dough—leave a margin of a half-inch or so around the edge.
7. Bake for 14 to16 minutes or until the cheese on top begins to brown slightly.
8. Combine the remaining butter with the garlic powder and brush it over the top of the bake as soon as it comes out of the oven. Slice it like a pizza into 8 pieces and serve hot.

• MAKES 8 PIECES.

•　•　•　•

RED LOBSTER PARROT BAY COCONUT SHRIMP

MENU DESCRIPTION: *"Jumbo butterflied shrimp hand-dipped in batter flavored with Captain Morgan Parrot Bay Rum & coconut flakes. Served with pina colada dipping sauce."*

Fans of this dish say the best part is the pina colada dipping sauce. And it's true; that sauce is so good you could eat it with a spoon. But the coconut shrimp is pretty awesome too, just on its own. Red Lobster's secret formula includes Captain Morgan's Parrot Bay rum, which sweetens the batter and adds a great coconut flavor (plus you can whip up a nice cocktail with it while you're cooking, if that's your thing). Panko breadcrumbs—which give a nice crunch to the batter—can be found in the aisle of your market where all the Asian foods are parked. This secret recipe makes two times the size of a serving you get at the Lobster, so there should be enough for everyone. The real thing comes with salsa on the side in addition to the pina colada sauce, but you may not even want to include it.

PINA COLADA DIPPING SAUCE

½ cup sour cream
¼ cup pina colada mix (liquid)
¼ cup crushed pineapple
   (canned)

2 tablespoons granulated
   sugar

SHRIMP

6 to 10 cups canola oil (amount required by fryer)

12 large shrimp, peeled and deveined (about ½ pound)

1 ½ cups all-purpose flour

2 tablespoons granulated sugar

¼ teaspoon salt

1 cup milk

2 tablespoons Captain Morgan's Parrot Bay coconut rum

1 cup panko Japanese breadcrumbs

½ cup shredded coconut

ON THE SIDE

salsa

1. Prepare pina colada dipping sauce first by combining all the ingredients. Cover this and let it chill out in the fridge while you make the shrimp.
2. Heat oil to 350 degrees.
3. Measure ¾ cup of flour into a medium bowl. In another medium bowl mix together the remaining ¾ cup flour, sugar, and salt. Stir milk and rum into flour mixture. Let this batter stand for five minutes. While the batter rests, combine panko breadcrumbs and shredded coconut into a third medium bowl.
4. Butterfly cut each shrimp before you start the battering: Use a sharp knife to slice through the top of the shrimp (where the vein was) so that you can spread the shrimp open. Leave the tail intact.
5. To batter the shrimp, dip each one in the flour, then the wet batter, then coat each shrimp with the panko/coconut mixture. Arrange the shrimp on a plate until all of them are battered.
6. Fry the shrimp by dropping six at a time into the hot oil for 2 to 3 minutes or until the shrimp are golden brown. Remove shrimp to a rack or paper towels to drain.
7. Serve shrimp with pina colada dipping sauce on the side, along with a small dish of your favorite salsa, if you like.

• SERVES 3 TO 4 AS AN APPETIZER.

• • • •

RED LOBSTER NEW ENGLAND CLAM CHOWDER

Considered one of Red Lobster's signature items, this dish has been screaming to be cloned for years now. The tiny screams, which sound like hundreds of little clams being plucked from their shells, could no longer be ignored. What's great about this clone recipe is that we don't have to do any of the plucking ourselves. Rather than going through the tedious (and expensive) task of steaming fresh clams and dicing up all the good parts, we can use the more affordable and convenient canned clams found in any supermarket. Just remember to not toss out the clam juice in the cans when you open them, since you'll need that flavorful liquid in the first step.

2 ½ cups water
3 6.5-ounce cans minced clams
    (plus liquid)
½ cup all-purpose flour
1 teaspoon minced fresh parsley
½ teaspoon salt
¼ teaspoon ground black pepper

1 bay leaf
dash dried thyme
2 white or red potatoes, peeled
    and diced (not russet or
    yellow potatoes)
1 cup heavy cream

1. Combine water and liquid drained from all 3 cans of clams in a large saucepan. Stir in flour, parsley, salt, pepper, bay leaf and thyme. Turn to medium heat.
2. When water begins to bubble, add the potatoes and simmer for 5 minutes. Stir often to keep the potatoes from sticking to the bottom of the pan.
3. Add the clams to the saucepan and simmer for 10 minutes, stirring often.
4. Add the cream and simmer for an additional 5 minutes. Watch the pan carefully to be sure the chowder doesn't bubble over. Turn down the heat if the soup begins to erupt.

• MAKES 5 SERVINGS.

TIDBITS

Some brands of canned clams seem to be saltier than others. Depending on the saltiness of the clams you choose, you may want to add a bit more salt. Start with an additional ¼ teaspoon of salt if you find the soup on the bland side.

•   •   •   •

RED LOBSTER TERIYAKI GLAZED FRESH FISH

Preheat your grill and put on your sandals for this great clone that's perfect when you've got a hankering for a tropical grilled fish dinner. Red Lobster lets you chose your favorite fish from the menu, then prepares it on the grill with a basting of tangy citrus and ginger teriyaki glaze. The delicious pineapple-mango salsa is the perfect finishing touch. Once you've got your favorite fresh fish from the market, you just need to prepare the sauce and salsa, and light the tiki torches.

TANGY CITRUS & GINGER TERIYAKI SAUCE

½ cup thick teriyaki glaze
   (Kikkoman)
⅓ cup orange juice
2 tablespoons honey
2 teaspoons vegetable oil

1 teaspoon lemon juice
¼ teaspoon fresh minced ginger

COOL PINEAPPLE-

MANGO SALSA

½ cup diced canned pineapple
½ cup diced fresh mango
¼ cup diced tomato

1 tablespoon chopped green onion
1 teaspoon diced canned jalapeno
1 teaspoon minced fresh cilantro

4 SERVINGS OF THE FISH OF YOUR CHOICE:
salmon, tilapia, rainbow trout,
  halibut, snapper, or swordfish

1. Prepare teriyaki sauce by combining all the ingredients in a blender until ginger is completely pureed. Chill until needed.
2. Prepare pineapple-mango salsa by combining the ingredients in a medium bowl. Cover and chill until needed.
3. Prepare fish by preheating your grill on high heat. Lightly salt and pepper the fish and grill it until done. Brush the fish with a coating of the teriyaki sauce just before it is removed from the heat. Carefully place each fish serving on the center of the plates. Spoon a garnish of the pineapple-mango salsa on top of each serving. Serve extra garnish and teriyaki on the side, if desired.

• MAKES 4 SERVINGS.

TIDBITS

The P. F. Chang's Mai Tai clone (found on page 257) makes a great companion cocktail for this dish, and the Red Lobster Parrot Bay Coconut Shrimp (on page 296) is the perfect appetizer if you're rolling with the tropical island theme.

•   •   •   •

RED ROBIN
SEASONING

Give yourself some time to make a tough decision when you get to this casual chain because there are nearly two dozen gourmet burgers on the Red Robin menu to pick from, not to mention scores of other fantastic food choices. Red Robin claims the steak fries served with your burger are world-famous. I'm not sure if that's been confirmed, but I do know one thing that makes the fries popular in my book: They come in an all-you-can-eat bottomless portion. Want more fries? Just ask, and you can have as many as your belly can pack in. As you're stuffing yourself, you may notice that the burgers and french fries at Red Robin have a secret ingredient in common that makes them taste so special. That's right, it's the seasoning blend. And I've got a clone for you right here that includes instant tomato soup mix as the secret ingredient. So, next time you make a burger, sprinkle some of this *TSR* version of the seasoning blend on the patty. When you cook up some frozen steak fries or french fries, sprinkle a little of this blend on them as soon as they come out of the oven or fryer. Soon, you'll discover all sorts of uses for this versatile spice blend. And the recipe here makes a portion that fits nicely into an empty spice bottle.

3 tablespoons salt
1 tablespoon instant tomato soup
    mix (Knorr tomato with basil
    works great)

2 teaspoons chili powder
¼ teaspoon ground cumin
¼ teaspoon ground black pepper

Combine the ingredients in a small bowl and stir well. Store in a covered container.

• MAKES ⅓ CUP.

•   •   •   •

RED ROBIN
5 ALARM BURGER

MENU DESCRIPTION: *"Crank up the heat with Pepper-Jack cheese, jalapenos, fresh tangy salsa, sliced tomato, crisp lettuce and chipotle mayo."*

According to Red Robin waiters, this spicy production is the second most popular choice from a list of 22 delicious designer burgers on the menu. If you like a peppery punch from your chow, this is the burger recipe to add to your grill-time repertoire. The hamburger patties on Red Robin burgers are huge, weighing in at ⅓ of a pound each, so get out your kitchen scale if you want a good clone. The restaurant chain uses its secret spice blend to season the patty, so whip that up first from the clone recipe on page 302 (or you can substitute seasoned salt, such as Lawry's). Fresh salsa or pico de gallo can usually be found in the deli section at the supermarket, and ground chipotle chile pepper (smoked red jalapenos) can be found next to the chili powder in the spice aisle. It's good stuff to have on hand in your spice cabinet since it's becoming a more popular ingredient these days.

CHIPOTLE MAYO

¼ cup mayonnaise
¼ teaspoon ground chipotle chile
   pepper
⅛ teaspoon paprika

1 5.5-ounce ground beef patty

¼ teaspoon (approx.) Red Robin
   Seasoning clone (on page
   302)
2 slices pepper Jack cheese
1 sesame seed hamburger bun

4 to 6 bottled jalapeno slices
   (nacho slices)
2 tablespoons fresh salsa or pico
   de gallo

⅓ cup shredded iceberg lettuce

1. Make the chipotle mayo spread by combining the ingredients in a small bowl. Cover and chill until you are ready to use it.
2. Preheat barbecue or indoor grill to medium heat.
3. Since the ground beef will shrink as it cooks, shape it into a round patty that is slightly larger than the sesame seed bun. Sprinkle a bit of the seasoning blend over both sides of the patty. Grill for 3 to 5 minutes per side, or until the patty is cooked the way you like it. About 1 minute before the burger is done place a couple slices of pepper Jack cheese on top of the patty to melt.
4. As the hamburger is grilling toast the face of the top and bottom sesame seed bun on an indoor griddle or skillet over medium heat.
5. Build your burger by first spreading approximately 2 teaspoons of the chipotle mayo on each of the toasted faces of the top and bottom bun.
6. Stack the hamburger patty on the bottom bun.
7. Stack 4 to 6 jalapeno slices on the patty.
8. Spoon 2 tablespoons of salsa or pico de gallo over the jalapeno slices.
9. Add about ⅓ cup of shredded lettuce on next, then finish the burger off with the top bun.

• MAKES 1 BURGER.

• • • •

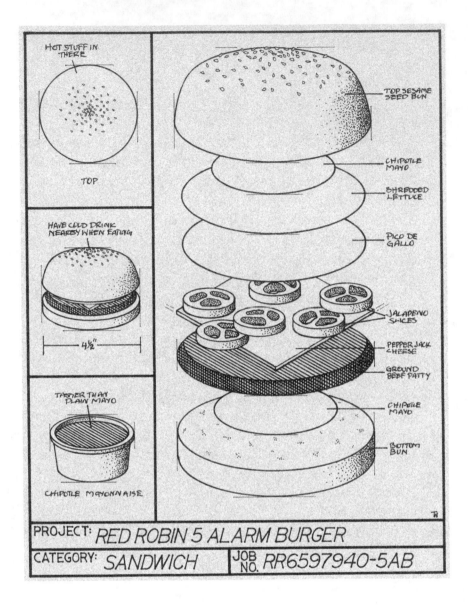

HOT STUFF IN THERE

TOP

TOP SESAME SEED BUN

CHIPOTLE MAYO

SHREDDED LETTUCE

PICO DE GALLO

JALAPENO SLICES

PEPPER JACK CHEESE

GROUND BEEF PATTY

CHIPOTLE MAYO

BOTTOM BUN

HAVE COLD DRINK NEARBY WHEN EATING

4½"

TASTIER THAN PLAIN MAYO

CHIPOTLE MAYONNAISE

PROJECT: *RED ROBIN 5 ALARM BURGER*

CATEGORY: *SANDWICH* | **JOB NO.** *RR6597940-5AB*

RED ROBIN
BANZAI BURGER

☆   ✌   💣   ✏   🎱   ✂   ☞

MENU DESCRIPTION: *"Marinated in teriyaki and topped with grilled pineapple, Cheddar cheese, lettuce, tomatoes, and mayo. Dude, you'll be like, ready to ride the pipeline on O'ahu's North Shore after you chomp on this!"*

Here's customer choice number one from Red Robin's huge burger menu. According to Red Robin servers, the beef they use for all their burgers is ground from Angus flank steak. That meat makes for a great burger to be sure, but it's tough to find in the market unless you grind your own. So if you're not up for some good old-fashioned meat-grinding fun, just pick up ground chuck for this recipe. If you can't find chuck, sirloin will have to do. Just make sure the fat content is at least 15 percent, since low-fat ground beef makes burgers that are just too dry and short on flavor. I tested a half-dozen popular teriyaki glazes in the stores and nothing comes close to the stuff they use at the restaurant, so I've included a recipe here to make your own. Be sure to watch your marinated meat and pineapple slices closely on the grill since the sugar in the teriyaki marinade could burn over the open flame. If you're grilling outside, keep the lid open. And don't hit the La-Z-Boy until this puppy's done.

TERIYAKI MARINADE

1 ¾ cups water
1 cup soy sauce
1 cup light brown sugar

½ teaspoon onion powder
½ teaspoon garlic
   powder

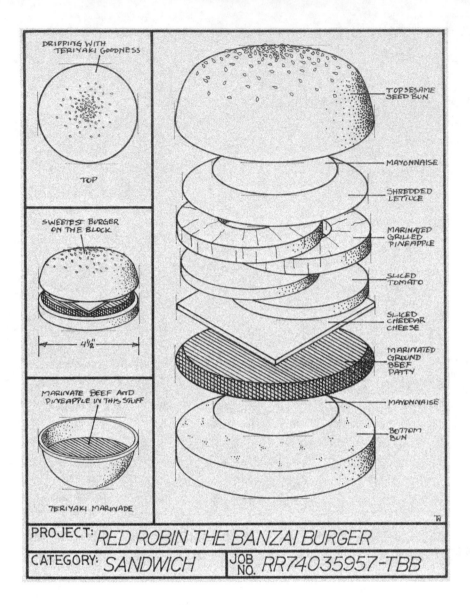

DRIPPING WITH
TERIYAKI GOODNESS

TOP

SWEETEST BURGER
ON THE BLOCK

4½"

MARINATE BEEF AND
PINEAPPLE IN THIS STUFF

TERIYAKI MARINADE

TOP SESAME
SEED BUN

MAYONNAISE

SHREDDED
LETTUCE

MARINATED
GRILLED
PINEAPPLE

SLICED
TOMATO

SLICED
CHEDDAR
CHEESE

MARINATED
GROUND
BEEF
PATTY

MAYONNAISE

BOTTOM
BUN

PROJECT: *RED ROBIN THE BANZAI BURGER*

CATEGORY: *SANDWICH*   JOB NO. *RR74035957-TBB*

1 5.5-ounce ground beef patty
2 canned pineapple slices
2 slices Cheddar cheese
1 sesame seed hamburger bun

4 teaspoons mayonnaise
2 tomato slices
⅓ cup shredded iceberg lettuce

1. Make teriyaki marinade by combining all the ingredients in a small saucepan over medium/high heat. Bring mixture to a boil then reduce heat and simmer for 10 minutes or until sauce thickens. Cover and chill marinade in the refrigerator for at least 30 minutes.

2. Form your ground beef into a round patty that is slightly larger in diameter than the sesame seed bun. Pour a little of the teriyaki glaze into a plastic container with a lid (such as Tupperware), then carefully drop in your patty. Add enough teriyaki glaze to cover the patty, then seal up the container and pop it into the fridge for at least 4 hours, but no more than 12 hours. Put the two pineapple slices into another container with a lid, add the remaining teriyaki glaze, cover it and chill the pineapple in the refrigerator for the same time as the burger.

3. When you are ready to make your hamburger, preheat barbecue or indoor grill to medium heat.

4. Start grilling the hamburger patty first. Cook it for 3 to 5 minutes per side or until it reaches your desired doneness. When you flip the burger add the pineapple slices to the grill. The pineapple will take about half as long to cook as the burger. You'll know the pineapple slices are done when they have some nice grill marks on each side. Be careful not to burn the burger or the pineapple. The teriyaki contains sugar, which may char if grilled too long. About 1 minute before the burger is done place 2 slices of Cheddar cheese on top of the patty to melt.

5. As the hamburger is grilling, toast the face of the top and bottom sesame seed bun on an indoor griddle or skillet over medium heat.

6. Build your burger by first spreading approximately 2 teaspoons

of mayo on each of the toasted faces of the top and bottom bun.

7. Stack the hamburger patty on the bottom bun.
8. Arrange the tomato slices on the patty.
9. Stack the grilled pineapple on top of the tomato slices.
10. Add about ⅓ cup of shredded lettuce on next, then finish the burger off with the top bun.

• MAKES 1 BURGER.

• • • •

RED ROBIN
TERIYAKI CHICKEN BURGER

MENU DESCRIPTION: *"A premium charbroiled chicken breast with sweet teriyaki sauce, grilled pineapple, Swiss cheese, lettuce, tomatoes & mayo. Why did the chicken cross the Pacific? Now you know."*

You're out there on the front line hanging over the grill. The smoke's in your eyes, the hair on your forearm is singed, and your sunburn is heading toward 2nd degree. But you don't care, because it's Saturday and you still get all of Sunday to heal. So whip out some chicken and grab the mallet—it's time to pound the flesh for this sweet chicken sandwich. With the kitchen mallet in hand, not only will you have an opportunity for further heroic injury, but you'll also be able to pound the chicken breast to a uniform thickness that works best when building sandwiches. The sweet and salty flavors of the custom secret teriyaki marinade go perfectly with the grilled pineapple and Swiss cheese (this recipe is for one sandwich but you'll have enough teriyaki marinade to make several sandwiches). Just be sure to watch the pineapple and chicken carefully while over the flames, since the teriyaki marinade has sugar in it and could cause charring from nasty flare-ups. Those small fires, while exciting, are just not good for your food.

TERIYAKI MARINADE

1 ¾ cups water
1 cup soy sauce
1 cup light brown sugar
½ teaspoon onion powder
½ teaspoon garlic powder

1 5-ounce skinless chicken breast
   fillet

2 canned pineapple slices
2 slices Swiss cheese
1 sesame seed hamburger bun
4 teaspoons mayonnaise
2 tomato slices
⅓ cup shredded iceberg
   lettuce

1. Make teriyaki marinade by combining all the ingredients in a small saucepan over medium/high heat. Bring mixture to a boil then reduce heat and simmer for 10 minutes or until sauce thickens. Cover and chill marinade in the refrigerator for at least 30 minutes.

2. Cover the chicken breast fillet with plastic wrap and pound on it with a kitchen mallet so that it is about ½-inch thick. The fillet should be a little larger than the diameter of your sesame seed bun. Pour a little of the teriyaki glaze into a plastic container with a lid (such as Tupperware), then drop the chicken in. Add enough teriyaki glaze to cover the chicken, but make sure you save some to marinate the pineapple slices. Seal up the container and pop it into the fridge for at least 4 hours, but no more than 12 hours. Put the two pineapple slices into another container with a lid, add the remaining teriyaki glaze, cover the container and chill it in the refrigerator for the same time as the chicken.

3. When you are ready to make your sandwich, preheat the barbecue or indoor grill to medium heat.

4. Start grilling the chicken breast first. Cook the chicken for 4 to 6 minutes per side or until it's done. When you flip the chicken add the pineapple slices to the grill. The pineapple will take less time to cook—about 3 or 4 minutes. You'll know the pineapple slices are done when they have some nice grill marks on each side. Be careful not to burn the chicken or the pineapple. The teriyaki contains sugar, which may char if

TOP

TOP SESAME
SEED BUN

MAYONNAISE

SHREDDED
LETTUCE

MARINATED
GRILLED
PINEAPPLE

SLICED
TOMATO

SLICED
SWISS
CHEESE

MARINATED
CHICKEN
BREAST
FILLET

MAYONNAISE

BOTTOM
BUN

4½"

TERIYAKI MARINADE

PROJECT:	RED ROBIN TERIYAKI CHICKEN BURGER	
CATEGORY: SANDWICH	JOB NO.	RR5940679-TCB

grilled too long. About 1 minute before the chicken is done place 2 slices of Swiss cheese on top of the fillet to melt.

5. As the chicken is grilling toast the face of the top and bottom sesame seed bun on an indoor griddle or skillet over medium heat.

6. Build your sandwich by first spreading approximately 2 teaspoons of the mayo on each of the toasted faces of the top and bottom bun.

7. Stack the chicken breast on the bottom bun.

8. Arrange the tomato slices on the chicken.

9. Stack the grilled pineapple on top of the tomato slices.

10. Add about ⅓ cup of shredded lettuce on next, then finish the sandwich off with the top bun.

• MAKES 1 SANDWICH.

• • • •

ROADHOUSE GRILL
ROADHOUSE RITA

If you want to keep this cocktail authentic you'll need to rustle up a 32-ounce jar. Bartenders at the Roadhouse Grill mix this delicious, yet potent libation in a large mason jar normally used for canning. You say you don't have one of those lying around? You have yet to enter the canning phase of your life? Not to worry. Just wash out a hefty mayonnaise jar—the large size. Those big mayo jars weigh in at exactly 32-ounces and provide you with an excuse for finally ditching the yellow gunk that's been fermenting in the back of the fridge for the last two years. For non-purists, any 32-ounce drinking glass or mug will do. Just be sure to fill your glass nearly to the top with ice before you mix. The salt on the rim is optional, but aspirin after a couple of these babies could prove to be essential.

3 ounces Jose Cuervo Gold Tequila (2 shots)
1 ½ ounces Triple Sec (1 shot)
¾ cup sweet-and-sour mix
¾ cup orange juice
1 ½ ounces Bud Light (1 shot)
wedge of lime

OPTIONAL
margarita salt (for rim of glass)

1. If you want salt on the rim of your glass, moisten the rim of a 32-ounce mason jar (a cup or glass is fine) and dip it in margarita salt.
2. To make the drink, fill the jar with ice. Add a couple shots of tequila, a shot of Triple Sec, then some sweet-and-sour mix and orange juice (in equal amounts) to within a half-inch of the top of the glass. Stir.
3. Splash a shot of beer over the top of the drink.
4. Add a wedge of lime and serve with a straw.

- MAKES 1 SERVING.

•   •   •   •

ROADHOUSE GRILL ROADHOUSE CHEESE WRAPS

MENU DESCRIPTION: *"Our original 'eggrolls' stuffed with Cheddar and Monterey Jack cheese, green onions and a touch of jalapeño peppers. Served with marinara."*

This variation on the popular fried cheese sticks appetizer conceals spicy jalapeno peppers and green onions in the middle, and then it's all wrapped up in large spring roll wrapper before frying. The marinara sauce on the side is perfect for dipping the cheesy tidbit, but you might also try your favorite salsa. To save time—and we all like that—use your favorite bottled marinara sauce for dipping so you won't need to whip up something from scratch.

8 thin slices Monterey Jack cheese
8 thin slices Cheddar cheese
1 jalapeno pepper, seeded and
    diced
1 green onion, diced

4 large spring roll wrappers
1 beaten egg
6 to 10 cups vegetable oil (as
    required by your fryer)

ON THE SIDE
marinara sauce

1. Use a sharp knife to make 8 thin slices each from the end of standard-size hunks of Cheddar and Monterey Jack cheeses.
2. Arrange 2 slices of Cheddar and 2 slices of Jack on your hand, then sprinkle about 1 teaspoon of diced jalapeno on top of the cheese. Sprinkle about ¼ teaspoon of diced green onion on next. Sandwich the peppers and green onion between the cheeses and roll it all up. Fold the cheese and squeeze it all together so that the peppers and green onion are sealed into the middle of the cheeses.
3. Lay a spring roll wrapper with one corner pointing away from you. Arrange the cheese lengthwise on the center of the wrapper.
4. Fold one of the side corners over the cheese filling. Brush a little beaten egg on the tip of the other side corner and fold it over the first corner so that it sticks. Brush some beaten egg on the corner pointing away from you. Fold the bottom corner up and over the filling. Roll the wrapper up, keeping it tight, until it rolls over the top corner with the egg on it. It should stick. Repeat with the remaining ingredients, then cover all the wraps and chill for at least 30 minutes. This will be long enough to heat up the oil in a deep fryer or large saucepan to 350 degrees.
5. When the oil is hot, fry the rolls for 2½ to 3 minutes or until the outside is golden brown. Drain the rolls on a rack or paper towels for 2 minutes before serving with your favorite marinara sauce on the side for dipping.

• SERVES 2 TO 4 AS AN APPETIZER.

•   •   •   •

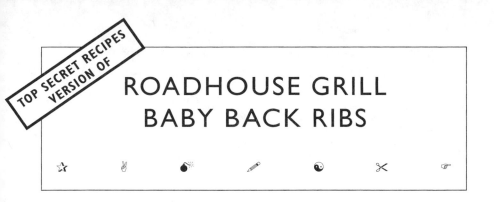

ROADHOUSE GRILL
BABY BACK RIBS

MENU DESCRIPTION: *"Our award-winning Baby Back Ribs are slow-roasted, then basted with Jim Beam Bourbon BBQ Sauce and finished on our Mesquite grill."*

When your crew bites into these baby backs they'll savor meat so tender and juicy that it slides right off the bone. The slow braising cooks the ribs to perfection, while the quick grilling adds the finishing char and smoky flavor. But the most important component to any decent rack of ribs is a sauce that's filled with flavor, and this version of Roadhouse Grill's award-wining sauce is good stuff. I ordered the ribs naked (without sauce) so that I could see if there was any detectable rub added before cooking and I didn't find anything other than salt and a lot of coarse black pepper. So that's the way I designed the recipe, and it works. You may also wish to add a little sauce to the ribs before they go into the oven as a great variation on the technique.

2 large racks of pork baby back ribs	salt
	coarse ground black pepper

SAUCE

2 tablespoons vegetable oil	½ cup apple cider vinegar
¼ cup minced fresh onion	½ cup brown sugar
1 ½ cups water	2 tablespoons honey
½ cup tomato paste	1 tablespoon Worcestershire sauce

1 ¾ teaspoon salt
1 teaspoon liquid mesquite smoke
1 teaspoon Jim Beam whiskey
¼ teaspoon coarse ground black
    pepper

⅛ teaspoon garlic powder
⅛ teaspoon paprika

1. To make the ribs, cut each large rack of ribs in half so that you have 4 half-racks. Sprinkle a light coating of salt and a more generous portion of coarse pepper over the top and bottom of each rack. Wrap the ribs in aluminum foil and bake in a preheated 300 degree oven for 2½ hours.

2. As the ribs cook, make the sauce by heating the oil in a medium saucepan over medium/high heat. Sauté the onions for 5 minutes or until they start to brown. Add the remaining ingredients and bring mixture to a boil then reduce heat and simmer for 1¼ hours, uncovered, or until sauce thickens. Remove from heat and set aside until the ribs are ready. Preheat your barbecue grill.

3. When ribs are finished in the oven, the meat should have pull back about ½-inch from the cut-ends of the bones. Remove the ribs from the oven, let them sit for 10 minutes or so, then remove the racks from the foil and put them on the grill. Grill the ribs for 3 to 4 minutes per side. They should be slightly charred in a few spots when they're finished. Brush barbecue sauce on the ribs while they're grilling, just before you serve them. Don't add the sauce too early or it may burn.

• SERVES 2 (FULL-RACKS) TO 4 (HALF-RACKS).

• • • •

ROMANO'S MACARONI GRILL CHICKEN PORTOBELLO

MENU DESCRIPTION: *"Grilled chicken breast with Portobello mushrooms, smoked mozzarella and demi glace, with a spinach orzo pasta."*

Fire up the grill for this take on one of Romano's most popular entrees. After you grill a couple of portobello mushroom caps, slice them thinly at an extreme angle to make wide slices that fit perfectly on top of grilled chicken breasts that have been rubbed with stone ground mustard (the kind with the whole mustard seeds in it). Romano's delicious demi glace is made from reduced veal stock, but a nice substitute can be made from a combination of canned beef broth and chicken broth. With plenty of garlic, rosemary and thyme in there, you'll have sauce that will get everyone in the house drooling as it simmers on the stove. The fresh julienned spinach tossed into the orzo pasta just before it's served scores extra points.

2 portobello mushroom caps

DEMI GLACE

1 tablespoon extra virgin olive oil
6 cloves garlic, crushed

3 cups beef broth
2 cups chicken broth

1 tablespoon cornstarch
2 teaspoons chopped fresh
    rosemary

½ teaspoon chopped fresh thyme
¼ teaspoon ground black pepper

ORZO PASTA

1 pound orzo pasta
1 tablespoon extra virgin oil
2 tablespoons minced garlic
    (4 cloves)
¾ cup diced red bell pepper
    (½ pepper)
1 cup chicken broth
4 tablespoons butter (½ stick)
1 teaspoon salt

½ teaspoon ground black pepper
4 cups julienned fresh spinach

4 skinless chicken breast fillets,
    halved (or 8 small fillets)
8 slices smoked mozzarella cheese

8 teaspoons stone ground
    mustard (such as Inglehoffer)

1. Preheat your grill to high. Remove the stems from the Porto-
    bello mushrooms and brush the caps with a coating of olive
    oil. Sprinkle salt and pepper on the underside of each cap,
    then grill for about 3 minutes per side. Remove the mush-
    room caps from the grill to cool for about 5 minutes. Slice
    the mushrooms at an extreme angle with a very sharp knife
    so that you get very wide slices. You want the knife almost
    parallel to the cutting surface so that your slices will cover
    the chicken breast. Take 8 of the biggest slices, cover them,
    then chop up the left over mushroom to use in the sauce.
2. Prepare the demi glace sauce by heating 1 tablespoon of extra
    virgin olive oil in a medium saucepan over medium/low heat.
    Crush 6 cloves of garlic with the palm of your hand and toss
    them into the oil along with the chopped mushroom pieces.
    Sweat the garlic and mushroom (slowly cook without
    browning) for 10 minutes. Add beef broth and chicken broth,
    then whisk in cornstarch. Add rosemary, thyme and black
    pepper and simmer for 40 minutes, then remove sauce from
    heat and cover it.
3. Prepare the orzo pasta by boiling it in a large pot of water.
    You want it al dente, which means it should be slightly tough

(we'll be cooking it more later). That should take about 7 minutes. Drain pasta.

4. Heat up 1 tablespoon of oil in a large stockpot or use the same pot you used for cooking the pasta. Add 2 tablespoons of minced garlic and the diced red bell pepper and sauté for 1 minute. Add the drained orzo pasta, 1 cup chicken broth, 4 tablespoons butter, 1 teaspoon salt, and ½ teaspoon ground black pepper. Cook for 10 minutes over medium heat, stirring occasionally.

5. Pound the chicken breasts a bit so that they are uniform in thickness. Rub ½ teaspoon stone ground mustard on each side of each chicken piece, then rub each with some oil. Grill the chicken for 4 to 5 minutes per side or until done. About 2 minutes before the chicken is done lay a slice of portobello mushroom on each piece. Lay a slice of mozzarella on the mushroom on each breast and finish grilling the chicken. When the cheese is melted, remove the chicken from the grill.

6. To serve dish, stir spinach into orzo and immediately spoon an equal helping onto each of four plates. Arrange two chicken pieces on each of the plates, then spoon the demi glace over the chicken and serve.

- MAKES 4 SERVINGS.

•   •   •   •

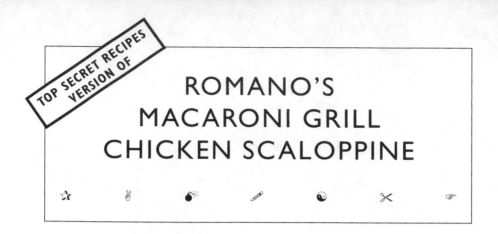

ROMANO'S MACARONI GRILL CHICKEN SCALOPPINE

MENU DESCRIPTION: *"Chicken breast, mushrooms, artichokes, capers & smoked prosciutto in lemon butter with pasta."*

Mushrooms, artichoke hearts, and prosciutto in a creamy lemon butter sauce surround sautéed chicken breasts and angel hair pasta for this unique and satisfying take on a traditional dish. This clone ranks in the top three most requested recipes on my hit list from the 227-unit Romano's Macaroni Grill. The successful Italian chain is part of the Brinker group of restaurants that controls several other high-profile casual eateries including Border Mexican Grill, Maggiano's, and Chili's.

SAUCE

1 tablespoon white wine
2 teaspoons lemon juice
1 cup salted butter (2 sticks)
⅓ cup heavy cream

1 pound angel hair pasta (or
    pasta of your choice)
4 skinless chicken breast fillets
½ cup all-purpose flour
3 tablespoons light olive oil

2 tablespoons butter
½ teaspoon lemon juice
2 cups sliced mushrooms
1½ cups canned artichoke
    hearts, sliced
    (1 14-ounce can)
⅓ cup thick-sliced smoked
    prosciutto, chopped (about
    1½ ounces)
2 tablespoons capers

GARNISH
4 teaspoons minced fresh parsley

1. Make the lemon butter sauce by pouring white wine and lemon juice into a saucepan over medium/low heat. Add butter and stir occasionally until it's melted. When the butter is melted, add the cream and whisk thoroughly. Bring mixture to a simmer, stirring frequently. Simmer for 5 to 6 minutes or until the sauce is thick. Remove it from the heat and set it aside.
2. Fold plastic wrap over each chicken breast and pound them with a mallet until the chicken is about ⅛-inch thick. Slice each flattened breast in half, then lightly salt and pepper each piece. Pour flour onto a plate then coat each chicken piece with a light layer of flour. If you haven't already done it, this is a good time to start boiling your pasta. Follow the directions on the package to cook the pasta al dente, or just slightly tough.
3. Preheat oven to 250 degrees. Heat 2 tablespoons of light olive oil, 2 tablespoons of butter, and ½ teaspoon of lemon juice in a large skillet over medium heat. Add the chicken breast pieces, four at a time, to the skillet and sauté for about 5 minutes per side or until the chicken is light brown. Place finished chicken on a baking sheet and keep it warm in the oven until you are ready to assemble your dish.
4. Rinse out the skillet and place it back over medium heat. Add 1 tablespoon of olive oil to the pan. When the oil is hot add the mushrooms, artichoke hearts, prosciutto, and capers and sauté for 3 to 4 minutes or just until you see some slight browning on the mushrooms and artichoke hearts. Pour the lemon butter sauce into the skillet and remove it from the heat.

5. Prepare each dish by piling pasta on one side of the plate. Sprinkle fresh parsley over the pasta. Arrange 2 chicken pieces on each plate then spoon the mushroom/artichoke sauce over the chicken pieces and serve.

•   MAKES 4 SERVINGS.

TIDBITS

If you can't find smoked prosciutto, any prosciutto will do. If you can, have your deli slice it about ⅛-inch thick.

• • • •

ROMANO'S MACARONI GRILL PENNE RUSTICA

☆   ✌   ●   ✏   ☯   ✂   ☞

MENU DESCRIPTION: *"Shrimp, grilled chicken & smoked prosciutto and Parmesan baked in a creamy cheese sauce."*

Romano's top-requested item is so popular they've even trade-marked the name. Grilled chicken, shrimp, prosciutto, and penne pasta bathed in a creamy gratinata sauce is topped with cheese and paprika, and baked until the top is a crispy brown. There's a distinct smoky flavor that comes from the smoked prosciutto used by the chain, and you might have a hard time finding such a unique item at your deli. No big deal. Just use regular prosciutto, and have the deli cut it pretty thick—⅛-inch will do. The dish will still work since you'll get smoky hints from the grilled chicken and shrimp. The chain serves up the entree in a wide, shallow baking dish that comes to you straight from the salamander (overhead oven/broiler). If you don't have any baking dishes like that, try using 9-inch glass pie dishes. These make for a great presentation, especially when served hot right to the table, garnished with a sprig of rosemary and a few sliced pimentos on top. Be sure to get the sliced pimentos, not diced. You want long pieces just like those they use at the restaurant.

GRATINATA SAUCE

3 tablespoons butter
2 tablespoons minced garlic
3 tablespoons Marsala wine
2 cups heavy cream
1 cup grated Parmesan cheese
½ cup milk
½ cup chicken broth
1 tablespoon cornstarch
1 tablespoon Grey Poupon Dijon
    mustard
2 teaspoons minced fresh
    rosemary

½ teaspoon salt
½ teaspoon minced fresh thyme
¼ teaspoon ground cayenne
    pepper

1 pound penne rigate pasta
12 medium shrimp, peeled and
    deveined
2 skinless chicken breast fillets
½ cup (about 2 ounces) thick-
    sliced smoked prosciutto,
    chopped

TOPPING

3 tablespoon grated Parmesan
    cheese

1 ½ teaspoons paprika

GARNISH

12 slices pimentos

4 sprigs rosemary

1. Preheat barbecue grill to high.
2. Prepare gratinata sauce by melting 3 tablespoons of butter over medium/low heat. Add garlic and sweat it for about 5 minutes. Be sure the garlic doesn't brown. Add the Marsala wine and cook for another 5 minutes. Add the remaining ingredients for the sauce and whisk well until smooth. Bring mixture to a simmer and keep it there for 10 minutes or until it's thick. Cover sauce and remove it from the heat.
3. Cook pasta following directions on the package (7 to 9 minutes in boiling water). You want the pasta tender, but not mushy (al dente). Drain pasta and set it aside when it's done.
4. Pound the thick end of your chicken breasts a bit with a kitchen mallet to make them a uniform thickness. Rub chicken

with olive oil, then sprinkle on a bit of salt and pepper. Spear the shrimp on skewers (6 per skewer should work fine), then rub them with oil, and sprinkle with salt and pepper.

5. Grill chicken for 5 to 6 minutes per side. Grill shrimp for 2 minutes per side. When chicken is done, slice each breast into strips.

6. Preheat oven to 500 degrees. Build each dish in a large, shallow baking dish. Or you can use a 9-inch glass or ceramic pie plate. Load 3 cups of pasta into each baking dish. Add one-quarter of the chicken, 3 shrimp and 2 tablespoons of prosciutto onto each serving. Spoon ¾ of a cup of gratinata sauce on each serving and toss to coat. Combine 3 tablespoons of grated Parmesan cheese with 1½ teaspoons paprika, then sprinkle about 1 tablespoon of this mixture over the top of each serving. Bake the dishes for 10 to 12 minutes, or until tops begin to brown. Arrange three pimento slices on the top of each serving, then jab a sprig of rosemary into the center and serve.

- Makes 4 servings.

• • • •

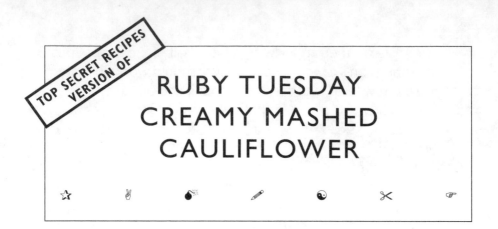

RUBY TUESDAY CREAMY MASHED CAULIFLOWER

The low-carb craze is influencing menus of America's restaurant chains, but no chain has embraced the trend as enthusiastically as Ruby Tuesday. *Nation's Restaurant News* awarded the chain "Best Healthy Choice Menu Selection for 2004," based on more than 30 new low-carb dishes added to the menu, including low-carb cheesecake, burgers in high-fiber tortilla wraps, and other low-carb stand-ins such as Creamy Mashed Cauliflower. This most talked-about of the new selections is a side dish stunt double for mashed potatoes, with a carb count coming in at a measly 9 net carbs per ¾-cup serving, according to the menu. The spices and cream that are added to steamed and pureed cauliflower give this dish the taste, texture and appearance of America's favorite side. Serve this up with any entrée that goes well with mashed potatoes, and you'll never miss the spuds.

1 head cauliflower
¾ cup water
1 tablespoon cornstarch
⅓ cup heavy cream
1 teaspoon granulated sugar

¾ teaspoon salt
¼ teaspoon ground white pepper
⅛ teaspoon garlic powder
⅛ teaspoon onion powder

1. Divide a head of cauliflower into florets that are all roughly the same size. Steam cauliflower pieces over boiling water for 15 to 20 minutes, or until the cauliflower is tender. Drain the cauliflower and toss it in a bowl of ice water to bring the cooking process to a screeching halt.
2. When the cauliflower has cooled, put the florets in a food processor along with ½ cup of water. Puree the cauliflower on high speed until smooth, but with some very small pieces of cauliflower remaining in the mix for just a bit of texture.
3. Pour all of the pureed cauliflower into a medium saucepan. Dissolve the cornstarch in the remaining ¼ cup of water and add the solution to the cauliflower.
4. Add the cream, salt, white pepper, garlic powder and onion powder to the cauliflower and stir. Set the saucepan over medium heat and cook, stirring often, for 5 to 10 minutes, or until thick.

- MAKES THREE ¾-CUP SERVINGS.

• • • •

TGI FRIDAY'S
BLACK BEAN SOUP

If you start making black bean soup in the morning using other recipes out there, you're lucky to be slurping soup by lunchtime. That's because most recipes require dry beans that have to re-hydrate for at least a couple hours, and many recipes say "over-night." But you know, tomorrow's just too far away when you're craving soup right now. So, for this often requested clone recipe, I sped up the process by incorporating canned black beans, rather than the dry ones. That way, once you get all the veggies chopped, you'll be souped up in less than an hour. Fridays' version of this soup has a slightly smoky flavor that's easily duplicated here with just a little bit of concentrated liquid smoke flavoring found in most markets. Just be sure to get the kind that says "hickory flavor."

2 tablespoons vegetable oil
¾ cup diced white onion
¾ cup diced celery
½ cup diced carrot
¼ cup diced green bell pepper
2 tablespoons minced garlic
4 15-ounce cans black beans

4 cups chicken broth
2 tablespoons apple cider vinegar
2 teaspoons chili powder
½ teaspoon cayenne pepper
½ teaspoon ground cumin
½ teaspoon salt
¼ teaspoon liquid hickory smoke

GARNISH

*shredded Cheddar/Monterey
    Jack cheese blend*

chopped green onion

1. Heat 2 tablespoons of oil in a large saucepan over medium/low heat. Add onion, celery, carrot, bell pepper, and garlic to the oil and simmer slowly (sweat) for 15 minutes or until the onions are practically clear. Keep the heat low enough that the veggies don't brown.
2. While you cook the veggies, pour the canned beans into a strainer and rinse them under cold water.
3. Measure 3 cups of the drained and rinsed beans into a food processor with 1 cup of chicken broth. Puree on high speed until smooth.
4. When the veggies are ready, pour the pureed beans, the whole beans, the rest of the chicken broth, and every other ingredient in the list (down to the liquid smoke), to the pot. Bring mixture to a boil, then reduce heat and simmer uncovered for 50 to 60 minutes or until soup has thickened and all the ingredients are tender. Serve the soup topped with a couple tablespoons of the cheese blend and a teaspoon or so of chopped green onion.

- MAKES SIX 1-CUP SERVINGS.

• • • •

T.G.I. FRIDAY'S BROCCOLI CHEESE SOUP

So good, and yet so easy. Now you can recreate this one at home just by tossing a few ingredients into a saucepan. Try to find one of the large 32-ounce cartons of chicken broth from Swanson—there's four cups in there, so it's perfect for this recipe. One big head of broccoli should provide enough florets to get you set. Use only the florets and ditch the stem, but be sure to cut the florets into bite-size pieces before dropping them in.

4 cups chicken broth
1 cup water
1 cup half-and-half
4 slices Kraft Cheddar Singles
½ cup all-purpose flour

½ teaspoon dried minced onion
¼ teaspoon ground black pepper
4 cups broccoli florets (bite-size pieces)

GARNISH
½ cup shredded Cheddar cheese

2 teaspoons minced fresh parsley

1. Combine chicken broth, water, half-and-half, cheese, flour, onion and pepper in a large saucepan. Whisk to combine and to break up any lumps of flour, then turn heat to medium/high.
2. Bring soup to a boil, then reduce heat to low.

3. Add broccoli to soup and simmer for 15 to 20 minutes or until broccoli is tender but not soft.
4. For each serving spoon one cup of soup into a bowl and garnish with a tablespoon of shredded cheese and a pinch of parsley.

• MAKES 6 SERVINGS.

•   •   •   •

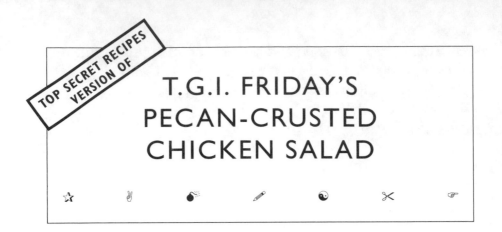

T.G.I. FRIDAY'S PECAN-CRUSTED CHICKEN SALAD

MENU DESCRIPTION: *"Pecan-crusted chicken, served sliced and chilled on salad greens tossed with Balsamic Vinaigrette dressing, topped with mandarin oranges, sweet-glazed pecans, celery, dried cranberries and Bleu cheese."*

With dried cranberries, mandarin orange wedges, bleu cheese, pecan-crusted chicken breast, and a delicious sweet and sour balsamic vinaigrette, it's no wonder this salad is the top pick at one of America's first casual dining chains. And don't be intimidated by all the ingredients here. The dressing is a cakewalk since you just pour everything (except the garlic) into a blender. The pecan-crusted chicken is a simple breading procedure, and the chicken cooks up in a snap. You'll be spending most of your time at the chopping block as you hack pecans into little pieces and get the lettuce, garlic and celery ready. I've made this recipe to serve four, but if there are only two of you, you can easily cut it in half.

PECAN-CRUSTED CHICKEN

4 skinless chicken breast fillets
½ cup finely chopped pecans
½ cup corn flake crumbs
¾ teaspoon salt

1 cup milk
2 eggs, beaten
1 cup all-purpose flour
½ cup canola oil

BALSAMIC VINAIGRETTE

1 cup canola oil

⅓ cup balsamic vinegar

4 teaspoons Grey Poupon Dijon
  mustard

4 teaspoons granulated sugar

½ teaspoons salt

2 teaspoons minced garlic
  (2 cloves)

1 cup dried cranberries

3 tablespoons dark brown sugar

½ cup finely chopped pecans

12 cups chopped romaine lettuce
  (2 heads)

1 cup sliced celery (2 stalks)

2 11-ounce cans mandarin
  orange segments, drained

½ cup crumbled bleu cheese

1. We'll make the pecan-crusted chicken first since it is
    served cold. Pound each chicken fillet to about ½-inch
    thick. You can do this easily by covering each chicken breast
    in plastic wrap, and pounding away with a kitchen mallet.
    Combine ½ cup finely chopped pecans, corn flake crumbs,
    and ¾ teaspoon salt in a shallow bowl. Combine milk with
    beaten eggs in another shallow bowl. Dump the flour into
    another shallow bowl. Bread each chicken breast by coating
    each with flour. Dip the flour-dusted chicken into the egg
    mixture, and then coat the chicken with a thick coating of the
    pecans and corn flake crumbs. Preheat ½ cup of canola oil in
    a large skillet over medium/low heat. When the oil is hot,
    sauté the chicken fillets for 3 to 4 minutes per side or until
    golden brown. Cool chicken on a rack or paper towels. When
    you can handle the chicken, cover it and refrigerate for at
    least two hours.

2. As the chicken chills, you can make the balsamic vinaigrette by
    combining 1 cup canola oil, balsamic vinegar, mustard, granu-
    lated sugar and ½ teaspoon salt in a blender. Blend on low
    speed for just a few seconds, or until the dressing begins to
    thicken. Don't blend too long or your vinaigrette will get too
    thick, like mayonnaise. Pour vinaigrette into a small bowl and
    mix in minced garlic. Chill this until you're ready to use it.

3. When you're ready to build your salads, toss lettuce and celery with about ¾ cup of the balsamic vinaigrette.
4. Arrange the lettuce on four plates, then sprinkle the cranberries over the lettuce (about ¼ cup per serving).
5. Combine the 3 tablespoons of brown sugar with ½ cup finely chopped pecans. Sprinkle 2 tablespoons of this mixture on each salad.
6. Sprinkle about ½ can of drained mandarin segments over each salad, followed by about 2 tablespoons of crumbled bleu cheese.
7. Sliced each chicken fillet into thin strips. Arrange one sliced chicken fillet on top of each salad and serve.

• MAKES 4 SERVINGS.

• • • •

T.G.I. FRIDAY'S
SIZZLING SHRIMP

The T.G.I. Friday's chain engineered a system-wide rejuvenation by upgrading the look of the restaurants and replacing many old menu items with new, creative dishes including several Atkins-approved low-carb selections. Though not low-carb (because of the potatoes) this new menu addition is still a healthy entree choice, and the presentation is very cool with the dish coming to your table in a sizzling iron skillet just like fajitas. This clone recreates that same sizzling presentation in a large serving for two (If you want to serve more, simply add another 8 to 10 shrimp to the dish—there are plenty of peppers and other stuff in there so the recipe still works). All you have to do is pop an oven-safe skillet into the oven as the potatoes are baking. This way, when the dish is ready to serve, you simply transfer it to this blazing hot pan before bringing it to the table. Ah, nice sizzle. Since this pan will be heating up in a very hot oven, be sure not to use a skillet with a plastic handle that could melt. A large cast-iron skillet is the best choice, if you've got one. If you don't have an oven-safe pan, you can always heat up your skillet on the stovetop.

POTATOES

2 medium red potatoes
2 teaspoons light olive oil
2 pinches salt

2 pinches ground black pepper
2 pinches minced fresh parsley

1 tablespoon light olive oil
1 green bell pepper, sliced
1 red bell pepper, sliced
½ Spanish onion, sliced
1 teaspoon ground cumin
¾ teaspoon Italian seasoning
   (herb blend)
¾ teaspoon salt
¾ teaspoon ground black pepper

¼ teaspoon cayenne pepper
1 14.5-ounce can diced
   tomatoes
24 to 28 medium shrimp, peeled
   and deveined
4 cloves garlic, minced
   (2 tablespoons)
1 tablespoon lime juice

GARNISH

½ cup crumbled ranchero or cotija
   cheese

1 tablespoon minced fresh parsley

1. Preheat oven to 475 degrees. Make sure your oven has two racks so that you have room to heat up the serving skillet. Place a large cast iron skillet or an oven-safe skillet (that does not have plastic handles) on the lower rack of the oven. This is the pan that will make the shrimp sizzling hot. Slice each of the potatoes lengthwise into 8 wedges. Toss the potatoes in a bowl with 2 teaspoons olive oil, plus a couple pinches each of salt, ground black pepper and minced parsley. Arrange the potato wedges in a non-stick baking pan (or in a pan lined with parchment paper), and bake for 25 to 30 minutes or until potatoes turn golden brown. When the potatoes are done, take them out and turn off the oven. Keep the empty skillet in there on the lower rack. We'll use that at the end.

2. Heat 1 tablespoon of olive oil in a large skillet over medium heat. When the oil is hot, add the red and green bell peppers, and onion. Stir in the cumin, ¾ teaspoon salt, ¾ teaspoon ground black pepper, Italian seasoning, and cayenne pepper. Sauté the vegetables for 8 minutes, stirring often.

3. When peppers and onions have sautéed for 8 minutes, add the can of diced tomatoes, including the liquid to the skillet.

Add the shrimp, garlic and lime juice. Cook for another 5 minutes, stirring often.

4. Use a thick hot pad to carefully remove the hot skillet from the oven. Pour the entire contents of the dish into the hot skillet, then arrange the potato wedges around the edge of the dish. Quickly sprinkle crumbled ranchero or cotija cheese over the center of the dish, followed by about a tablespoon of minced fresh parsley. Serve it up immediately—while it's still sizzling.

- SERVES 2.

• • • •

TONY ROMA'S BLUE RIDGE SMOKIES SAUCE

☆   ✌   💣   ✎   ☯   ✂   ☞

Of the four famous barbecue sauces served on those delicious, tender ribs at Tony Roma's, this is the only one that wasn't cloned in the first restaurant book, *Top Secret Restaurant Recipes*. This sweet, smoky sauce is great on pork spareribs cooked with the Tony Roma's clone recipe in that book, or you can use either of the techniques found in this book: For Chili's Baby Backs on page 105, and for Roadhouse Grill Baby Backs on page 319. Or you can use the sauce on a recipe of your own for pork or beef ribs, even chicken. Now Tony Roma's sells each of its four sauces at the restaurant chain, separately, or in gift sets. But if you don't have a Tony Roma's close by, or you just like to dabble, this is a good way to get that one-of-a-kind barbecue taste at home.

1 cup ketchup
1 cup red wine vinegar
½ cup brown sugar
¼ cup molasses
1 ½ teaspoons liquid hickory smoke

½ teaspoon salt
rounded ¼ teaspoon ground black pepper
¼ teaspoon garlic powder
¼ teaspoon onion powder

1. Combine all of the ingredients in a medium saucepan over high heat, and whisk until smooth.
2. Bring sauce to a boil, then reduce heat and simmer uncovered for 30 to 40 minutes or until sauce has thickened.

• MAKES 1 ½ CUPS.

•   •   •   •

TONY ROMA'S
BAKED POTATO SOUP

MENU DESCRIPTION: *"A house specialty full of baked potatoes and topped with cheddar cheese, bacon and green onions."*

The thick-and-creamy texture and rich taste of Tony Roma's best-selling soup is duplicated with a little flour, some half-and-half, and most notably, instant mashed potatoes. Give yourself an hour to bake the potatoes and around 30 minutes to prepare the soup. Garnish each serving with shredded cheese, crumbled bacon and green onions, and then humbly await your due praise.

2 medium russet potatoes
3 tablespoons butter
1 cup diced white onion
2 tablespoons all-purpose flour
4 cups chicken broth
2 cups water
¼ cup cornstarch

1 ½ cups instant mashed
    potatoes, dry
1 teaspoon salt
¾ teaspoon ground black pepper
½ teaspoon dried basil
⅛ teaspoon dried thyme
1 cup half-and-half

GARNISH

½ cup shredded Cheddar cheese
¼ cup crumbled cooked bacon

2 green onions, chopped
    (green part only)

1. Preheat oven to 400 degrees and bake the potatoes for 1 hour or until done. When potatoes have cooked remove them from the oven to cool.
2. As potatoes cool prepare soup by melting butter in a large saucepan, and sauté onion until light brown. Add the flour to the onions and stir to make a roux.
3. Add broth, water, cornstarch, mashed potato flakes, and spices to the pot and bring to a boil. Reduce heat and simmer for 5 minutes.
4. Cut potatoes in half lengthwise and scoop out contents with a large spoon. Discard skin. Chop baked potato with a large knife to make chunks that are about ½-inch in size.
5. Add chopped baked potato and half-and-half to the saucepan, bring soup back to a boil, then reduce heat and simmer the soup for another 15 minutes or until it is thick.
6. Spoon about 1½ cups of soup into a bowl and top with about a tablespoon of shredded Cheddar cheese, a half tablespoon of crumbled bacon and a teaspoon or so of chopped green onion. Repeat for remaining servings.

- SERVES 6 TO 8.

• • • •

TONY ROMA'S
MAPLE SWEET POTATOES

Here's a clone for a new menu item at Tony Roma's that's served alongside the Carolina Honeys BBQ Salmon (cloned in the preceding recipe on page 347). With maple syrup, cinnamon and pecans in there, this is a great new way for you to easily prepare sweet potatoes that everyone at the table will surely scarf down with unbridled glee.

1 large sweet potato
1 tablespoon butter
¼ of a white onion, chopped
   (about ½ cup)

3 tablespoons finely chopped
   pecans
3 tablespoons maple syrup
¼ teaspoon cinnamon

1. Bake sweet potato for 40 to 45 minutes at 400 degrees. This will bake the potato nearly all the way through, while still leaving it firm enough to slice when cool. Remove the sweet potato from the oven and let it cool so that you can handle it. When the sweet potato has cooled, remove the skin and slice it into 1-inch bite-size cubes.

2. Melt 1 tablespoon of butter in a large skillet. Add onion and pecans and sauté for a couple minutes or until onion begins to brown.

3. Add cubed sweet potato, maple syrup and cinnamon and sauté for 3 to 5 minutes, stirring often, or until the sweet potato pieces are hot and tender.

• SERVES 2 TO 4.

• • • •

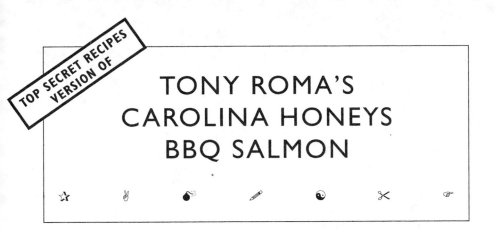

TONY ROMA'S CAROLINA HONEYS BBQ SALMON

Take one of Tony Roma's famous sauces, brush it over some grilled salmon and you've got a bravo moment. But it's not just about saucing up the fish. The salmon is first rubbed with a secret seasoning blend before it's grilled. The sauce doesn't appear in the show until the end. For your encore, serve this dish along with the next recipe for Maple Sweet Potatoes on the side just like in the restaurant, and absorb the applause.

SAUCE

1 cup ketchup
1 cup white vinegar
½ cup molasses
½ cup honey
1 teaspoon liquid hickory smoke

½ teaspoon salt
¼ teaspoon garlic powder
¼ teaspoon onion powder
¼ teaspoon Tabasco pepper
   sauce

SEASONING

1 teaspoon salt
½ teaspoon ground black pepper
¼ teaspoon paprika
¼ teaspoon garlic powder

¼ teaspoon cayenne pepper
4 6-ounce salmon fillets (without
   skin)
canola or olive oil non-stick spray

1. Combine all ingredients for the sauce in a saucepan over medium/high heat. Blend the ingredients with a whisk until smooth. When the mixture comes to a boil, reduce heat and simmer uncovered for 30 minutes or until mixture thickens. Remove from heat.
2. Combine all ingredients for seasoning in a small bowl. Pre-heat barbecue or indoor grill to high heat.
3. Sprinkle seasoning lightly over both sides of the salmon, spray each fillet lightly with olive or canola oil non-stick spray. Grill the salmon for about 3 minutes then rotate it 90 degrees to make criss-crossing grill marks. Grill for another 3 minutes then turn the salmon over for 3 minutes and rotate it again to make criss-crossing grill marks on that side. Grill until done. Remove salmon fillets from the grill, brush with the sauce and serve.

• SERVES 4.

•　•　•　•

WAFFLE HOUSE WAFFLES

It was two friendly Atlanta, Georgia neighbors who got together in 1955 to build the first Waffle House in their eventual 1479-restaurant chain. With the dimpled breakfast hotcake as a signature item (and this is 3 years before IHOP was founded!), the privately held chain grew into 20 Southern U.S. states. Today tasty food at rock-bottom prices, plus 24-hours-a-day service, makes Waffle House a regular stop for devoted customers any time of the day or night. And don't even think about referring to your server as a waitress; they're called "associates."

For the best clone of the 50-year-old secret formula for these waffles you really should chill this batter overnight in the fridge as they do in each of the restaurants. But hey, sometimes you just can't wait. If you need instant gratification, the recipe still works fine if you cook up the waffles the same day. At least wait for 15 to 20 minutes after you make the batter so that it can rest and thicken a bit. That'll give you time to dust off the waffle iron and heat it up.

1 ½ cups all-purpose flour
1 teaspoon salt
½ teaspoon baking soda
1 egg
½ cup plus 1 tablespoon
    granulated sugar
2 tablespoons butter, softened

2 tablespoons vegetable
    shortening
½ cup half-and-half
½ cup milk
¼ cup buttermilk
¼ teaspoon vanilla extract

1. Combine flour, salt and baking soda in a medium bowl. Stir to combine.
2. Lightly beat the egg in another medium bowl. Add the sugar, butter, and shortening and mix well with an electric mixer until smooth. Add the half-and-half, milk, buttermilk and vanilla. Mix well.
3. Add the wet mixture to the dry mixture while beating. Mix only briefly. It's okay if there are small lumps in the batter since over beating could produce waffles that are too tough.
4. Cover and chill overnight. (You can use batter right away if you like, but a good 12-hour chill makes a better batter.)
5. Rub a light coating of vegetable oil on your waffle iron or use a non-stick oil spray. Preheat the waffle iron. Leave the batter out of the refrigerator to warm up a bit as your waffle iron is preheating.
6. Spoon ⅓ to ½ cup of batter into the waffle iron and cook for 3 to 4 minutes or until the waffles are brown.

• MAKES 6 WAFFLES.

•   •   •   •

Classic Restaurant Recipes

APPLEBEE'S QUESADILLAS

☆　✌　💣　✏　☯　✂　☞

MENU DESCRIPTION: *"Two cheeses, bacon, tomatoes, onions & jalapenos grilled between tortillas with guacamole, sour cream & salsa."*

When Bill and T.J. Palmer opened their first restaurant in Atlanta, Georgia, in 1980, they realized their dream of building a full-service, reasonably-priced restaurant in a neighborhood setting. They called their first place T.J. Applebee's Edibles & Elixirs, and soon began franchising the concept. In 1988 some franchisees bought the rights to the name and changed it to Applebee's Neighborhood Grill & Bar. By that time, there were 54 restaurants in the organization. Today there are over 650, making Applebee's one of the fastest-growing restaurant chains in the world.

According to waiters at the restaurant, the easy-to-make and slightly spicy quesadillas are one of the most popular appetizers on the Applebee's menu. The recipe calls for 10-inch or "burrito-size" flour tortillas, which can be found in most supermarkets, but any size can be used in a pinch. Look for the jalapeño "nacho slices" in the ethnic or Mexican food section of the supermarket. You'll find these in jars or cans. Cilantro, which is growing immensely in popularity, can be found in the produce section near the parsley, and is also called fresh coriander or Chinese parsley.

2 10-inch ("burrito-size") flour
　　tortillas
2 tablespoons butter, softened

⅓ cup shredded Monterey Jack
　　cheese
⅓ cup shredded Cheddar cheese

½ medium tomato, chopped
2 teaspoons diced onion
I teaspoon diced canned jalapeño
("nacho slices")

I slice bacon, cooked
¼ teaspoon finely chopped fresh
cilantro
dash salt

ON THE SIDE

sour cream
guacamole

salsa

1. Heat a large frying pan over medium heat.
2. Spread half of the butter on one side of each tortilla. Put one tortilla, butter side down, in the hot pan.
3. Spread the cheeses evenly onto the center of the tortilla in the pan. You don't have to spread the cheese all the way to the edge. Leave a margin of an inch or so all the way around.
4. Sprinkle the tomato, onion, and jalapeño over the cheese.
5. Crumble the slice of cooked bacon and sprinkle it over the other ingredients.
6. Sprinkle the cilantro and a dash of salt over the other ingredients.
7. Top off the quesadilla with the remaining tortilla, being sure that the buttered side is facing up.
8. When the bottom tortilla has browned, after 45 to 90 seconds, flip the quesadilla over and grill the other side for the same length of time.
9. Remove the quesadilla from the pan, and, using a sharp knife or pizza cutter, cut the quesadilla three times through the middle like a pizza, creating 6 equal slices. Serve hot with sour cream, guacamole, and salsa on the side.

• SERVES I OR 2 AS AN APPETIZER.

• • • •

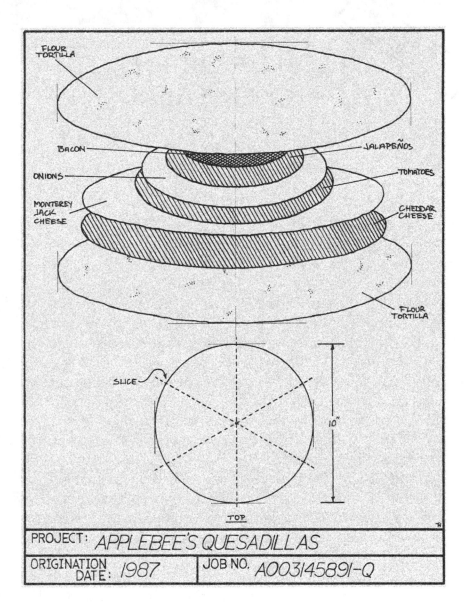

FLOUR TORTILLA

BACON

ONIONS

MONTEREY JACK CHEESE

JALAPEÑOS

TOMATOES

CHEDDAR CHEESE

FLOUR TORTILLA

SLICE

10"

TOP

PROJECT: *APPLEBEE'S QUESADILLAS*

ORIGINATION DATE: *1987*

JOB NO. *A003145891-Q*

353

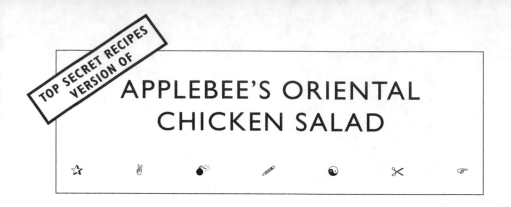

APPLEBEE'S ORIENTAL CHICKEN SALAD

MENU DESCRIPTION: *"Crisp Oriental greens topped with chunks of crunchy Chicken Fingers, toasted almonds & crispy rice noodles tossed in a light Oriental vinaigrette."*

Applebee's 60-item menu is revised at least twice a year. That means about 40 percent of the entire menu changes on a regular basis, with those selections varying from location to location. The other 60 percent are items found on menus in all of the Applebee's restaurants, and they seldom change. This practice of constant menu retooling is becoming more frequent in all of the large restaurant chains these days. As competition grows, the chains find they must alter their menus regularly to keep discriminating customers interested.

Even though the Oriental Chicken Salad, which is considered one of the restaurant's signature items, has been on the menu for some time now, it's possible that by the time you are reading this book it has been replaced by another salad selection. If that happens, here's the only way you can still enjoy this salad creation—by making your own. You'll love the Oriental dressing with the unique, nutty flavor of roasted sesame oil. This type of oil is becoming quite popular today and can be found in the supermarket near the other oils or where the Asian food is displayed.

ORIENTAL DRESSING

3 tablespoons honey
1 ½ tablespoons white vinegar
4 teaspoons mayonnaise

1 tablespoon Grey Poupon Dijon
   mustard
⅛ teaspoon sesame oil

SALAD

2 to 4 cups vegetable oil for frying
1 egg
½ cup milk
½ cup all-purpose flour
½ cup cornflake crumbs
1 teaspoon salt
¼ teaspoon ground black pepper
1 skinless chicken breast fillet

3 cups chopped romaine lettuce
1 cup chopped red cabbage
1 cup chopped napa cabbage
½ carrot, julienned or
   shredded
1 green onion, sliced
1 tablespoon sliced almonds
⅓ cup chow mein noodles

1. Using an electric mixer, blend together all the ingredients for the dressing in a small bowl. Put the dressing in the refrigerator to chill while you prepare the salad.
2. Preheat the oil in a deep fryer or frying pan over medium heat. You want the temperature of the oil to be around 350 degrees. If using a frying pan, the oil should be around ½ inch deep. More oil can be used in a deep fryer so that the chicken is immersed.
3. In a small, shallow bowl beat the egg, add the milk, and mix well.
4. In another bowl, combine the flour with the cornflake crumbs, salt, and pepper.
5. Cut the chicken breast into 4 or 5 long strips. Dip each strip of chicken first into the egg mixture then into the flour mixture, coating each piece completely.
6. Fry each chicken finger for 5 minutes or until the coating has darkened to brown.
7. Prepare the salad by tossing the romaine with the red cabbage, napa cabbage, and carrot.

8. Sprinkle the green onion on top of the lettuce mixture.
9. Sprinkle the almonds over the salad, then the chow mein noodles.
10. Cut the chicken into bite-size chunks. Place the chicken on the salad, forming a pile in the middle. Serve with the salad dressing on the side.

• • • •

THE CHEESECAKE FACTORY AVOCADO EGGROLLS

MENU DESCRIPTION: *"Chunks of Fresh Avocado, Sun-Dried Tomato, Red Onion and Cilantro Deep Fried in a Crisp Chinese Wrapper."*

In 1995, Forbes Magazine named the Cheesecake Factory in its list of the 200 best small companies in America. At 20 stores now, the Cheesecake Factory plans to grow at a modest rate of about 5 new restaurants per year, and still does not franchise.

Here's something different that I think you'll really like. The Avocado Eggrolls are one of the most popular appetizers on the menu at the Cheesecake Factory, and it's not hard to see why. The combination of hot avocado, sun-dried tomatoes, and the cilantro-tamarind sauce is one of the most unique and tasty flavors I've enjoyed at any of the restaurant chains. The trickiest part might be finding the tamarind pulp at your market. It's a brown, sticky pulp that looks sort of like puréed prunes, and can be found in the spice section or near the ethnic foods—or try a Middle Eastern market. The pulp often contains the large seeds of the fruit, so be sure to remove them before measuring. If you can't find the tamarind, you can get by substituting smashed raisins or prunes.

EGGROLLS

1 large avocado

2 tablespoons chopped sun-dried
   tomatoes (bottled in oil)

1 tablespoon minced red onion

½ teaspoon chopped fresh
   cilantro

pinch salt

3 eggroll wrappers

1 egg, beaten

vegetable oil for frying

DIPPING SAUCE

¼ cup chopped cashews

⅔ cup chopped fresh cilantro

2 cloves garlic, quartered

2 green onions, chopped

1 tablespoon granulated sugar

1 teaspoon ground black pepper

1 teaspoon ground cumin

4 teaspoons white vinegar

1 teaspoon balsamic vinegar

½ teaspoon tamarind pulp

½ cup honey

pinch ground saffron

¼ cup olive oil

1. After you peel the avocado and remove the pit, dice it into bite-size pieces.

2. In a small bowl, gently combine the avocado with the tomatoes, red onion, ½ teaspoon cilantro, and a pinch of salt. Be careful not to smash the avocado.

3. Prepare the eggrolls by spooning ⅓ of the filling into an eggroll wrapper. With the wrapper positioned so that one corner is pointing toward you, place the filling about 1 inch from the bottom corner and 1 inch from each side. Roll the bottom corner up over the filling, then roll the filling up to about the middle of the wrapper. Brush the remaining corners and edges of the wrapper with the beaten egg. Fold the left and right corners over the filling and "glue" the corners to the wrapper. Finish by rolling the wrapper and filling up over the top corner. Press on the wrapper to ensure it is sealed. Repeat these steps with the remaining two eggrolls and keep them covered in the refrigerator while you make the dipping sauce.

4. Prepare the sauce by combining the cashews, cilantro, garlic,

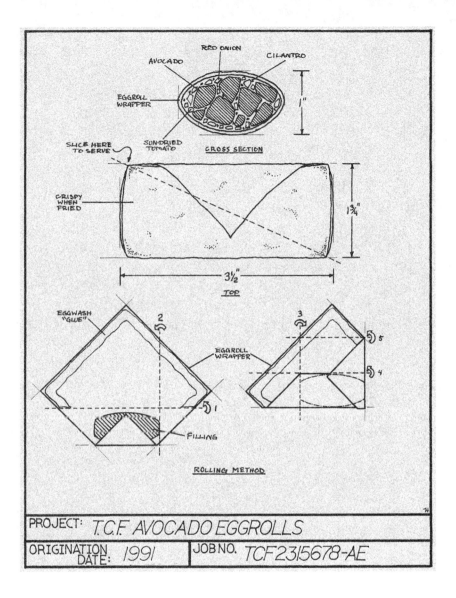

RED ONION

AVOCADO

CILANTRO

EGGROLL
WRAPPER

1"

SLICE HERE
TO SERVE

SUN-DRIED
TOMATO

CROSS SECTION

CRISPY
WHEN
FRIED

1¾"

3½"

TOP

EGGWASH
"GLUE"

2

EGGROLL
WRAPPER

3

5

1

4

FILLING

ROLLING METHOD

PROJECT: *T.C.F. AVOCADO EGGROLLS*

ORIGINATION
DATE: *1991*

JOB NO. *TCF2315678-AE*

green onions, sugar, black pepper, and cumin in a food processor or blender. Blend with short bursts until the mixture is well blended, and the cashews and garlic have been chopped into pieces about half the size of a grain of rice.

5. Combine the vinegars, honey, tamarind, and saffron in a small bowl. Heat the mixture for about 1 minute in a microwave, then stir until the tamarind pulp dissolves completely.

6. Pour the tamarind mixture into the blender or food processor with the cashew mixture and mix with short bursts until well combined (about 20 seconds).

7. Pour the blended sauce into a small bowl. Add the oil and stir by hand. Cover and refrigerate the sauce for at least 30 minutes before serving.

8. Heat oil in a deep fryer or a deep pan over medium heat. You want the oil to be deep enough to cover the eggrolls.

9. When the oil is hot, fry the eggrolls for 3 to 4 minutes or until golden brown. Drain on paper towels.

10. When the eggrolls can be safely touched, slice once diagonally across the middle of each one and serve them arranged around a sauce dish filled with the dipping sauce.

• SERVES 1 OR 2 AS AN APPETIZER.

• • • •

CHILI'S GRILLED CARIBBEAN CHICKEN SALAD

MENU DESCRIPTION: *"Grilled, marinated chicken breast, mixed greens, pico de gallo, pineapple chunks, tortilla strips & honey-lime dressing."*

Larry Levine started building his chain of Chili's restaurants in Dallas in 1975. At that time Chili's was basically a hamburger joint with a gourmet touch, dining room service and booze. Even though the menu then offered only eleven items, the restaurant was so popular that throngs of hungry customers waited patiently in lines extending into the parking lots. This caught the eye of the persuasive restaurateur Norman Brinker, who, in 1983, convinced Larry to sell his chain of Chili's restaurants, which by then had grown to a total of thirty.

Before Norman had stepped into the picture, more than 80 percent of Chili's business was in hamburgers. Today a much larger menu reflects the current trends in food, and salads are some of the best-selling items. These days the Grilled Caribbean Salad with the tasty honey-lime dressing is the salad of choice.

HONEY-LIME DRESSING

¼ cup Grey Poupon Dijon
   mustard
¼ cup honey
1 ½ tablespoons granulated sugar

1 tablespoon sesame oil
1 ½ tablespoons apple cider
   vinegar
1 ½ teaspoons lime juice

Blend all the ingredients in a small bowl with an electric mixer. Cover and chill.

PICO DE GALLO

2 medium tomatoes, diced
½ cup diced Spanish onion
2 teaspoons chopped fresh
    jalapeño pepper, seeded and
    de-ribbed

2 teaspoons finely minced fresh
    cilantro
pinch of salt

Combine all the ingredients in a small bowl. Cover and chill.

SALAD

4 skinless chicken breast fillets
½ cup teriyaki marinade, store
    bought or your own (page
    307)
4 cups chopped iceberg lettuce

4 cups chopped green leaf lettuce
1 cup chopped red cabbage
1 5.5-ounce can pineapple chunks
    in juice, drained
10 tortilla chips

1. Marinate the chicken in the teriyaki for at least 2 hours. You can use a resealable plastic bag for this. Put the chicken into the bag and pour in the marinade, then toss it into the fridge.
2. Prepare the barbecue or preheat a stovetop grill. Grill the chicken for 4 to 5 minutes per side or until done.
3. Toss the lettuce and cabbage together, then divide the greens into two large individual-serving salad bowls.
4. Divide the pico de gallo and pour it in two even portions over the greens.
5. Divide the pineapple and sprinkle it on the salads.
6. Break the tortilla chips into large chunks and sprinkle half on each salad.
7. Slice the grilled chicken breasts into thin strips, and spread half the strips onto each salad.
8. Pour the dressing into two small bowls and serve with the salads.

- SERVES 2 AS AN ENTRÉE

• • • •

CHILI'S PEANUT BUTTERCUP CHEESECAKE

MENU DESCRIPTION: *"Chocolate & vanilla marbled cheesecake on a chocolate cookie crust, topped w/fudge & Reese's Peanut Butter Cup pieces."*

If I had to pick one person in the restaurant business with the most respected and distinguished career, it would have to be Norman Brinker. The 65-year-old CEO of Brinker International is still building on a success story that spans four decades, and recently detailed his life in an autobiography, *On the Brink*. Back in the fifties, Norman took a job with Robert Peterson, who had just a few years earlier opened the first Jack-in-the-Box in San Diego, California. By the age of 34, Norman owned 20 percent of Jack-in-the-Box, giving him enough capital to set out on his own venture. In 1964 he opened a fifties-style coffee shop in downtown Dallas called Brinks. He sold that eatery a year later for $6,000 and sank that cash into a new chain that would become one of his most successful ventures. Norman opened the first Steak and Ale in 1966, took the chain public in 1971, then 10 years later sold the whole kit-and-caboodle for $100 million to the Pillsbury Company (that's some serious dough, boy). Pillsbury kept him on to run the operation, but Norman needed new action. In 1983, he purchased Chili's from founder Larry Levine and within 12 years built the chain into a billion-dollar company. Today Norman continues to watch Brinker International grow as new concepts like Cozymel's and Romano's Macaroni Grill are added to his long list of restaurant chain successes.

Speaking of rich, here's a tasty dessert for anyone who digs cheesecake and peanut butter cups. Use an 8-inch springform pan for this recipe if you have one. If not, you can also use two 9-inch pie pans and make two smaller cheesecakes. For the Oreo cookie crumbs, you can crumble three Oreo cookies, after removing the filling, or you can find packaged Oreo crumbs in the baking section of your supermarket near the graham cracker crumbs.

1 cup graham cracker crumbs
¼ cup Oreo chocolate cookie
    crumbs (3 cookies with filling
    removed)
⅓ cup butter, melted (⅔ stick)
¼ cup creamy peanut butter
3 8-ounce packages cream
    cheese, softened
3 eggs

1 cup sour cream
1 cup granulated sugar
1½ teaspoons vanilla extract
¼ cup chocolate syrup
1 cup fudge topping
4 chilled regular-size Reese's
    peanut butter cups
    (not bite-size)

1. Preheat the oven to 375 degrees.
2. In a medium bowl combine the graham cracker crumbs, chocolate cookie crumbs, and melted butter.
3. Press the crumbs firmly over just the bottom of an 8-inch springform pan. Bake for 6 to 8 minutes.
4. When the crust is cool, spread the peanut butter in a circle in the center of the crust. (You may soften the peanut butter for 30 seconds in the microwave to make it easier to spread.) You don't need to spread the peanut butter to the edge—leave about an inch margin all around.
5. You'll need two separate bowls for the two fillings, one larger than the other. In the larger bowl, with an electric mixer, beat together the cream cheese, eggs, sour cream, sugar, and vanilla until smooth.
6. Remove 1 cup of the cream cheese mixture and pour it into the smaller bowl. Add the chocolate syrup to this mixture and combine.

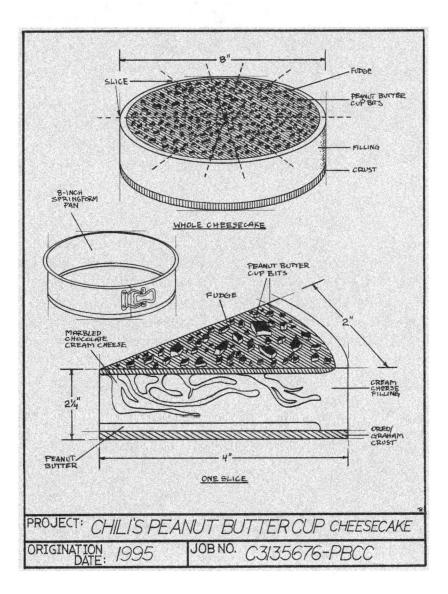

8"

SLICE

FUDGE

PEANUT BUTTER
CUP BITS

FILLING

CRUST

8-INCH
SPRINGFORM
PAN

WHOLE CHEESECAKE

PEANUT BUTTER
CUP BITS

FUDGE

2"

MARBLED
CHOCOLATE
CREAM CHEESE

CREAM
CHEESE
FILLING

2¼"

OREO/
GRAHAM
CRUST

PEANUT
BUTTER

4"

ONE SLICE

PROJECT: *CHILI'S PEANUT BUTTER CUP CHEESECAKE*

ORIGINATION
DATE: *1995*

JOB NO. *C3135676-PBCC*

7. Pour the large bowl of filling into the pan and spread it evenly over the crust.
8. Pour the chocolate filling onto the other filling and spread it out. Using the tip of a knife, swirl the chocolate into the white filling beneath it. A couple of passes should be enough.
9. Lower the oven temperature to 350 degrees. Bake the cheesecake for 70 to 80 minutes or until it becomes firm in the center. Remove from the oven and allow it to cool.
10. When the cheesecake is completely cool, soften the fudge topping in a double boiler or the microwave for about 45 seconds, then spread it out evenly over the cheesecake. Be sure to cover the entire surface of the filling.
11. Unwrap the peanut butter cups and chop them into small chunks.
12. Sprinkle the peanut butter cup pieces and any crumbs over the top of the cheesecake. Chill.
13. Slice the cake 5 times through the middle to make 10 slices.

• SERVES 10.

•　•　•　•

CRACKER BARREL HASH BROWN CASSEROLE

MENU DESCRIPTION: *"Made from scratch in our kitchens using fresh Grade A Fancy Russet potatoes, fresh chopped onion, natural Colby cheese and spices. Baked fresh all day long."*

In the late sixties Dan Evins was a Shell Oil "jobber" looking for a new way to market gasoline. He wanted to create a special place that would arouse curiosity, and would pull travelers off the highways. In 1969 he opened the first Cracker Barrel just off Interstate 40 in Lebanon, Tennessee, offering gas, country-style food, and a selection of antiques for sale. Today there are over 260 stores in 22 states, with each restaurant still designed as a country reststop and gift store. In fact, those stores (which carry an average of 4,500 different items apiece) have made Cracker Barrel the largest retailer of American-made finished crafts in the United States.

Those who know Cracker Barrel well love the restaurant for its delicious home-style breakfasts. This casserole, made with hash browns, Colby cheese, milk, beef stock, and spices is served with many of the classic breakfast dishes at the restaurant. The recipe here is designed for a skillet that is also safe to put in the oven. If you don't have one of those, you can easily transfer the casserole to a baking dish after it is done cooking on the stove.

1 26-ounce bag frozen country-
    style hash browns
2 cups shredded Colby cheese
¼ cup minced onion
1 cup milk

½ cup beef broth
2 tablespoons butter, melted
dash garlic powder
1 teaspoon salt
¼ teaspoon ground black pepper

1. Preheat the oven to 425 degrees F.
2. Combine the frozen hash browns, cheese, and onion in a large bowl.
3. Combine the milk, beef broth, half the melted butter, the garlic powder, salt, and black pepper in another bowl. Mix until well blended, then pour the mixture over the hash browns and mix well.
4. Heat the remaining butter in a large, ovenproof skillet over high heat.
5. When the skillet is hot, spoon in the hash brown mixture. Cook the hash browns, stirring occasionally, until hot and all of the cheese has melted (about 7 minutes).
6. Put the skillet into the oven and bake for 45 to 60 minutes or until the surface of the hash browns is dark brown.

TIDBITS

If your skillet isn't ovenproof (because it has a plastic handle, for example), you can also spoon the potatoes into a glass 9 x 9-inch baking dish and microwave the potatoes until they are hot and the cheese has melted. Then put that baking dish into the 425 degree oven until the surface of the hash browns has browned.

If you can't find Colby cheese, you can also use Cheddar cheese for this recipe. Colby, however, is preferred.

• SERVES 4 TO 6 AS A SIDE DISH

•   •   •   •

CRACKER BARREL
CHICKEN & DUMPLINS

MENU DESCRIPTION: *"We use only the 'best of the breast' chicken tenderloin in our recipe. Our dumplins are made from scratch, then hand rolled and cut into strips before simmering to perfection in chicken stock."*

By 1977 there were 13 Cracker Barrel stores located in Georgia and Tennessee, with all of them based on founder Dan Evins's original concept of a restaurant and store built around gasoline pumps. But with the oil embargo and energy crisis of the mid-seventies, Cracker Barrel started building stores that did not offer gas. Soon all of the original 13 stores were converted so that today not one Cracker Barrel lets you "filler-up" while you fill yourself up.

Another old-time favorite at Cracker Barrel is the Chicken & Dumplins on the lunch and dinner menu. The nice thing about this version of the popular classic dish is that it creates its own tasty gravy. As the "dumplins" dissolve some, the flour thickens the stock into a creamy sauce. Just remember to let your dough rest a bit before rolling it to cut out the dumplins. This will allow the gluten in the flour to work much better. Use extra flour on your cutting board and rolling pin if the dough is too tacky, and try not to roll the dough too thin.

CHICKEN AND STOCK

3 quarts water
1 3- to 4-pound chicken, cut up
1 ½ teaspoons salt
1 small onion, sliced
2 stalks celery, chopped
1 clove garlic, peeled and
    quartered

1 bay leaf
4 to 6 whole parsley leaves
1 teaspoon coarse ground black
    pepper
1 tablespoon lemon juice

"DUMPLINS"

2 cups all-purpose flour
1 tablespoon baking powder

1 ¼ teaspoons salt
1 cup plus 2 tablespoons milk

1. Bring the water to a boil in a large pot. Add the chicken, 1 teaspoon of salt, onion, celery, garlic, bay leaf, and parsley to the pot. Reduce the heat to simmer and cook the chicken, uncovered, for 2 hours. The liquid will reduce by about one third.

2. When the chicken has cooked, remove it from the pot and set it aside. Strain the stock to remove all the vegetables and floating scum. You only want the stock and the chicken, so toss everything else out.

3. Pour 1½ quarts (6 cups) of the stock back into the pot (keep the leftover stock, if any, for another recipe—it can be frozen). You may also want to use a smaller pot or a large saucepan for this. Add pepper, the remaining ½ teaspoon salt, and the lemon juice, then reheat the stock over medium heat while preparing the dumplins.

4. For dumplins, combine the flour, baking powder, 1¼ teaspoons salt, and milk in a medium bowl. Stir well until smooth, then let the dough rest for to 5 to 10 minutes. Roll the dough out onto a floured surface to about a ½-inch thickness.

5. Cut the dough into ½-inch squares and drop each square into the simmering stock. Use all of the dough. The dumplins will first swell and then slowly shrink as they partially dissolve

to thicken the stock into a white gravy. Simmer for 20 to 30 minutes until thick. Stir often.

6. While the stock is thickening, the chicken will have become cool enough to handle. Tear all the meat from the bones and remove the skin. Cut the chicken meat into bite-size or a little bigger than bite-size pieces and drop them into the pot. Discard the skin and bones. Continue to simmer the chicken and dumplins for another 5 to 10 minutes, but don't stir too vigorously or the chicken will shred and fall apart. You want big chunks of chicken in the end.

7. When the gravy has reached the desired consistency, ladle four portions onto plates and serve hot. Serve with your choice of steamed vegetables, if desired.

• SERVES 4 AS AN ENTREE.

•   •   •   •

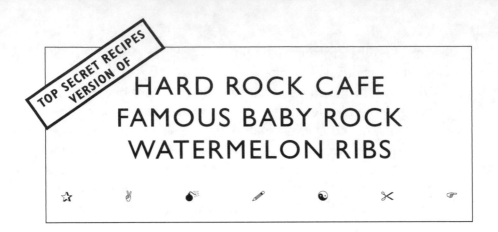

HARD ROCK CAFE FAMOUS BABY ROCK WATERMELON RIBS

TOP SECRET RECIPES VERSION OF

MENU DESCRIPTION: *"Texas style ribs basted in our special watermelon B.B.Q. sauce, grilled and served with fries and a green salad."*

The collection of rock and roll memorabilia is different in each Hard Rock Cafe. You may find artifacts that come from recording stars of the fifties, like Elvis Presley and Fats Domino, to more contemporary artists such as Prince, Pearl Jam, and Nirvana. Usually there are several gold and platinum records donated from artists, sequined stage costumes, and famous guitars, some even left in a smashed condition as they were donated straight from a performance. The Hard Rock also collects movie memorabilia, such as Tom Cruise's pilot helmet from the movie *Top Gun* and the Indiana Jones jacket from *Raiders of the Lost Ark.*

In 1995, Hard rock cofounder Peter Morton opened the world's first rock-and-roll hotel, The Hard Rock Hotel and Casino, in Las Vegas. Peter now operates the hotel and his swank restaurant Morton's in Hollywood, California—the famous location of many a celebrity power meal over the years.

I thought these ribs with a barbecue sauce made from watermelon rind had a unique and memorable flavor begging to be duplicated at your next power meal. The sauce is sweet and slightly tangy, and the ribs are so tender they melt in your mouth. It's the slow-cooking process that makes them that way. Throwing them on the grill at the last minute is not meant to cook them so much as it is to add the smoky flavor and slight charring that good ribs require. If possible, make the watermelon barbecue sauce a day ahead so the ribs can marinate in it overnight. If you don't have time for that, at least marinate the ribs for a couple of hours.

Watermelon rind from about ½ of a small watermelon
1 cup dark corn syrup
½ cup water
¼ cup tomato ketchup
¼ cup white vinegar

¾ teaspoon crushed red pepper flakes
½ teaspoon liquid hickory smoke
¼ teaspoon ground black pepper

4 pounds baby back ribs

1. For the puréed watermelon rind, you want to cut off the green skin and about half an inch of the hard white part, keeping the part of the watermelon that is lighter red to white. This is the tender part of the rind. Try to stay away from the harder, white rind just inside the green skin. Put the rind into a food processor and purée for only about 10 seconds. Strain the liquid from the pulp and use 1 cup of pulp, measured after straining.

2. Combine the watermelon pulp with the remaining ingredients for the sauce in a medium saucepan over high heat. Bring the mixture to a boil, then reduce the heat and simmer, covered, for about 1 hour or until it's as thick as you like it.

3. Cut racks of ribs into plate-size portions of about 6 or 7 rib bones each. Brush the ribs with the barbecue sauce and wrap each rack individually in aluminum foil. Be sure to save some sauce for later. Let the ribs marinate in the refrigerator for a couple of hours at least. (Overnight is best.)

4. Preheat the oven to 300 degrees. To cook the ribs, set them with the seam of the foil facing up, into the oven. Bake for 2 to 2½ hours or until the rib meat has pulled back from the cut end of the bones by about ½ inch. They should be very tender.

5. Remove the ribs from the foil and brush on some additional sauce. Grill the ribs on a hot barbecue for 2 to 4 minutes per

side or until you see several spots of charred sauce. Be sure to watch the ribs so that they do not burn. Serve with left-over sauce on the side.

- SERVES 2 TO 4 AS AN ENTREE.

• • • •

HOOTERS
BUFFALO
CHICKEN WINGS

MENU DESCRIPTION: *"Nearly world famous. Often imitated, hardly ever duplicated."*

"Hooters is to chicken wings what McDonald's is to hamburgers," claims promotional material from the company. True, the six fun-loving midwestern businessmen who started Hooters in Clearwater, Florida, on April Fool's Day in 1983 chose a classic recipe for chicken wings as their feature item. But while some might say it's the Buffalo Wings that are their favorite feature of Hooters, others say it's the restaurant chain's trademark Hooters girls—waitresses casually attired in bright orange short-shorts and skin-tight T-shirts. Apparently it's a combination that works.

Today there are nearly 200 Hooters across the United States serving more than 150 tons of chicken wings every week. I've tasted lots of chicken wings, and I think these are some of the best wings served in any restaurant chain today. The original dish can be ordered in 10-, 20- or 50-piece servings; or if you want to splurge, there's the "Gourmet Chicken Wing Dinner" featuring 20 wings and a bottle of Dom Perignon champagne, for only $125. To further enhance the Hooters experience when you serve these messy wings, throw a whole roll of paper towels on the table, rather than napkins, as they do in the restaurants.

vegetable oil for frying
¼ cup butter (½ stick)
¼ cup Crystal Louisiana Hot
    Sauce or Frank's Red Hot
    Cayenne Sauce
dash ground black pepper
dash garlic powder

½ cup all-purpose flour
¼ teaspoon paprika
¼ teaspoon cayenne pepper
¼ teaspoon salt
10 chicken wing pieces thawed if
    frozen

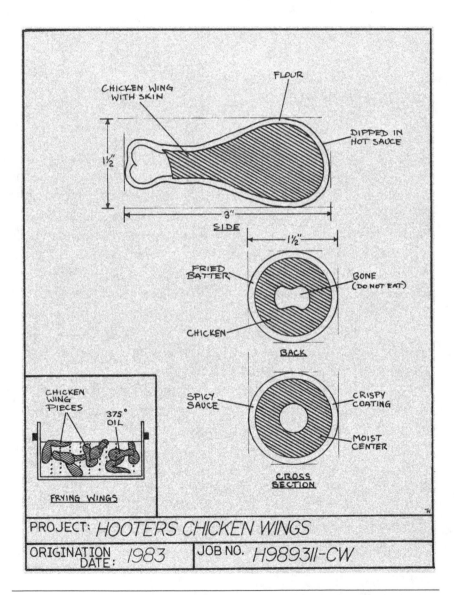

PROJECT: *HOOTERS CHICKEN WINGS*

ORIGINATION DATE: *1983*

JOB NO. *H989311-CW*

ON THE SIDE
bleu cheese dressing   *celery sticks*

1. Combine the butter, hot sauce, ground pepper, and garlic powder in a small saucepan over low heat. Heat until the butter is melted and the ingredients are well-blended.
2. Combine the flour, paprika, cayenne pepper, and salt in a small bowl.
3. Dry the wings. Put the wings into a large bowl and sprinkle the flour mixture over them, coating each wing evenly. Put the wings in the refrigerator for 60 to 90 minutes. (This will help the breading to stick to the wings when fried.)
4. While the wings are resting, heat oil in a deep fryer to 375 degrees. You want just enough oil to cover the wings entirely—an inch or so deep at least.
5. Put all the wings into the hot oil and fry them for 10 to 15 minutes or until some parts of the wings begin to turn dark brown.
6. Remove the wings from the oil to a paper towel to drain. But don't let them sit too long, because you want to serve the wings hot.
7. Quickly put the wings into a large bowl. Add the butter and hot sauce mixture and stir, coating all of the wings evenly. You could also use a large plastic container (such as Tupperware) with a lid for this. Put all the wings inside the container, add the sauce, put on the lid, then shake. Serve with bleu cheese dressing and celery sticks on the side.

• SERVES 3 TO 5 AS AN APPETIZER.

•　•　•　•

HOOTERS
BUFFALO GRILLED SHRIMP

MENU DESCRIPTION: *"It don't get no batter than this."*

With the double-entendre name and female servers (many of whom, off-duty, are models), Hooters has become a company with critics. Several years ago a group of Hooters Girls in Minneapolis sued the company on grounds of sexual harassment, saying that the uniforms featuring shorts and tight T-shirts or tank tops were demeaning. Ultimately, the women dropped the suit. But more recently, the Equal Employment Opportunity Commission ordered the company to hire men on the foodservice staff. Hooters countered with a sarcastic million-dollar advertising campaign featuring a mustachioed man named "Vince" dressed in Hooters Girl getup. Once again, that suit was dropped.

Vice president of marketing Mike McNeil told *Nation's Restaurant News* "Hooters Girls are actually wearing more clothing than what most women wear at the gym or the beach. It's part of the concept. I don't think the world would be a better place if we had guys be Hooters Girls." You may agree or disagree, but the fact is that Hooters is currently the country's thirteenth largest dinner house chain and one of the fastest growing, with an increasing number of diners discovering Buffalo Shrimp, a delicious spin-off of Buffalo Chicken Wings.

vegetable oil for frying
¼ cup butter (½ stick)
¼ cup Crystal Louisiana Hot
    Sauce or Frank's Red Hot
    Cayenne Sauce
dash ground black pepper

dash garlic powder
⅛ teaspoon paprika
12 uncooked large shrimp
1 egg, beaten
½ cup milk
1 cup all-purpose flour

ON THE SIDE
lemon wedges

1. Combine the butter, hot sauce, ground pepper, garlic powder, and paprika in a small saucepan over low heat. Heat until the butter is melted and the ingredients are well blended.
2. Prepare the shrimp by cutting off the entire shell, leaving only the last segment of the shell and the tailfins. Remove the vein from the back and clean the shrimp. Then, with a paring knife, cut a deeper slice where you removed the vein (down to the tail), so that you can fan the meat out. Be careful not to cut too deep. This will butterfly the shrimp.
3. Combine the egg with the milk in a small bowl. Put the flour into another bowl.
4. Dredge each shrimp in the milk mixture, then coat it with the flour. Make sure each shrimp is evenly coated. When you have coated all of the shrimp with flour, let them sit for about 10 minutes in the refrigerator before frying.
5. Meanwhile, heat oil in a deep fryer to 375 degrees. You want the oil deep enough to cover the shrimp completely.
6. Fry the shrimp in the hot oil for 7 to 10 minutes or until the tip of each tail begins to turn dark brown. Remove the shrimp from the oil to paper towels briefly, to drain.
7. Quickly put the shrimp into a large bowl, add the butter and hot sauce mixture and stir, coating each shrimp evenly. You

could also use a large plastic container with a lid for this. Put all the shrimp inside, add the sauce, put on the lid, then gently turn the container over a few times to coat all of the shrimp. Serve with wedges of lemon on the side.

- SERVES 3 TO 4 AS AN APPETIZER

• • • •

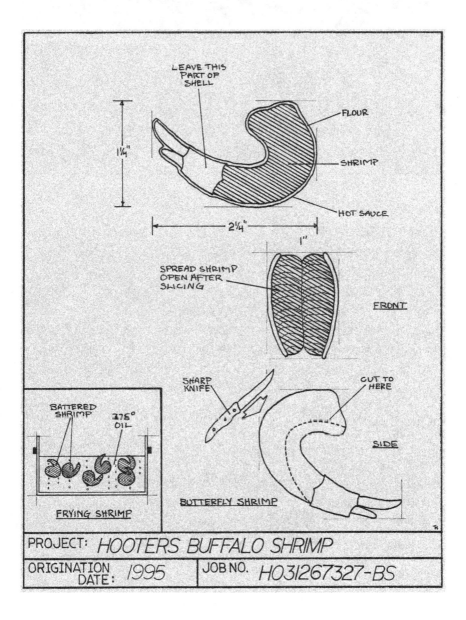

LEAVE THIS
PART OF
SHELL

FLOUR

SHRIMP

HOT SAUCE

$1\frac{1}{4}''$

$2\frac{1}{4}''$

$1''$

SPREAD SHRIMP
OPEN AFTER
SLICING

FRONT

SHARP
KNIFE

CUT TO
HERE

SIDE

BATTERED
SHRIMP

375°
OIL

FRYING SHRIMP

BUTTERFLY SHRIMP

PROJECT: *HOOTERS BUFFALO SHRIMP*

ORIGINATION
DATE: *1995*

JOB NO. *H031267327-BS*

IHOP
FAJITA OMELETTE

MENU DESCRIPTION: *"Seasoned chicken or beef with onions, diced green peppers, cheese, and chile salsa."*

Pancakes are obviously the signature entree, but IHOP serves a variety of breakfast selections—more than 65 items! Along with a cup of coffee from the trademarked "Never Empty Coffee Pot," diners can choose from about a dozen different omelette selections including the Santa Fe Omelette, International Omelette, Chorizo and Cheese Omelette, and the delicious Fajita Omelette.

   In my version of the original favorite, you can use either chicken or beef.

1 skinless chicken breast fillet or
    6-ounce flank steak
	¼ medium Spanish onion, diced
	    (about ½ cup)

½ teaspoon vegetable oil	1 small tomato, diced
½ teaspoon lime juice	(about ½ cup)
¼ teaspoon chili powder	2 teaspoons butter
⅛ teaspoon salt	5 large eggs, beaten
⅛ teaspoon ground cumin	1 cup shredded Cheddar cheese
dash garlic powder	⅓ cup salsa
dash ground black pepper	2 tablespoons sour cream
½ green bell pepper, diced (about ½ cup)	

1. Pound the chicken breast or flank steak between sheets of plastic wrap until about ¼ inch thick, then cut the meat into bite-size pieces.
2. Pour the oil into a medium skillet over high heat. Add the meat and sauté it for a couple of minutes until it starts to brown.
3. Add the lime juice to the meat. Blend the spices together in a small bowl, then add this mixture to the meat. Mix well until blended in.
4. Add the pepper and onion to the meat and simmer for 5 to 10 minutes over medium heat or until the veggies begin to turn brown. Add the tomato and cook another 2 minutes.
5. Set a large skillet over medium heat. Add 1 teaspoon of butter to the pan.
6. When the butter has melted, add half of the beaten eggs to the pan and swirl to coat the entire bottom of the pan.
7. Cook the eggs for a minute or so or until the top surface is beginning to get firm. Be sure the bottom is not getting too brown before the top cooks. If you notice this happening, turn down the heat.
8. Sprinkle about ¼ cup of cheese down the center of the eggs.
9. Spoon a heaping tablespoon of salsa over the cheese.
10. Spoon one-fourth of the meat and vegetables onto the salsa.
11. Fold the edges over the center of the omelette and let it cook for another minute or so.
12. Carefully flip the omelette over in the pan with the seam side down. Let it cook for another minute or two, then slide it out onto a serving plate. Keep this omelette hot in a slow oven while you prepare the other one.
13. When both omelettes are done, spoon the remaining meat and vegetables over each of the omelettes.
14. Sprinkle a couple tablespoons of cheese over the other topping.
15. Add 2 tablespoons of salsa.

16. Then add a 1-tablespoon dollop of sour cream to the salsa on the middle of the omelette.

• SERVES 2.

• • • •

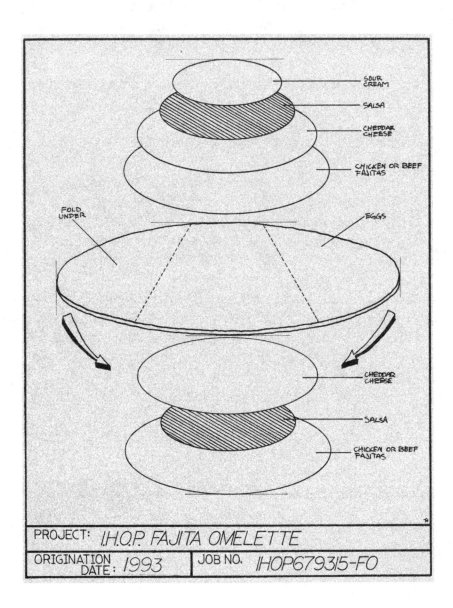

PROJECT: *I.H.O.P. FAJITA OMELETTE*

ORIGINATION DATE: *1993*   JOB NO. *IHOP67931S-FO*

LONE STAR STEAKHOUSE BLACK BEAN SOUP

This restaurant boasts a unique "Texas roadhouse" ambiance. When you walk into any Lone Star restaurant, the first thing you'll notice is the crackling of peanut shells beneath your feet. When you're seated you get your own free bucket of peanuts to munch on, and you just flip the shells onto the wood plank floors. Western music plays over the speakers, and every hour or so the wait staff breaks into a funky little honky tonk line dance next to your table while the crunching peanut shells add a unique percussion element.

The spicy black bean soup is a popular item on the Lone Star menu. Here's a way to make a version of your own that can be served as an appetizer or as a meal in itself. It's great with a garnish of freshly diced red onion, jalapeños, and sour cream on top.

2 15-ounce cans black beans
¼ cup diced red onion
2 teaspoons chopped pickled
   jalapeño slices ("nacho
   slices")
1 teaspoon granulated sugar

1 teaspoon cider or wine vinegar
2 cloves garlic, minced
¼ teaspoon salt
¼ teaspoon cayenne pepper
½ teaspoon chili powder

GARNISH

4 teaspoons chopped red onion   I tablespoon sour cream
6 to 8 jalapeño slices

1. Pour the canned beans along with the liquid into a medium saucepan. Add the remaining soup ingredients and mix.
2. Bring the soup to a boil, then reduce the heat to low and simmer, covered, for about I hour, adding water if necessary or until it's as thick as you like.
3. Serve each bowl of soup with a garnish of red onion, jalapeño slices, and sour cream arranged carefully in the center of the soup.

TIDBITS

This soup is also very good with a bit of chopped fresh cilantro added to it while simmering and/or as a garnish. You may want to try some shredded Cheddar or Monterey Jack cheese on top as well.

- SERVES 4 AS AN APPETIZER, 2 AS AN ENTREE

•   •   •   •

LONE STAR STEAKHOUSE SWEET BOURBON SALMON

MENU DESCRIPTION: *"Fresh salmon filet, marinated and mesquite grilled."*

It is said that Americans eat an estimated 63 pounds of beef per capita, and we get a lot of it in chain restaurants. But for those of you who want something other than beef, Lone Star has additional selections including the Sweet Bourbon Salmon.

Don't worry if you can't mesquite grill your salmon, it's the sweet bourbon marinade that makes this dish so tasty. Not only is this marinade good on salmon, but on other fish and chicken as well. If you do happen to use a charcoal grill and have some mesquite smoking chips on hand, soak a handful of chips in water for a couple hours and then arrange them on the red-hot coals. This will give your salmon a taste even closer to the original.

SWEET BOURBON MARINADE

¼ cup pineapple juice

2 tablespoons soy sauce

2 tablespoons brown sugar

1 teaspoon Kentucky bourbon

¼ teaspoon cracked black pepper

⅛ teaspoon garlic powder

½ cup vegetable oil

2 8-ounce salmon fillets (without skin)

2 teaspoons snipped fresh chives

1. Combine the pineapple juice, soy sauce, brown sugar, bourbon, pepper and garlic powder in a medium bowl. Stir to dissolve the sugar. Add the oil.
2. Be sure all of the skin is removed from the salmon. Place the fillets in a shallow dish and pour the bourbon marinade over them, saving a little to brush on the fish as it cooks. Put a lid over the fish and refrigerate for at least an hour. A few hours is even better.
3. Preheat your barbecue or stovetop grill over medium/high heat.
4. Cook the fish for 5 to 7 minutes per side or until each fillet is cooked all the way through. Regularly brush the fillets with the marinade.
5. Arrange the fillets on each plate with the chives sprinkled over the top.

• SERVES 2 AS AN ENTREE.

• • • •

OLIVE GARDEN
TOSCANA SOUP

MENU DESCRIPTION: *"Spicy sausage, russet potatoes, and cavolo greens in a light creamy broth."*

For two years after the first Olive Garden restaurant opened in 1982, operators were still tweaking the restaurant's physical appearance and the food that was served. Even the tomato sauce was changed as many as 25 times.

This soup blends the flavors of potatoes, kale, and Italian sausage in a slightly spicy chicken and cream broth. When I first tried the soup at the restaurant I was surprised at how good it was. I'd never had any soup with the leafy, healthy, spinach-like kale in it (found in most produce sections), and the combination of flavors was addicting. When you try this version for yourself I think you'll agree.

2¾ cups chicken broth
¼ cup heavy cream
1 medium russet potato
2 cups chopped kale

½ pound spicy Italian sausage
¼ teaspoon salt
¼ teaspoon crushed red pepper
   flakes

1. Combine the stock and cream in a saucepan over medium heat.
2. Slice the unpeeled potato into ¼-inch slices, then quarter the slices and add them to the soup.
3. Add the kale.

4. Grill or sauté the sausage. When cooked and cooled, cut the sausage at an angle into slices about ½ inch thick. Add the sausage to the soup.
5. Add the spices and let the soup simmer for about 1 hour. Stir occasionally.

• SERVES 4 AS AN APPETIZER, 2 AS AN ENTREE.

•   •   •   •

OUTBACK STEAKHOUSE ALICE SPRINGS CHICKEN

MENU DESCRIPTION: *"Grilled chicken breast and bacon smothered in mushrooms, melted Monterey Jack and Cheddar cheeses, with honey mustard sauce."*

In the late eighties, as the public's concern about eating beef was growing, the restaurant industry saw a big shift toward chicken meals. In the midst of a poultry-crazy country, that last thing you'd expect anyone to do is open a steakhouse. But that's exactly what the boys who founded Outback Steakhouse did. And by the time their restaurant had become the sixth largest dinnerhouse chain in the country, they had proven that what many people still want is a big honkin' slab of beef.

    With a menu dominated by beef items, it's nice to find that the restaurant can do great things with chicken meals as well, such as the Alice Springs Chicken. You'll love the mushrooms, bacon, cheese, and honey mustard piled on a chicken breast that's been grilled on the "barbie."

HONEY MUSTARD MARINADE

½ cup Grey Poupon Dijon mustard   1 ½ tablespoons vegetable oil
½ cup honey   ½ teaspoon lemon juice

4 skinless chicken breast fillets
1½ tablespoons vegetable oil
2 cups sliced mushrooms
   (10 to 12 mushrooms)
2 tablespoons butter
salt
pepper

dash of paprika
8 slices bacon, cooked
1 cup shredded Monterey Jack
   cheese
1 cup shredded Cheddar cheese
2 teaspoons finely chopped fresh
   parsley

1. Use an electric mixer to combine the Dijon mustard, honey, 1½ teaspoons oil, and lemon juice in a small bowl. Whip the mixture for about 30 seconds.
2. Pour about two-thirds of the marinade over the chicken breasts and marinate them, covered, in the refrigerator for about 2 hours. Chill the remaining marinade until later.
3. After the chicken has marinated, preheat the oven to 375 degrees and heat up an ovenproof frying pan large enough to hold all four breasts and 1 tablespoon of oil over medium heat. (If you don't have an ovenproof skillet, transfer the chicken to a baking dish for baking.) Sear the chicken in the pan for 3 to 4 minutes per side or until golden brown. Remove the pan from the heat, but keep the chicken in the pan.
4. As the chicken is cooking, in a small frying pan sauté the sliced mushrooms in the butter.
5. Brush each seared chicken breast with a little of the reserved honey mustard marinade (*not* the portion that the chicken soaked in), being sure to save a little extra that you can serve on the side later with the dish.
6. Season the chicken with salt, pepper, and a dash of paprika.
7. Stack two pieces of cooked bacon, crosswise, on each chicken breast.
8. Spoon the sautéed mushrooms onto the bacon, being sure to coat each breast evenly.
9. Spread ¼ cup of Monterey Jack cheese onto each breast followed by ¼ cup of Cheddar.

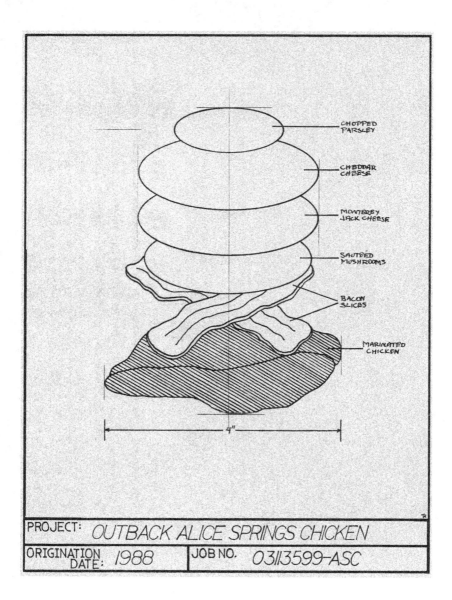

CHOPPED PARSLEY

CHEDDAR CHEESE

MONTEREY JACK CHEESE

SAUTEED MUSHROOMS

BACON SLICES

MARINATED CHICKEN

4"

PROJECT: OUTBACK ALICE SPRINGS CHICKEN

ORIGINATION DATE: 1988

JOB NO. 03113599-ASC

10. Bake the pan of prepared chicken breasts for 7 to 10 minutes or until the cheese is thoroughly melted and starting to bubble.
11. Sprinkle each chicken breast with ½ teaspoon parsley before serving. Put extra honey mustard marinade into a small bowl to serve on the side.

- SERVES 4 AS AN ENTREE.

• • • •

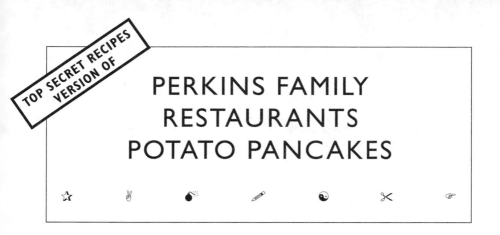

PERKINS FAMILY RESTAURANTS POTATO PANCAKES

MENU DESCRIPTION: *"Hearty pancakes made with grated potatoes, onions and parsley."*

When Matt and Ivan Perkins tasted the food at Smitty's Pancake House in Seattle, they were smitten. Soon they had purchased the rights to William Smith's recipes, which had been perfected at his renowned restaurant since it opened just after World War II. In 1958, the brothers realized their dream and opened a Smitty's restaurant of their own in Cincinnati, Ohio. When the brothers decided to give the chain an identity all its own, all of the Smitty's were changed to Perkins, and business continued to thrive through the years.

If you've never tried potato pancakes from Perkins or any restaurant, now's the time. This is a tasty classic, breakfast recipe that doesn't necessarily have to be for breakfast. I've given you the option to make the pancakes with frozen hash brown potatoes or with fresh potatoes you shred by hand. The fresh potatoes obviously taste better, but if you're in a rush, go with frozen. It may sound strange if you haven't tried it, but maple or maple-flavored syrup goes great on these hotcakes. At least I think so. You may just want some butter and powdered sugar on top.

1 cup all-purpose flour
1 cup whole milk
4 eggs
3 tablespoons butter, melted
3 tablespoons granulated sugar
¼ teaspoon baking powder
½ teaspoon salt

1 tablespoon chopped fresh
   parsley
1 tablespoon minced onion
2½ cups frozen hash browns
   (thawed) or shredded fresh
   potatoes (3 to 4)

ON THE SIDE
butter   *syrup*

1. Combine all of the ingredients, except the potatoes, in a large mixing bowl. Beat by hand or with an electric mixer until smooth.
2. Add the potatoes to the batter and mix by hand until the potatoes are well combined.
3. Let the batter rest while you preheat a skillet or griddle to about medium heat. Grease the pan with a little butter. You may also use nonstick spray.
4. Ladle ¼-cup dollops of batter into the pan. Cook as many at a time as will fit comfortably in your pan. Cook each pancake for 1½ to 2 minutes per side until brown. Serve in a fanned-out stack with a pat of butter on top. Serve syrup on the side, if desired.

TIDBITS

Because fresh shredded potatoes have more moisture than frozen, you may need to add a couple tablespoons more flour to the batter if you decide to shred your own spuds.

- SERVES 3 TO 4 AS A BREAKFAST OR SIDE DISH.

•   •   •   •

PLANET HOLLYWOOD CHICKEN CRUNCH

MENU DESCRIPTION: *"A basket of tender chicken breaded with Cap'n Crunch and seasonings, served with Creole mustard sauce."*

The Orlando, Florida Planet Hollywood, which had its big opening in 1994, pulls in yearly sales receipts totaling around $50 million, making it the highest volume restaurant in America. If you've never tried the Chicken Crunch at Planet Hollywood, you're missing a treat. Sliced chicken breast fingers are coated with a crunchy, slightly sweet breading combination of Cap'n Crunch cereal and cornflake crumbs. The chicken is then deep-fried to a golden brown and served with a tasty dipping sauce made from mayonnaise, horseradish, and Dijon mustard. You've probably tasted nothing like it.

CREOLE MUSTARD SAUCE

2 tablespoons Grey Poupon
   Country Dijon mustard
3 tablespoons mayonnaise
1 teaspoon yellow mustard

1 teaspoon cream-style
   horseradish
1 teaspoon honey

vegetable oil for frying
2 skinless chicken breast fillets
2 cups Cap'n Crunch cereal
½ cup cornflake crumbs
½ teaspoon onion powder

½ teaspoon garlic powder
½ teaspoon salt
¼ teaspoon ground white pepper
1 egg, beaten
1 cup milk

1. Preheat oil in a deep pan or deep fryer to 375 degrees. You want to use enough oil to completely cover the chicken 1 to 2 inches deep.
2. Combine all of the ingredients for the Creole mustard sauce in a small bowl and chill the sauce while the chicken is prepared.
3. Cut each chicken breast, lengthwise, into 5 long slices (chicken fingers).
4. Smash the Cap'n Crunch into crumbs using a food processor, or put the cereal into a plastic bag and start pounding.
5. Combine the cereals, onion powder, garlic powder, salt, and pepper in a medium bowl.
6. Combine the egg with the milk in a separate bowl.
7. Dredge each piece of chicken in the milk mixture, then completely coat it with the dry mixture. Do this for all the chicken before frying.
8. When the oil is hot, fry the chicken for 4 to 6 minutes or until golden to dark brown and crispy. Remove to paper towels or a rack to drain. Serve hot with Creole mustard sauce on the side for dipping.

- SERVES 2 TO 4 AS AN APPETIZER OR SNACK.

• • • •

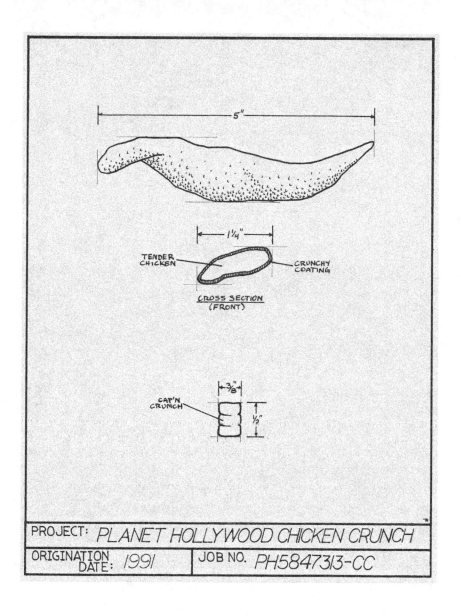

5"

TENDER
CHICKEN

CRUNCHY
COATING

1¼"

CROSS SECTION
(FRONT)

CAP'N
CRUNCH

3/8"

½"

PROJECT: PLANET HOLLYWOOD CHICKEN CRUNCH

ORIGINATION
DATE: 1991

JOB NO. PH5847313-CC

PLANET HOLLYWOOD POT STICKERS

MENU DESCRIPTION: *"Six pot stickers filled with fresh ground turkey meat seasoned with ginger, water chestnuts, red pepper and green onions. They are fried and served in a basket with spicy hoisin."*

Planet Hollywood is known for the film and television memorabilia displayed throughout the restaurants. Some of the items on display behind thick Plexiglas include the genie bottle from *I Dream of Jeannie,* Val Kilmer's bat suit from *Batman Forever,* Tom Hanks' costume from *Forrest Gump,* Judy Garland's dress from *The Wizard of Oz,* and the painting from the set of the television show *Friends.* In addition to the memorabilia is a wall at the entrance to each restaurant that displays handprints in plaster from the likes of Mel Gibson, Jimmy Stewart, Harrison Ford, Demi Moore, Samuel L. Jackson, Paul Newman, Goldie Hawn, Patrick Swayze, and many others.

Pot stickers are a popular Asian dumpling that can be fried, steamed, or simmered in a broth. Planet Hollywood has customized its version to make them crunchier than the traditional dish, and it's a tasty twist. Since hoisin sauce would be very difficult to make from scratch, you can use a commercial brand found in most stores.

¼ *pound ground turkey*
½ *teaspoon minced fresh ginger*
I *teaspoon minced green onion*

I *teaspoon minced water chestnuts*
½ *teaspoon soy sauce*
½ *teaspoon ground black pepper*

¼ teaspoon crushed red pepper
    flakes (no seeds)
¼ teaspoon salt
⅛ teaspoon garlic powder

1 egg, beaten
12 wonton wrappers
    (3 x 3-inch size)
vegetable oil for frying

ON THE SIDE

hoisin sauce

1. In a small bowl, combine all the ingredients except the egg, wrappers, and oil. Add 1 tablespoon of the beaten egg. Save the rest of the egg for later.
2. Invert a small bowl or glass with a 3-inch diameter on the center of a wonton wrapper and cut around it to make a circle. Repeat for the remaining wrappers. Preheat oil in a deep fryer or a deep saucepan to 375 degrees. Use enough oil to cover the pot stickers—1 to 2 inches should be enough.
3. Spoon ½ tablespoon of the turkey filling into the center of one wrapper. Brush a little beaten egg around half of the edge of the wrapper and fold the wrapper over the filling. Gather the wrapper as you seal it, so that it is crinkled around the edge. Repeat with the remaining ingredients.
4. Deep-fry the pot stickers, six at a time, in the hot oil for 3 to 6 minutes or until they are brown. Drain on a rack or paper towels. Serve with the hoisin sauce for dipping. If you want a spicier sauce, add some more crushed red pepper or cayenne pepper to the sauce.

TIDBITS

If you can't find wonton wrappers, you can also use eggroll wrappers for this recipe. Eggroll wrappers are much bigger, so you will be wasting more of the dough when you trim the wrappers to 3-inch-diameter circles. But in a pinch, this is a quick solution.

Pot sticker wrappers can also be found in some supermarkets, but I've found the wonton wrappers and eggroll wrappers, when fried, taste more like the restaurant version.

- SERVES 3 TO 6 AS AN APPETIZER OR SNACK

• • • •

RED LOBSTER STUFFED SHRIMP AND STUFFED MUSHROOMS

Bill Darden was only 19 when he started his restaurant career in 1939 by opening a 25-seat lunch counter called The Green Frog in Waycross, Georgia. From the start Bill's business was a hopping success. That success helped Bill to springboard into other restaurant acquisitions throughout the years including 20 Howard Johnson's restaurants. Then, in 1968, as he reached his mid-fifties, Bill took another gamble and opened a seafood restaurant in Lakeland, Florida. When deciding on a name for the new restaurant, someone suggested that since he had great luck with the name "Green Frog" in the past, why not name this one "Red Lobster." And so it was.

Here are a couple of great dishes to serve as appetizers or on the side with an entree such as broiled lobster or fish. These recipes include a stuffing that varies in the restaurants only in the type of seafood used—the stuffed shrimp contains crabmeat and the stuffed mushrooms contain lobster meat. If you like, you can use the stuffings interchangeably in the mushrooms caps and shrimp.

STUFFED SHRIMP

½ cup water

3 tablespoons butter

1 tablespoon minced celery

1 tablespoon minced onion

1 tablespoon finely chopped red chili pepper

1 tablespoon finely chopped green chili pepper

¼ teaspoon dried parsley

½ teaspoon salt

dash pepper

½ tablespoon granulated sugar

¾ cup cornbread crumbs (Pepperidge Farm cornbread stuffing mix is good)

1 cup lump crab meat (fresh, frozen, or one 6-ounce can)

1 egg, beaten

20 large shrimp

¼ to ½ pound Cheddar cheese, thinly sliced

paprika

1. Preheat the oven to 375 degrees.
2. Boil the water and 2 tablespoons butter in a medium saucepan.
3. Add the celery, onion, peppers, parsley, salt, pepper, and sugar.
4. Reduce the heat to low and let it simmer for 5 minutes.
5. Add the bread crumbs and remove from the heat.
6. Mix the crab meat with the beaten egg. Add to the breadcrumb mixture, cover, and let it sit for 5 minutes.
7. In the meantime, prepare each shrimp by cutting along the back to remove the vein and removing all of the shell except the last joint and the tip of the tail. Cut deep into the shrimp where the vein was, but not all of the way through, and spread the meat open (butterfly slice) so that each shrimp will sit in a roasting pan, cut side up, with its tail sticking up. Repeat for all of the shrimp and arrange in a baking dish.
8. Scoop about 1 tablespoon of stuffing onto the top of the spread-out portion of each shrimp.
9. Melt the remaining tablespoon of butter and brush it over the surface of each stuffed shrimp. Scoot all the shrimp close together after you do this.

10. Spread thin slices of Cheddar cheese evenly over the entire surface of all of the shrimp. Sprinkle on a dash of paprika.

11. Bake the shrimp for 15 to 20 minutes or until the shrimp are completely cooked. Broil for an additional 1 to 2 minutes to brown the cheese just slightly.

PROJECT: *RED LOBSTER STUFFED SHRIMP/SHROOMS*

ORIGINATION DATE: 1976/1986 JOB NO. RL5555317-SSS

STUFFED MUSHROOMS

1. Follow the above directions for the stuffing, but substitute 1 cup cooked lobster meat for the crab meat. If you broil the tail from a live lobster for another recipe, such as the one on page 407, you can use the meat from the legs and claws for this recipe. Simply cook the remaining lobster in the shell for 15 to 20 minutes in rapidly boiling salted water. Use a nut cracker to remove the meat. You may also use canned lobster meat for this recipe, although fresh lobster meat tastes much better.
2. Instead of shrimp, use 20 to 24 (about 1 pound) mushrooms with stems removed.
3. Fill the mushroom caps with 2 to 3 teaspoons of stuffing, brush with melted butter, and top with slices of Monterey Jack cheese rather than Cheddar.
4. Season lightly with paprika, then bake the mushrooms in a roasting pan or baking dish in a preheated oven set on 375 degrees for about 12 minutes, or until the cheese is melted. Broil for 1 to 2 minutes to slightly brown the cheese.

• SERVES 4 TO 6 AS AN APPETIZER.

•　•　•　•

RED LOBSTER
BROILED LOBSTER

The namesake of the Red Lobster chain is the delicious broiled lobster, lightly seasoned, served with lemon and melted butter. Two varieties are most often available at the restaurant: Maine lobster and rock lobster. The Maine lobsters are purchased live, while rock lobster tails come frozen; and both are available in stores across the country. Rock lobsters, also known as spiny lobsters, are found in warmer waters. They have no claws, which is why you only get rock lobster tails. Each Red Lobster restaurant has a special device that bakes and broils the lobsters without burning them. Since these special broilers don't come with most homes, I've created a cooking method using a conventional oven that produces broiled lobster just like that which you can enjoy at the restaurant.

2 6-ounce rock lobster or Maine lobster tails	dash ground black pepper
melted butter	dash cayenne pepper
¼ teaspoon salt	dash ground allspice
¼ teaspoon paprika	lemon wedges

1. Thaw lobster tails if frozen, then preheat the oven to 425 degrees.
2. Each tail is prepared differently for cooking. The meat from the rock lobster is fully exposed on top of the shell for

broiling, while the meat of the Maine lobster is left in the shell.

To prepare the rock lobster, use a kitchen scissors to cut along the top of the shell down to the tail. Crack the ribs of the shell underneath so that you can spread the shell open on top and pull the meat out down to the tail. You may have to use a spoon to pull the meat away from inside of the shell so that it will come free. Leave the end of the meat attached to the shell when you pull it out, then close the shell underneath it. Now you should be able to rest the meat back down on top of the shell. Cut about ¼ inch deep down the center of the meat so that you can pull the colored part of the meat over, exposing the white center. This may have already happened when you cut the shell open.

For the Maine lobster, slice down the top of the shell to the tail. Crack the ribs in the center along the bottom of the tail so that you can hinge the shell open from the top. Use a spoon to pull the meat away from the inside of the shell so that it is easy to eat when cooked, but leave the meat inside the shell. Slice down the middle of the meat so that you can spread open the colored part. This may have already happened when you cut the top of the shell open.

3. Brush the lobster meat with melted butter.
4. Combine the salt, paprika, peppers, and allspice in a small bowl. Sprinkle a dash of this spice combination on the top of each lobster.
5. Bake in the oven on a broiling pan for 15 minutes.
6. Turn the oven to broil and broil for an additional 6 to 8 minutes or until the meat or shell just begins to turn a light brown on top. Be careful not to burn the lobster meat. Remove from the broiler and serve with melted butter and a lemon wedge.

TIDBITS

If you like, you can take the Maine lobster meat out of the shell as explained in the method for the rock lobster. That's not the way Red Lobster does it, but, hey, you're not eating at Red Lobster.

• SERVES 2 AS AN ENTREE

• • • •

RED LOBSTER
SCALLOPS AND BACON

At the time I was researching this book there were two ways you could have your bacon and scallops at Red Lobster: wrapped and broiled, or grilled on a skewer. The former is a smaller portion to be served as an appetizer, while the skewers may be served as a main entree or part of one. I've included recipes to clone both versions.

BROILED
BACON-WRAPPED SCALLOPS

4 medium sea scallops
2 slices bacon
melted butter
salt
paprika

ground black pepper
1 tablespoon warm bottled clam
    juice
4 toothpicks

1. Preheat the broiler to high.
2. Boil 2 to 3 cups of water in a small pan over high heat. Salt the water.
3. Boil the scallops in the water for 3 to 4 minutes, or until they firm up. Drain the scallops when they're done.
4. Cook the bacon slices for a couple minutes per side. Don't cook until crispy or you won't be able to fold the bacon around the scallops.

5. When the scallops are cool enough to touch, cut or tear a piece of partially cooked bacon in half and wrap one half over the top of the scallop so that it meets itself underneath. Put a toothpick through the bacon to stick it in place. If you have a problem wrapping your bacon (story of my life) because it is too crispy, dip the bacon into hot or boiling water to make it more flexible. Repeat this with the remaining scallops.
6. Put the scallops on their side in an oven-safe dish and brush with melted butter.
7. Lightly season the scallops with salt, paprika, and a dash of ground pepper.
8. Broil the scallops for 5 to 6 minutes, or just until the edges begin to brown.
9. Remove the scallops from the oven and add warm clam juice to the bottom of the baking dish. Serve in the same dish.

- Serves 2 as an appetizer.

GRILLED SCALLOP AND BACON SKEWERS

1 teaspoon salt
16 sea scallops
4 round zucchini slices, ½ inch thick
2 slices bacon, cooked soft

1 tablespoon melted butter
4 8-inch skewers
dash of salt
dash of paprika
dash of ground black pepper

ON THE SIDE
brown rice

1. Preheat the barbecue grill to medium/high heat.
2. In a large saucepan, heat 3 to 4 cups of water until boiling. Add a teaspoon or so of salt to the water.
3. Boil the scallops for 4 minutes or until they firm up.
4. Remove the scallops from the water and drain.

ZUCCHINI

SCALLOPS

TOOTHPICK

BACON

BACON

WOOD
SKEWER

GRILLED SCALLOP
& BACON SKEWER

8"

1½"

1¼"

TOP

SIDE
(CROSS SECTION)

BACON

SCALLOP

BROILED BACON-
WRAPPED SCALLOP

PROJECT: RED LOBSTER SCALLOPS & BACON

ORIGINATION DATE: 1994   JOB NO. RL 897313-SB

5. When the scallops have cooled enough to handle, begin building your 4 skewers.
6. Cut a zucchini slice in half and pierce it, round edge first, onto the skewer.
7. Slide the zucchini to the end until there's about 1 inch left on the end of the skewer.
8. Slide one scallop on next, piercing through the rounded edges.
9. Cut the bacon into quarters and slide one piece of bacon on next.
10. Add two more scallops, one more piece of bacon, another scallop, and the other half of the zucchini slice (this one goes cut side first).
11. Make three more skewers exactly the same way.
12. Generously brush the skewers with melted butter.
13. Lightly season with salt, paprika, and a dash of black pepper.
14. Grill the skewers for 4 to 5 minutes per side or until the zucchini has softened. Serve the skewers over a bed of brown rice.

TIDBITS

For a healthier alternative, try turkey bacon with either of these recipes as a substitute for the pork bacon.

• SERVES 2 AS AN ENTREE.

• • • •

MENU DESCRIPTION: *"Full-flavored jalapeños stuffed with cool cream cheese and deep-fried in a cracker-crumb coating. Served with sweet jalapeño jelly & sour cream."*

Red Robin was one of the first restaurant chains to serve No-Fire Peppers, an item which can be found on many restaurant menus today under a variety of different names. The cream cheese–filled, battered and fried jalapeño peppers are actually called Poppers by their creators, Anchor Foods, a restaurant food supply company which manufactures Poppers and a variety of other appetizers for sale to restaurant chains everywhere. According to *Restaurants and Institutions* magazine, Poppers were the #1 food item added to restaurant menus in 1995, with restaurants purchasing over 700 million of the little suckers.

It's important when you make these that you allow time for them to freeze. The freezing stage ensures that the coating stays on when the peppers are fried and prevents the cream cheese from squirting out as it heats up.

4 large, fresh jalapeño peppers
¼ pound cream cheese
2 eggs
¾ teaspoon salt
1 teaspoon vegetable oil
⅔ cup self-rising flour

⅛ teaspoon garlic powder
dash paprika
dash onion powder
½ cup cornflake crumbs
vegetable oil for frying

ON THE SIDE

hot pepper jelly   *sour cream*

1. Remove the stems from the jalapeños, then slice each one down the middle lengthwise and remove the seeds and inner membranes. Be careful to wash your hands afterward.
2. Poach the jalapeño halves in a saucepan half-filled with boiling water for 10 to 15 minutes or until tender. Drain and cool.
3. Blot with a cloth or paper towel to dry the inside of each jalapeño slice, then use a teaspoon to spread about ½ ounce of cream cheese into each jalapeño half.
4. Beat the eggs in a small, shallow bowl, then add ¼ teaspoon salt and the oil and combine with a whisk.
5. In another shallow bowl, combine the flour, ½ teaspoon salt, garlic powder, paprika, and onion powder.
6. Add the cornflake crumbs to a third shallow bowl.
7. Working one at a time, dip each stuffed jalapeño into the egg mixture, then into the flour mixture. Repeat, by again dipping the jalapeño into the egg and then back into the flour. Finally, dip the jalapeño back into the egg, then into the cornflake crumbs.
8. Put the coated peppers side by side on a plate and into the freezer for at least 2 hours. This way when the peppers are fried, the breading won't fall off and the cheese in the center won't ooze out.
9. When the peppers are frozen, heat vegetable oil in a deep fryer or deep saucepan to about 350 degrees. Use enough oil to cover the jalapeños when frying. Fry the peppers for 3½ to 4 minutes or until the outside is a dark golden brown. Drain on a rack or paper towels. Serve hot with pepper jelly and sour cream on the side.

TIDBITS

You can also make these ahead of time by frying them for only 1½ minutes and then refreezing them until you are ready to serve them. Then cook the frozen jalapeños in hot oil for 3½ minutes or until they are hot all the way through. You may also bake the frozen jalapeños in a 450 degrees oven on a greased baking pan for 10 to 15 minutes, turning them over halfway through the heating time.

• SERVES 2 TO 4 AS AN APPETIZER.

•   •   •   •

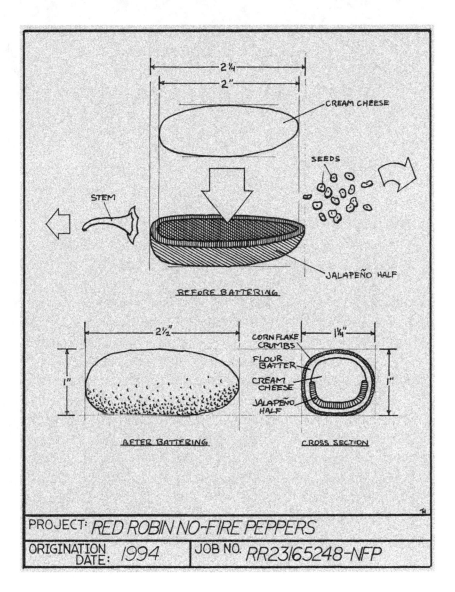

2¼"

2"

CREAM CHEESE

SEEDS

STEM

JALAPEÑO HALF

BEFORE BATTERING

2½"

1"

CORN FLAKE CRUMBS

FLOUR BATTER

CREAM CHEESE

JALAPEÑO HALF

1¾"

1"

AFTER BATTERING

CROSS SECTION

PROJECT: *RED ROBIN NO-FIRE PEPPERS*

ORIGINATION DATE: *1994*

JOB NO. *RR23165248-NFP*

RED ROBIN
BBQ CHICKEN SALAD

☆　　✌　　💣　　✏　　☯　　✂　　☞

MENU DESCRIPTION: *"Breast of chicken basted with BBQ sauce & topped with cheddar cheese, tomato, fresh avocado, and black beans. Served with Ranch dressing & garlic cheese bread."*

In 1969, Gerald Kingen bought a beat-up 30-year-old bar called Red Robin in Seattle across the road from the University of Washington. The pub did a booming business with the college and local crowd, but in 1973 building officials gave their opinion of the bar: Either fix it up or shut it down. Jerry not only fixed up the 1200-square-foot building, but also expanded it to three times its old size, to 3600 square feet, and added a kitchen to start making food. Red Robin soon became popular for its wide selection of gourmet burgers in addition to the designer cocktails served in kooky glasses. Jerry says he set out to create a chain of restaurants that would be recognized as "the adult McDonald's and poor man's Trader Vic's."

2 cups chopped romaine lettuce
2 ups chopped green leaf or
　　iceberg lettuce
½ cup chopped red cabbage
1 small tomato, chopped (¼ cup)
1 skinless chicken breast fillet
⅓ cup barbecue sauce (Bulls' Eye
　　or K.C. Masterpiece work well)

½ cup canned refried black beans
½ cup shredded Cheddar cheese
¼ cup French's French
　　Fried Onions (onion straws)
3 avocado slices (¼ avocado)
¼ cup ranch dressing

1. Toss the lettuces and cabbage together and arrange on a large plate.
2. Arrange the tomato on the lettuce mixture at the bottom of the plate.
3. Grill the chicken breast on a hot barbecue grill for 4 to 5 minutes per side or until done. Brush a generous coating of barbecue sauce over the chicken as it grills.
4. Heat the black beans in the microwave or in a saucepan over medium heat.

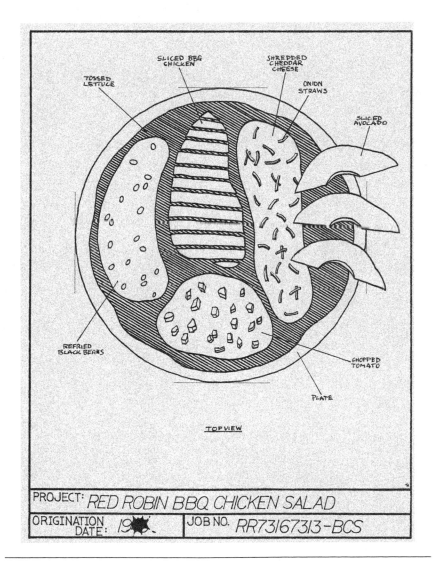

SLICED BBQ CHICKEN

SHREDDED CHEDDAR CHEESE

TOSSED LETTUCE

ONION STRAWS

SLICED AVOCADO

REFRIED BLACK BEANS

CHOPPED TOMATO

PLATE

TOP VIEW

PROJECT: RED ROBIN BBQ CHICKEN SALAD

ORIGINATION DATE: 19⬛.

JOB NO. RR73167313-BCS

5. Spread the black beans over the lettuce on the left side of the plate.
6. Slice the warm chicken into bite-size pieces and arrange them neatly over the lettuce in the center of the plate.
7. Sprinkle the cheese over the lettuce on the right side of the plate.
8. Sprinkle the onion straws over the cheese.
9. Garnish the salad with 3 slices of avocado arranged side by side on the right rim of the plate. Serve with the ranch dressing and the remaining barbecue sauce on the side.

TIDBITS

You can also make the onion straws yourself by following this simple recipe:

ONION STRAWS

2 cups vegetable oil
¼ cup very thinly sliced white onion
½ cup all-purpose flour

½ teaspoon baking soda
¼ teaspoon salt
⅔ cup cold water

1. Heat the oil in a wide saucepan to 350 degrees.
2. Slice the onion into very thin onion rings and then cut the rings in half, making long strips or straws. Try to slice the onion as thin as possible.
3. Combine the flour, baking soda, and salt in a large bowl. Add the cold water and whisk until the batter is smooth.
4. When the oil is hot, drop the onions into the batter. Remove the onions one at a time, let them drip off a bit, and then place them into the hot oil. You will want to cook these for about 2 minutes apiece, or until you see them turn a golden brown. Drain the onion straws on a paper towel.

• SERVES 1 AS AN ENTREE (CAN BE DOUBLED).

• • • •

RED ROBIN
MOUNTAIN HIGH MUDD PIE

Gerald Kingen is a man with a mission. In 1985 he sold his successful Red Robin chain of restaurants to Tokyo-based Skylark Co. Ltd. Unhappy with the changes the new owners were implementing, Jerry and a partner purchased a "substantial equity position" of the Irvine, California–based Red Robin in March of 1996. Now Jerry is once again at the helm of the company, with a goal of reviving old menu items and living up to the old slogan as "the world's greatest gourmet burger maker & most masterful mixologists."

A unique signature dessert item is the Mountain High Mudd Pie, which servers claim is one of the most ordered desserts on the menu. Save some room for this giant-size sundae made from chocolate and vanilla ice cream with peanut butter, caramel, and fudge sauce. There are several stages of freezing, so give yourself at least seven hours to allow for these steps. This dessert is big and serves at least a dozen, so it's good for a small party or gathering, or makes a unique birthday cake. If there's only a few of you, leftovers can be frozen in a sealed container for several weeks and enjoyed later.

6 cups chocolate ice cream
1 cup peanut butter cookie
    pieces
6 cups vanilla ice cream
1⅔ cups creamy peanut butter

4 chocolate-flavored graham
    crackers
1 cup fudge topping
1 20-ounce squirt bottle chocolate
    topping

1 20-ounce squirt bottle caramel
    topping
1 can whipped cream

¾ cup chopped peanuts
12 maraschino cherries, with
    stems

1. Soften the chocolate ice cream and load it into the bottom of a 2½- to 3-quart mixing bowl. Make sure the surface of the ice cream is smooth and leveled.
2. Spread the peanut butter cookie pieces evenly over the top of the ice cream, then cover the bowl and put it back into the freezer for at least 1 hour. (If you can't find packaged peanut butter cookies, use the recipe in "Tidbits.")
3. Soften the vanilla ice cream and spread it over the chocolate ice cream and cookie pieces. Again, be sure to smooth and level the surface of the ice cream. Cover the bowl with plastic wrap and put it back into the freezer for at least 1 hour.
4. Use a spatula to spread ⅔ cup of peanut butter over the surface of the ice cream. Be sure the ice cream has hardened before you do this or it could get sloppy.
5. Crush the chocolate graham crackers into crumbs and spread them evenly over the peanut butter. Put the bowl back into the freezer for at least 1 hour.
6. Remove the bowl from the freezer and hold it in a sink filled with warm water for about 1 minute. You want the ice cream around the edges to soften just enough that you can invert the ice cream onto a plate.
7. Turn a large plate upside down and place it on top of the bowl. Flip the bowl and plate over together, and tap gently on the bowl until the ice cream falls out onto the plate. You may have to put the bowl back into the water if it's stubborn. Once the ice cream is out, cover it with plastic wrap and place it back in the freezer for another 1 or 2 hours.
8. Without heating it up, spread the fudge evenly over the entire surface of the ice cream mountain. Put the fudge-coated ice cream back into the freezer for 1 hour.
9. When the fudge has hardened, spread the remaining 1 cup

of peanut butter over the entire surface as well. Once again, back into the freezer for at least 1 hour. We're almost there.

10. Slice the ice cream with a warm knife into 12 pieces. Put wax paper between the cuts so that when you serve it later, it is easy to divide. Then slip it back into the freezer, covered.

PEANUT BUTTER
FUDGE TOPPING
CHOCOLATE ICE CREAM
PEANUT BUTTER COOKIE
VANILLA ICE CREAM
PEANUT BUTTER
CHOCOLATE GRAHAM CRUST

4"
5"

CROSS SECTION

3 QUART BOWL

BOWL MOLD

NUTS
WHIPPED CREAM
PLATE
MARASCHINO CHERRY
PIE SLICE
CARAMEL SYRUP
CHOCOLATE SYRUP

PRESENTATION
(TOP VIEW)

PROJECT: RED ROBIN MOUNTAIN HIGH MUDD PIE
ORIGINATION DATE:
JOB NO. RR443160265-MHMP

423

11. When serving, first coat a plate with a criss-cross pattern of chocolate and caramel sauce. Make three parallel lines down the plate with the squirt bottle of chocolate sauce. Then three parallel horizontal lines made with the bottle of caramel sauce.
12. Place the slice of ice cream upright onto the plate toward the back of the design.
13. Spray whipped cream on top and down the curved edge of the ice cream slice, onto the plate over the sauces. Be generous.
14. Sprinkle about a tablespoon of chopped nuts over your creation.
15. Add a cherry to the top. Marvel at the beauty, then dig in or serve it before it melts. Repeat for the remaining slices.

TIDBITS

If you would like to make your own peanut butter cookies, rather than buying them pre-made, here is a recipe that makes about 2 dozen tasty cookies—more than enough for the ice cream dessert.

PEANUT BUTTER COOKIES

½ cup butter, softened (1 stick)
½ cup granulated sugar
½ cup firmly packed brown
  sugar
½ cup creamy peanut butter

1 egg
1 ¼ teaspoons vanilla extract
1 ½ cups all-purpose flour
1 teaspoon baking soda
½ teaspoon salt

1. Preheat the oven to 325 degrees.
2. Use an electric mixer to combine the butter with the sugars in a large bowl until creamy.
3. Add the peanut butter, egg, and vanilla and mix until smooth.
4. Sift together the flour, baking soda, and salt, and combine with the moist ingredients in the large bowl. Mix the dough until all of the ingredients are smooth and well blended.

5. Drop rounded tablespoons of the dough onto an ungreased cookie sheet. Press the dough flat with a fork and bake for 15 to 18 minutes, until the edges of the cookies begin to turn light brown.

- SERVES 12.

• • • •

SHONEY'S
COUNTRY FRIED STEAK

MENU DESCRIPTION: *"Tender steak, lightly breaded and golden fried. Smothered with country milk gravy."*

Alex Schoenbaum opened the doors to his first restaurant, Parkette, a drive-in in Charleston, West Virginia, in 1947, at the start of a boom in popularity of the classic American drive-in restaurants many of us now know only from reruns of *Happy Days*. Schoenbaum's restaurant did very well and he decided, in 1951, to purchase a Big Boy franchise, the fastest growing chain at the time. In 1953, Parkette changed its name to Shoney's Big Boy.

Today Shoney's is no longer affiliated with Big Boy, but maintains a menu that features the Southern homestyle favorites that have made it so successful for so long. One of the old-time favorites is the Country Fried Steak smothered in peppered milk gravy. The technique here is to freeze the steaks after they have been breaded with flour. This way the coating won't wash off when the steaks are fried—the same technique the restaurants use.

2 cups all-purpose flour	2 cups water
1 tablespoon salt	4 4-ounce cube steaks
¼ teaspoon ground black pepper	vegetable oil for frying

COUNTRY GRAVY

1 ½ tablespoons ground beef	¼ teaspoon coarse ground black
¼ cup all-purpose flour	pepper
2 cups chicken broth	¼ teaspoon salt
2 cups whole milk	

1. Prepare the steaks at least several hours before you plan to serve this meal. First, sift the flour, salt, and pepper together into a large, shallow bowl. Pour the water into another shallow bowl.
2. Trim the steaks of any fat, then use your hand to press down firmly on each cube steak on a hard surface to flatten it out a bit. You don't want the steaks too thick.
3. Dredge each steak, one at a time, first in the water and then in the flour. Repeat this one more time so that each steak has been coated twice.
4. When all four steaks have been coated, place them on waxed paper and put them into the freezer for several hours until they are solid. This is the same technique used at the restaurant chain to ensure that the flour coating won't fall off when frying the steaks.
5. About 10 minutes before you are ready to cook the steaks, prepare the gravy by browning the ground beef in a small frying pan. Crumble the meat into tiny pieces as you cook it.
6. Transfer the meat to a medium saucepan over medium heat. Add ¼ cup flour and stir it in with the ground beef. Add the remaining ingredients for the gravy and bring to a boil, stirring often. Cook for 10 to 15 minutes until thick. Reduce the heat to low to keep the gravy warm while the steaks are prepared.
7. As the gravy is cooking, heat oil in a deep fryer or a deep frying pan over medium/high heat to 350 degrees. You want enough oil to cover the steaks when frying.
8. When the oil is hot, drop the steaks, one at a time, into the oil. Fry for 8 to 10 minutes or until golden brown, then drain on paper towels.
9. Serve the steaks with gravy poured over the top, with a side of mashed potatoes, grits, or steamed vegetables, if desired.

- SERVES 4 AS AN ENTREE.

•   •   •   •

T.G.I. FRIDAY'S SPICY CAJUN CHICKEN PASTA

MENU DESCRIPTION: *"Fettuccine tossed with sautéed chicken, mushrooms, onions and red and green peppers in Friday's own spicy, tomato Creole sauce."*

There are over 549 T.G.I. Friday's restaurants in 47 states and 54 countries, all serving this Cajun-style chicken pasta. This dish is a bit like a jambalaya except the rice has been replaced with pasta.

Use a large pan for this recipe, and note that for the chicken stock or broth, you can also use a chicken bouillon cube dissolved in boiling water.

This recipe makes two large restaurant-size portions, but could easily serve a family of four.

4 tablespoons butter (½ stick)
1 green bell pepper, chopped
    (1 cup)
1 red bell pepper, chopped
    (1 cup)
½ white onion, sliced and
    quartered (1 cup)
1 clove garlic, pressed
2 skinless chicken breast fillets

2 teaspoons olive oil
1 medium tomato, chopped
4 to 6 mushrooms, sliced
    (1 ¼ cups)
1 cup chicken broth
salt
¼ teaspoon cayenne pepper
¼ teaspoon paprika
¼ teaspoon ground white pepper

¼ teaspoon dried thyme

4 to 6 quarts water

1 12-ounce box fettuccine

2 teaspoons chopped fresh
    parsley

1. Melt 2 tablespoons of the butter in a large skillet over medium/high heat.
2. Sauté the bell peppers, onions, and garlic in the butter for 8 to 10 minutes or until the vegetables begin to soften slightly.
3. As the vegetables are cooking, cut the chicken breasts into bite-size pieces.
4. Prepare a medium-size pan over high heat with the olive oil. When the pan is hot, add the chicken and cook, stirring, for 5 to 7 minutes or until the chicken shows no pink.
5. When the vegetables are soft (about 10 minutes) add the chicken to the pan.
6. Add the tomatoes, mushrooms, chicken stock, ¼ teaspoon salt, cayenne pepper, paprika, white pepper, and thyme and continue to simmer for 10 to 12 minutes until it thickens.
7. In the meantime bring the water to a boil in a large pot. If you like, add a half tablespoon of salt to the water. Cook the fettuccine in the boiling water until done. This will take 10 to 12 minutes.
8. When the noodles are done, drain them and add the remaining 2 tablespoons of butter. The butter should melt quickly on the hot noodles. Toss the noodles to mix in the butter.
9. Serve the dish by dividing the noodles in half onto two plates. Divide the chicken and vegetable sauce evenly and spread it over the top of the noodles on each plate. Divide the parsley and sprinkle it over each serving.

If you want a thicker sauce, combine ½ teaspoon arrowroot or cornstarch with 2 tablespoons of white wine in a small bowl and stir to dissolve. Remove the pan from the heat before adding this thickener, stir it in, then put it back on the heat.

• SERVES 2 AS A LARGE ENTREE.

• • • •

Bonus Recipes

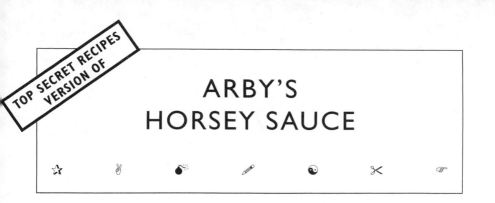

ARBY'S
HORSEY SAUCE

☆   ✌   💣   ✏   ☯   ✂   ☞

Even though Arby's has diversified its menu with wraps and deli sandwiches on sliced whole wheat bread, it's the thinly-sliced roast beef piled high on hamburger buns that made this chain famous. Since roast beef and horseradish go beautifully together, Arby's created a delicious mayo-based horseradish sauce, which happens to be great on most homemade sandwiches, too. But it just isn't cool to hoard handfuls of the blister packs to take home. So, with the help of this secret formula, you can clone as much Horsey sauce as you want. Get out the blender, since you'll need it to puree the horseradish in the mix so that the sauce is smooth like the real deal.

1 tablespoon white vinegar
4 teaspoons granulated sugar
⅛ teaspoon salt

1 cup mayonnaise
2 tablespoons plus 2 teaspoons
    prepared horseradish

1. In a small dish, dissolve the sugar and salt in the vinegar.
2. Measure mayonnaise and horseradish into a blender. Add the vinegar solution, then turn blender on medium speed for about 10 seconds.
3. Pour sauce into a covered container and chill it for at least a couple hours to let the flavors mingle.

- MAKES 1 CUP.

•   •   •   •

BAJA FRESH
SALSA BAJA

As Baja Fresh continues its rapid expansion across the country, more and more requests are coming in for a clone of the chain's signature salsa, which is made fresh from scratch every day at the Mexican grill. Its medium spiciness, smoky flavor and deep black color make the salsa unique and mysterious. That is, until now, since I've got the *Top Secret* formula for you right here. But the recipe wasn't as easy to create as I first thought. I figured the tomatoes would have to be extremely blackened over a hot grill, but I wasn't sure how to get them dark enough to turn the salsa black without the tomatoes getting all mushy and falling apart on the barbecue.

So, I went back to Baja Fresh before they opened to peer through the window to see if I could catch some hot salsa production action. I waited and waited. After several hours as the lunch rush was beginning to wind down and no fresh salsa was in the pipeline, it was time for extreme measures to get things moving. I went in and ordered 30 tubs of Salsa Baja to go, and that did it. I ended up with a big bag filled with 2 gallons of salsa (thankfully they poured those 8-ounce portions into bigger bowls), and the restaurant went immediately into "salsa red alert" to replenished the now-dwindling salsa reserve. It was perfect! As I was grabbing my bag, a dude come out from the kitchen with a huge box of tomatoes to slam on the hot grill. I ordered a giant Diet Pepsi and parked myself at a close table to watch the process. That's when I discovered the secret. For super-charred tomatoes they start with firm, chilled tomatoes, that aren't too big or too ripe. I also found out that the tomatoes must start roasting on the grill with the stem-side down. The rest was simple . . .

7 firm medium tomatoes, cold
1 jalapeno
1 clove garlic
1 teaspoon salt

1 ½ cups water
juice of 1 lime
2 tablespoons diced white onion
2 tablespoons chopped cilantro

1. Preheat barbecue grill to high heat.
2. Place 6 of the tomatoes, stem-side-down (remove any stems), directly on the grill. Allow the tomatoes to roast over the flame for 20 to 30 minutes. When the tomatoes are very charred and blackened on the first side, flip them over and continue to grill for another 20 to 30 minutes until most of the surface of each tomato is black. When you flip over the tomatoes, add the jalapeno pepper to the grill (take the stem off first). The jalapeno skin will blacken like the tomatoes. Turn the pepper as it cooks so that the entire surface darkens.
3. Take the tomatoes and pepper off the grill and put them in a bowl to cool for 10 or 15 minutes. Dump the tomatoes and pepper and any liquid in the bowl into a blender. Add a clove of garlic and the salt and blend on high speed until pureed. Add water and lime juice and blend again on high speed for 30 to 45 seconds. As the blacked bits of tomato are chopped finer, the sauce will darken.
4. Pour the mixture into a bowl. Dice the remaining tomato and add it to the salsa. Add the onion and cilantro, then cool the mixture in the refrigerator.

• MAKES 3 CUPS.

• • • •

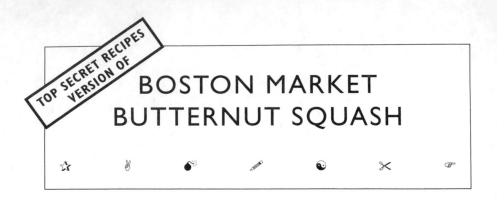

BOSTON MARKET
BUTTERNUT SQUASH

Here's a great way to make flavorful butternut squash that's easy and quick. Most of your time will be spent cutting the squash into 1-inch cubes so that you can steam it. You can also use the microwave to cook the squash (see Tidbits), but I tend to prefer the texture from good, old-fashioned steaming. After the squash is cooked, mash it up, mix in the other ingredients and you've got a great side that fits right in with many meals, especially spicy dishes. Since these squashes come in varying sizes, you may want to start with just ¼ teaspoon of salt, give it a taste, then add more to suit you.

1 medium butternut squash
2 tablespoons butter, melted
2 tablespoons light brown sugar
½ teaspoon salt

¼ teaspoon ground nutmeg
¼ teaspoon ground allspice
⅛ teaspoon ground black pepper

1. Cut squash into quarters. Remove the seeds and slice off the skin, then chop the squash into 1-inch cubes. Put squash in a steamer rack in a large saucepan over boiling water and cover. Steam for 30 minutes or until the squash is tender.
2. When squash has cooked, use a potato masher to mash squash until smooth in a large bowl. Add remaining ingredients and continue mashing until everything is mixed in. Let the squash sit for at least 10 minutes so that the flavors can

mesh. Reheat in the microwave for a minute or so before serving.

- MAKES 4 SERVINGS.

TIDBITS

If you want to cook the squash in the microwave poke several deep slices in the whole squash with a paring knife. Microwave the squash on high for 20 minutes or until you see all of the tough outer skin change color. The entire surface of the squash should be tender. Let it cool for 15 minutes, then slice it in half and scoop out the seeds with an ice cream scoop. Toss those, then scoop the good stuff into a bowl and proceed with the recipe from step #2.

• • • •

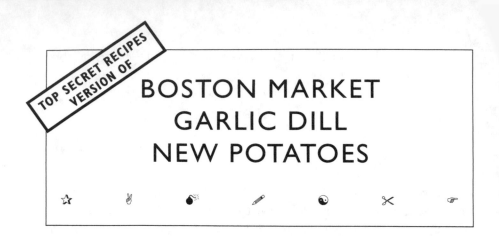

BOSTON MARKET
GARLIC DILL
NEW POTATOES

Technically speaking, "new potatoes" can be any young potato. Boston Market, however, uses red potatoes for this particular dish, and they're actually not all that young. So, for this recipe you need some common, medium-size red potatoes. After cutting the potatoes into bite-size slices, you simply steam them on a steamer rack or basket in a large, covered saucepan over boiling water. When the potatoes are done, toss them with a delicious mix of melted butter, fresh dill and garlic, and you've got a quick clone that could stand up to any taste test.

8 medium red potatoes
3 tablespoons butter, melted
1 tablespoon chopped fresh dill

2 teaspoons minced garlic
  (about 2 cloves)
¼ teaspoon salt

1. Cut the potatoes in half, cut the halves in half, then cut the quarters in half, so that you have eight wedges from each potato. Steam the sliced potatoes on a steamer rack over boiling water in a large, covered saucepan for 10 minutes, or until the tip of a knife encounters just a little resistance when stuck into the potatoes. The potatoes will cook a bit more after they come off the heat, so you want to be sure not to overcook them.

2. Combine the melted butter, dill, garlic, and salt in a small bowl.
3. When the potatoes are cooked, dump them into a medium bowl. Pour the garlic butter over the potatoes, then gently toss the potatoes until they are well-coated. Be careful not to toss the potatoes too much or they may start to fall apart, and you're not making mashed potatoes.

• MAKES 4 TO 6 SERVINGS.

• • • •

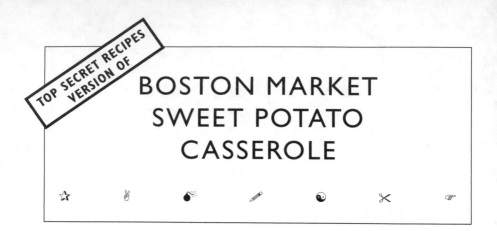

BOSTON MARKET
SWEET POTATO
CASSEROLE

Sure, this often requested clone from Boston Market may be considered a side dish, but it seems more like dessert. The brown sugar, cream, marshmallows and oatmeal streusel give this casserole a taste similar to sweet potato pie, yet the dish goes great alongside meals as varied as low-key chicken dinners or festive holiday banquets. And the great part is, if you're planning to use this for entertaining, you can make everything but the streusel a day ahead so you won't be stressed at crunch time. Just cover the filled baking dish and pop it in the fridge. Take it out a few hours before you plan to bake it so the casserole can come close to room temperature, then you simply make your streusel and pop the whole thing in the oven.

6 cups mashed sweet potatoes
   (5 to 6 potatoes-see step #1)
¾ cup dark brown sugar
½ cup heavy cream

¼ cup melted butter (½ stick)
¼ teaspoon ground cinnamon
¼ teaspoon salt
2 cups mini marshmallows

OATMEAL STREUSEL

¼ cup rolled oats
2 tablespoons dark brown sugar
1 tablespoon all-purpose flour

⅛ teaspoon ground cinnamon
2 tablespoons cold butter

1. Rub a little vegetable oil on the skin of each sweet potato and bake them in a preheated 400 degree oven for 60 to 70 minutes or until they are tender. When the potatoes are cool enough to handle, scrape out the insides and use an electric mixer on high speed to beat the potatoes until they are mashed and smooth. Measure exactly 6 cups of the mashed sweet potato into a large bowl.
2. Add ¾ cup brown sugar, heavy cream, melted butter, ¼ teaspoon cinnamon, and salt into the sweet potatoes and mix well with the beater until all the ingredients are incorporated. Pour this mixture into an 8x8-inch baking dish.
3. Preheat oven to 350 degrees.
4. Make the oatmeal streusel by grinding the rolled oats to a fine flour using a food processor. A blender will also work.
5. Combine the oat flour with 2 tablespoons brown sugar, all-purpose flour, and ⅛ teaspoon cinnamon in a small bowl. Cut the cold butter into the dry mixture using a pastry knife or a fork. You should have a crumbly mixture with pea-size bits. Sprinkle this oatmeal streusel over the sweet potato mixture and pop it into the oven for 50 to 60 minutes or until the top begins to brown slightly.
6. When you remove the casserole from the oven immediately spread the marshmallows over the top. Let this sit for about 10 minutes. The heat from the casserole will melt the marshmallows, and then it's ready to serve.

- MAKES 6 TO 8 SERVINGS.

• • • •

CLIFF & BUSTER
COCONUT MACAROONS

While passing these out to each giddy audience member on her 2003 "Favorite Things" show, Oprah gushed, "Isn't that the best macaroon you've ever had?" The recipe for these delicious, yet easy-to-clone, coconut macaroons was passed down to Cliff Barsevich years ago from his grandmother, and they were served at the events serviced by Cliff and partner Ron Strle's catering business. When customers continued to rave about the cookies, the duo began selling the macaroons by the box in high-end stores such as Neiman Marcus. With a lot of help from *The Oprah Winfrey Show*, the cookies have become a huge success. Still, at 15 bucks a dozen, it's nice to have a clone that will satisfy your macaroon munchies at a fraction of the cost. It's the closest we'll ever get to a homemade version since Cliff says he's never sharing the recipe. He says when he dies he's taking the secret formula with him.

MACAROONS

3 cups unsweetened shredded coconut (about 8 ounces— see Tidbits)

⅓ cup sweetened condensed milk
¾ teaspoon vanilla extract
¾ teaspoon almond extract

CHOCOLATE GANACHE

½ cup semi-sweet chocolate chips

3 tablespoons heavy cream

1. Preheat oven to 350 degrees.
2. Dump the shredded coconut into a large bowl.
3. Stir vanilla and almond extract into the condensed milk.
4. Drizzle the condensed milk over the coconut while tossing the coconut to coat it thoroughly.
5. When the coconut and condensed milk are combined, use a 1¼-inch sorbet scoop to mold the macaroons. Press the macaroon mixture firmly into the scoop, then turn it out onto a sheet pan. Bake the macaroons for 12 to 15 minutes or until you see the top of the macaroons beginning to turn light brown. Remove the macaroons from the oven and let them cool.
6. As the macaroons cool, resist the temptation to eat them. Instead, prepare the chocolate ganache by combining the chocolate chips with the cream in a small glass or ceramic cup or bowl. Microwave this on 50 percent power for 1 minute, then gently stir the chocolate. If the chocolate is not completely melted after a couple minutes of stirring, microwave it again for another 30 seconds on half power and stir. Be careful not to overcook the chips or the chocolate will seize up and your ganache will be grainy instead of smooth. If that happens, start over. Sorry. Now you can have a macaroon.
7. When the chocolate is melted and smooth, pour it into a squirt bottle and drizzle it in thin streams over each macaroon. Let the macaroons sit out for a few hours. At a room temperature of 72 degrees the chocolate should set up in 3 or 4 hours. When the chocolate has set, store the macaroons in an airtight container for up to 14 days at room temperature or for up to 4 weeks in the fridge.

- MAKES 20 MACAROONS.

TIDBITS

The real Cliff & Buster's macaroons use a thinly shredded short flake unsweetened coconut which can be found in specialty stores such as Trader Joe's. If you can't track down this type of coconut, using the more common sweetened stuff found in just about every supermarket will still make an excellent cookie.

•   •   •   •

DEL TACO
CRISPY FISH TACO

☆   ✌   💣   ✎   ☯   ✂   ☞

Del Taco's latest release is a tasty double corn tortilla-wrapped fried halibut fish stick that's topped with cabbage, fresh salsa and a creamy "secret sauce." Thanks to the availability of breaded frozen fish sticks in just about every market, this clone is crazy simple. And if you can't find crispy halibut sticks, the more common breaded pollock works fine. If you're not into the breaded stuff, you can also use frozen fish portions that are grilled, not breaded. The real recipe requires two thin corn tortillas, but if your tortillas are on the thick side, the clone also works well with just one tortilla per taco.

SECRET SAUCE

¼ cup mayonnaise

1 tablespoon whole milk

½ teaspoon fresh lime juice

SALSA

2 medium tomatoes, diced (about 1 ½ cups)

½ medium Spanish onion, diced (about ¾ cup)

2 tablespoons chopped cilantro

1 teaspoon fresh lime juice

¼ teaspoon salt

¼ teaspoon ground black pepper

⅛ teaspoon cayenne pepper

8 frozen fish sticks   *16 small corn tortillas*
2 cups shredded cabbage

GARNISH
8 lime wedges

1. Make the secret sauce by combining mayonnaise, milk and lime juice in a small bowl. Whisk until smooth, then cover and chill until needed.
2. Make salsa by combining ingredients in a medium bowl. Cover and chill this as well until your fish is baked and you're ready to build the tacos.
3. Bake the frozen fish sticks as directed on the box.
4. Warm tortillas in the microwave in a tortilla warmer, or wrapped them in moist paper towels before nuking.
5. Build each taco using two tortillas per taco. Drop a fish stick into the center of the tortillas, then spoon about 1½ teaspoons of sauce over the fish. Add about ¼ cup of cabbage and top off the taco with a couple dollops of salsa. Serve each taco with a lime wedge.

• MAKES 8 TACOS.

•   •   •   •

HELLMAN'S/ BEST FOODS MAYONNAISE

One day in France in 1756, when Duke de Richelieu's chef couldn't find any cream for a sauce made with eggs and cream, he substituted oil. The thick emulsion that formed is now one of the basic sauces for our modern cuisine. A homemade version of this simple culinary breakthrough was an important ingredient on Richard Hellmann's salads in the deli he opened in New York City in 1905. When Richard started selling his mayonnaise by the jar at the deli, the bottles flew out the door. Before long Hellmann's ruled the East coast, while another company, Best Foods, was having success with mayonnaise west of the Rockies. In 1932, Best Foods bought Hellmann's, and today the two brands split the country with the Best Foods brand west of the Rockies and Hellmann's to the east. The mayonnaise recipes are nearly identical, although some people claim that Best Foods mayonnaise is a little tangier.

In this clone recipe you'll be creating an emulsion by whisking a stream of oil into a beaten egg yolk. The solution will begin to magically thicken and change color, and before you know it you'll be looking at a bowl of beautiful, off-white, fresh mayonnaise. I've found the best way to add the oil to the egg yolk a little bit at a time while whisking is to pour the oil into a plastic squirt bottle (like the kind used for ketchup or mustard). This will allow you to whisk continuously with one hand while squirting oil with the other. The real stuff is made with soybean oil, which can be hard to find in some areas. Fortunately common canola oil is a great substitute.

egg yolk	¼ teaspoon plus ⅛ teaspoon
¼ teaspoons white vinegar	granulated sugar
teaspoon water	¼ teaspoon bottled lemon juice
¼ teaspoon plus ⅛ teaspoon salt	I cup canola oil (or soybean oil)

1. Whisk the egg yolk by hand for 15 seconds.
2. Combine vinegar, water, salt, sugar, and lemon juice in a small bowl or glass measuring cup. Stir until salt and sugar are dissolved. Add half of this solution to the egg yolk and whisk for another 15 seconds.
3. Pour I cup of canola oil (or soybean oil) into a plastic squirt bottle. This bottle will allow you to dribble the oil into the egg yolk with one hand while whisking with the other. Squirt a few drops of oil into the yolk and whisk, and continue to add oil a little bit at a time while whisking non-stop. When you have used about half of the oil, your mayonnaise should be very thick. Add the remaining vinegar solution. Whisk. Now you can add the remaining oil in a steady stream while whisking until all of the oil has been added. Your mayonnaise should be thick and off-white in color.
4. Put the mayonnaise into an old mayonnaise jar and seal it with a lid. Keep up to 2 weeks in your refrigerator.

• MAKES I CUP.

TIDBITS

You can save a little elbow grease by dumping all the ingredients except the oil into a blender. Turn it on low speed and add the oil in a slow drizzle until mayonnaise thickens.

•   •   •   •

JACQUIN'S
PEPPERMINT SCHNAPPS

☆   ✌   💣   ✏   ☯   ✂   ☞

All you need to make this minty schnapps at home is four ingredients including inexpensive vodka and an empty bottle to store it in. This is a recipe that was created for *More Top Secret Recipes* many years ago but didn't make it into the final version. Now it finally has a home in a book.

⅓ cup granulated sugar
1 16-oz. bottle light corn syrup

2 cups 80-proof vodka
2 teaspoons peppermint extract

1. Combine sugar and corn syrup in a 2 quart pan over medium heat. Heat until sugar dissolves, stirring regularly (about 5 minutes).
2. When sugar has dissolved, remove mixture from the heat, add vodka, and cover tightly with a lid. Let it cool down before you take the lid off.
3. When the liquid has cooled down, add the peppermint extract and pour it all into a sealable bottle.

• MAKES 4 CUPS.

• • • •

JASON'S DELI CREAMY LIQUEUR FRUIT DIPPING SAUCE

When Joe Tortorice and Rusty Coco opened the first Jason's Deli in Beaumont, Texas in 1976, they could only dream of one day having more than 136 stores in 15 states. The original menu of 12 items has exploded to over 75, with many of the awesome sandwich selections paired up with a side order of assorted fruit and creamy liqueur fruit dipping sauce. The tasty sauce is easily cloned here with only three ingredients and can be customized for those of you watching the fat grams by substituting low-fat or fat-free sour cream. Serve this sauce along with a bowl of your favorite fresh fruit such as pineapple, strawberries, grapes or whatever happens to be in season.

1 cup sour cream
½ cup light brown sugar

4 teaspoons Grand Marnier
   liqueur

Whisk together all ingredients in a medium bowl until sugar is dissolved. Chill for an hour, then stir once before serving.

• MAKES 1 ½ CUPS.

• • • •

KRAFT
MIRACLE WHIP

Even though it looks like mayonnaise, Food and Drug Administration dudes say it has to be called "dressing." Miracle Whip was invented in 1933 as a sweeter, more flavorful alternative to mayonnaise, but it contains a few extra ingredients that the FDA says aren't suppose to be in mayonnaise, such as sugar, paprika and garlic powder. To clone it, you just need to make a simple emulsion with egg yolk and oil. With the addition of the other flavors you've got yourself a Miracle Whip clone that's way fresher than the stuff on store shelves.

1 egg yolk	¼ teaspoon bottled lemon juice
¼ teaspoon dry mustard	1 cup canola oil
5 teaspoons white vinegar	pinch paprika
4 teaspoons granulated sugar	pinch garlic powder
¼ teaspoon plus ⅛ teaspoon salt	

1. Whisk the egg yolk by hand for 15 seconds.
2. Combine vinegar, sugar, salt and lemon juice in a small bowl or glass measuring cup. Stir until salt and sugar is dissolved. Add half of this solution to the egg yolk and whisk for another 15 seconds.
3. Pour canola oil into a plastic squirt bottle. This bottle will allow you to dribble the oil into the egg yolk with one hand while whisking with the other. Squirt a few drops of oil into

the yolk and whisk, and continue to add oil a little bit at a time while whisking non-stop. When you are about halfway through the oil, your mayonnaise should be very thick. Whisk in the remaining vinegar solution and add the mustard, paprika and garlic powder. Now you can add the remaining oil in a steady stream while whisking until all of the oil has been added.

4. Put the dressing into an old mayonnaise jar and seal it with a lid. Keep up to 7 to 10 days in your refrigerator.

- MAKES 1 CUP.

•　•　•　•

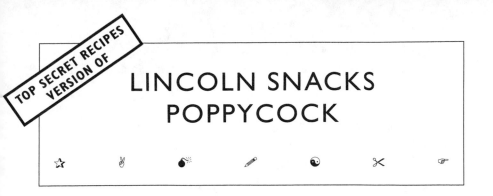

LINCOLN SNACKS
POPPYCOCK

☆　　✌　　💣　　✏　　☯　　✂　　☞

This Nebraska-based company grows a special kind of yellow mushroom popcorn that pops into fluffy round shapes for all its brands of candy-coated popcorn—Fiddle Faddle, Screaming Yellow Zonkers, and Poppycock—but we can use plain microwave popcorn for an easy clone. The Poppycock motto is, "It's our amazing glaze!" and it is pretty amazing. The butter-toffee glaze is flavored with maple syrup, and each box is packed with lots of nuts, unlike any other glazed popcorn brands. Clone the Poppycock flavor you prefer: All cashews, all pecans, or a combination of almonds and pecans. Of course, you can mix in any nuts you like as long as it comes to two cups worth (macadamia nuts is an awesome variation). Make sure the nuts are roasted, salted or unsalted nuts each work fine. You really need a candy thermometer for this recipe to get it perfect, but you can always wing it by drizzling some of the candy into a glass of cold water once you see the syrup begin to darken. If the candy forms brittle threads, it's ready. You coat the popcorn with the glaze by heating everything up in the microwave and stirring. There is also a way to do this in your oven (see Tidbits), but the microwave method is faster.

¾ cup light corn syrup
½ cup light brown sugar
½ cup salted butter (1 stick)
⅓ cup maple syrup

¼ cup water
2 tablespoons granulated sugar
¼ teaspoon salt
1 teaspoon vanilla extract

8 cups plain (not buttered)
microwave popcorn, popped

2 cups roasted nuts (pecans,
cashews, or almonds/pecans)

1. Combine corn syrup, sugars, butter, maple syrup, water and salt in a large saucepan over medium heat. Simmer the mixture and monitor it with a candy thermometer. Your target temperature is 290 degrees, or just before the hard crack stage. The temperature continues to rise a bit after you turn off the heat, so this is a good place to stop cooking.
2. While the candy cooks, pop the popcorn in the microwave and measure out 8 cups of popcorn. Make sure to remove any unpopped kernels. Pour the popcorn into a large microwave-safe glass bowl. Measure the nuts of your choice into a glass measuring cup. Just before the candy reaches 290 degrees, microwave the nuts in the measuring cup on high for 1 minute to warm them up.
3. When your candy hits 290 degrees, turn off the heat, add the vanilla and stir in the warm nuts. Immediately microwave the bowl of popcorn for 1 minute on high, then pour the candy and nuts mixture over the popcorn while stirring. Microwave the bowl for 1 more minute on high, then stir well to coat the popcorn and nuts with candy. You may want to go back into the microwave for an additional minute since the candy will begin to harden quickly. Stir well to coat all of the popcorn, then quickly pour the popcorn out onto wax paper or onto a silicon non-stick mat.
4. When the popcorn is cool, break it up and put it into a tightly sealed container to keep it fresh. This stuff gets sticky and stale pretty quickly in moist climates.

• MAKES 10 CUPS.

TIDBITS

To use your oven rather than the microwave to coat the popcorn and nuts, preheat it to 275 degrees while the candy is cooking.

Pour the nuts on a large buttered baking sheet. When the candy reaches 290 degrees, add the vanilla, then stir the warm nuts into the candy. Spread the popcorn on the baking sheet, drizzle with the hot candy syrup and stir. Put the popcorn back into the oven for 5 minutes, then take it out and stir to coat. Repeat if necessary, pour onto wax paper or a silicone mat, then go to step #4.

• • • •

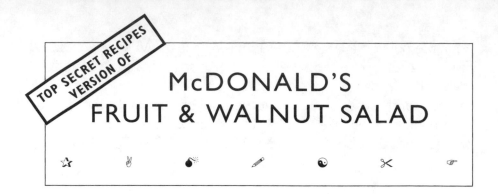

McDONALD'S FRUIT & WALNUT SALAD

McDonald's enlisted Destiny's Child, Venus Williams, and Bob Greene (Oprah's Trainer) to kick off its Balanced Lifestyles campaign in the spring of 2005, starting with this salad and the tagline "Get a fruit buzz." Most of the recipe is no big secret: Two kinds of sliced apples, red seedless grapes and low-fat vanilla yogurt. But this new product did inspire another way to candy walnuts. It's a quick technique that includes honey and peanut oil, along with some granulated sugar and a little vanilla. Also, you should know that McDonald's has to use a special preservative coating on the apple slices to keep them from turning brown in the ten minutes or so that it takes for sliced apples to turn brown. Copy this recipe at home, and you won't have to worry about such things.

CANDIED WALNUTS

1 teaspoon peanut oil
1 teaspoon honey
2 tablespoons granulated sugar
¼ teaspoon vanilla extract
⅛ teaspoon salt
¾ cup coarsely chopped walnuts

2 small Granny Smith apples, cored and cut into 16 slices each

2 small gala apples, cored and cut into 16 slices each
40 red seedless grapes
¾ cup Dannon low-fat vanilla yogurt

1. Make the candied walnuts by combining peanut oil, honey, sugar, vanilla, and salt in a medium skillet over medium heat in the order listed. When mixture begins to bubble, add chopped walnuts and stir constantly until sugar begins to smoke and/or caramelize. Immediately turn off heat and keep stirring the nuts so that they do not burn. After a minute of stirring off the heat, pour nuts out onto a plate. Toss nuts as they cool so that they don't stick together.
2. When nuts have cooled, build each salad by mixing 8 slices of Granny Smith apple, 8 slices of gala apple, 10 grapes, 3 tablespoons of yogurt, and 3 tablespoons of candied walnuts. Stir and serve.

- MAKES 4 SERVINGS.

• • • •

PANERA BREAD FRENCH ONION SOUP

The 825 Panera Bread outlets in 35 states are famous for fantastic sandwiches, but it's this delicious French onion soup that gets most of the cloning requests. The biggest difference I find with Panera's formula versus other onion soup recipes is the inclusion of a small, almost undetectable, bit of tomato sauce. So, rather than opening up a whole can of tomato sauce to use just one tablespoon, I discovered that a bit of ketchup works perfectly. Panera Bread also makes their soup special by using sweet cream butter to sauté the onions, and just a bit of Tabasco pepper sauce in the pot to wake everything up. The croutons on top of the soup appear to be made from the chain's foccacia bread that has been buttered, cubed, and toasted until crispy, but you can use any bread you may have on hand. As for the cheese on top, the menu says it's Asiago-Parmesan, but the cheese I tasted was more Asiago than Parmesan, so using plain Asiago cheese (that's been shaved using a potato peeler) works like a charm.

¼ cup unsalted butter
8 cups sliced white onions (4 to 5 medium onions)
2 14-ounce cans beef broth (I used Swanson)
¾ cup chicken broth (Swanson again)
3 tablespoons all-purpose flour
1 ½ cups water

1 tablespoon ketchup
1 ½ teaspoons ground black pepper
1 ½ teaspoons salt
¼ teaspoon dried thyme
¼ teaspoon garlic powder
couple drops Tabasco pepper sauce

GARNISH

croutons   *shaved Asiago cheese*
butter

1. Melt butter in a large saucepan over medium heat. When the butter is melted, add sliced onions and sauté for 15 to 20 minutes, stirring often, until onions turn brown.
2. Add remaining ingredients (but not the garnish) to the pan and stir to combine. Heat soup until it's boiling, then reduce heat and simmer uncovered for 20 minutes.
3. Make croutons for the top of the soup by slicing foccacia bread (or any bread you may have) into ¾-inch thick slices. Butter both sides of those slices, then cut the slices into bite-size cubes. Bake the bread in a 425 degree oven for 15 minutes or until crispy. Shave some Asiago cheese by simply dragging a potato peeler over the edge of a wedge of Asiago.
4. Serve the soup super hot with a handful of croutons floating on top followed by a couple tablespoons of shaved Asiago cheese.

• MAKES 8 CUPS.

•　　•　　•　　•

RONDELÉ GARLIC & HERB CHEESE SPREAD

The real thing found in the deli section of your market is often used on crackers; as a dip for raw vegetables; or even as a spread on sandwiches, burgers, and wraps. I've come up with an easy way to recreate the brand version using a 12-ounce tub of whipped cream cheese (which means you'll happily get 3 times the amount of the 4-ounce original!). Just be sure when mixing your version, that you don't over mix, or you will destroy the fluffiness of the whipped cheese. The Italian seasoning included here is a dried herb blend (usually marjoram, thyme, rosemary, savory, sage, oregano, and basil) found near the other bottled herbs and spices. I used McCormick brand for this clone, but any brand should work fine. Since the herbs are dry, the flavor is more subtle than fresh, even after the herbs soak up moisture from the cheese. And that's just want we want for a proper clone.

1 12-ounce tub Philadelphia
   whipped cream cheese
1 ½ teaspoons finely minced fresh
   garlic

¾ teaspoon Italian seasoning
¼ teaspoon plus ⅛ teaspoon salt
⅛ teaspoon onion powder

Gently stir garlic, Italian seasoning, salt, and onion powder into whipped cream cheese. Store the spread in your fridge for at least a couple hours. Overnight is even better. Stir once more before serving.

• MAKES 12 OUNCES.

• • • •

SONIC DRIVE-IN
HICKORY BURGER

I like barbecue sauce on everything—ribs, chicken, fish, French fries; probably even ice cream if I'd get up the nerve to try it—so naturally, I love this burger. Where there used to be mayonnaise is now a glob of delicious Kraft Hickory BBQ sauce. Gimme a pile of napkins, I'm in heaven.

¼ pound ground beef
1 large plain white hamburger
    bun
butter-flavored spray or melted
    butter
salt

ground black pepper
1 tablespoon Kraft Hickory BBQ
    Sauce
1 tablespoon chopped white onion
⅓ cup chopped lettuce

1. Shape the ground beef into a thin circle the same diameter as the bun. Cover the patty with wax paper and freeze.
2. When you're ready to prepare the burger, preheat a large skillet over medium heat.
3. Spray some butter spray or spread a thin layer of melted butter on the faces of the top and bottom bun. Lightly brown the faces of the bun in the skillet, then remove them and set them aside.
4. Grill the beef patty in the skillet, and lightly sprinkle it with salt and pepper. Cook the beef for 3 to 4 minutes per side until done.

5. As the patty cooks, build the burger by first spreading the BBQ sauce over the face of the bottom bun.
6. Sprinkle the chopped onion over the sauce.
7. Arrange the lettuce on the sandwich next.
8. When the beef is ready, stack it on top of the other condiments, and top off the sandwich with the top bun. If you'd like the sandwich hotter, microwave it on high for 10 to 15 seconds.

• MAKES 1 BURGER.

•　•　•　•

SONIC DRIVE-IN
JALAPEÑO BURGER

If you like mustard and dig spicy stuff then this is the burger choice for you. No ketchup or mayo here, just mustard. Add to that a big pile of jalapeno slices and you've got a burger so nice, it'll burn twice.

¼-pound ground beef
1 large plain white hamburger
    bun
butter-flavored spray or melted
    butter
salt

ground black pepper
1 ½ teaspoons yellow mustard
6 to 10 canned jalapeno slices
    (nacho slices)
⅓ cup chopped lettuce

1. Shape the ground beef into a thin circle the same diameter as the bun. Cover the patty with wax paper and freeze it.
2. When you're ready to prepare the burger, preheat a large skillet over medium heat.
3. Spray some butter spray or spread a thin layer of melted butter on the faces of the top and bottom bun. Lightly brown the faces of the bun in the skillet, then remove them and set them aside.
4. Grill the beef patty in the skillet, and lightly sprinkle it with salt and pepper. Cook the beef for 3 to 4 minutes per side until done.
5. As the patty cooks, build the burger by first spreading the mustard over the face of the bottom bun.

6. Arrange the jalapeno slices on the mustard.
7. Arrange the lettuce on the sandwich next.
8. When the beef is ready, stack it on top of the other condiments, and top off the sandwich with the top bun. If you'd like the sandwich hotter, microwave it on high for 10 to 15 seconds.

- MAKES 1 BURGER.

• • • •

SONIC DRIVE-IN NO. 1 BURGER

Driving through Louisiana in 1953, Troy Smith happened upon a cozy hamburger stand that had installed an intercom system to speed up ordering. Troy adapted the idea for his small chain of burger joints and hired nimble servers to quickly bring food out to customers. He called his new place Sonic, and the concept was a smash, with revenues for the chain doubling during the first week. Sonic was cashing in on the growing popularity of the automobile. Hungry patrons parked their cars in a stall, rolled down the window, and ordered from a two-way speaker box, then the food was quickly brought out to the car on a tray by a roller-skating carhop with excellent balance. Today Sonic has rejuvenated the carhop concept by serving customers the same way as in the '50s: with individual car stalls, speakers, and waitresses on wheels.

Sonic's signature hamburger is an old-school, made-in-American, no-frills hamburger with standard ingredients and great taste. Sometimes the old-fashioned way is the best way.

¼ pound ground beef
1 large plain white hamburger bun
butter-flavored spray or melted butter
salt
ground black pepper

2 teaspoons mayonnaise
3 dill pickle slices (hamburger slices)
1 tablespoon chopped white onion
⅓ cup chopped lettuce
2 tomato slices

1. Shape the ground beef into a thin circle the same diameter as the bun. Cover the patty with wax paper and freeze it.
2. When you're ready to prepare the burger, preheat a large skillet over medium heat.
3. Spray some butter spray or spread a thin layer of melted butter on the faces of the top and bottom bun. Lightly brown the faces of the bun in the skillet, then remove them and set them aside.
4. Grill the beef patty in the skillet, and lightly sprinkle it with salt and pepper. Cook the beef for 3 to 4 minutes per side until done.
5. As the patty cooks, build the burger by first spreading the mayonnaise over the browned face of the bottom bun.
6. Arrange the pickle slices on the mayonnaise.
7. Sprinkle the chopped onion over the pickles.
8. Arrange the lettuce on the sandwich next.
9. Stack the tomato slices on the lettuce.
10. When the beef is ready, stack it on top of the other condiments, and top off the sandwich with the top bun. If you'd like the sandwich hotter, microwave it on high for 10 to 15 seconds.

• MAKES 1 BURGER.

• • • •

SONIC DRIVE-IN PEANUT BUTTER SHAKE & PEANUT BUTTER FUDGE SHAKE

Here are a couple easy-to-make milkshake clones from Sonic's fountain in response to many requests stacking up at *TSR* central. The straight peanut butter version is crazy good if you like peanut butter, and when you add a little fudge to the recipe for the second clone you've got what tastes like a drinkable Reese's peanut butter cup.

PEANUT BUTTER SHAKE

2¼ cups vanilla ice cream
¼ cup whole milk

2 tablespoons creamy peanut butter

PEANUT BUTTER FUDGE SHAKE

2¼ cups vanilla ice cream
¼ cup whole milk
2 tablespoons creamy peanut butter

1 tablespoon chocolate fudge

1. Combine the ingredients for the shake of your choice in a blender. Be sure to pack the ice cream into the measuring cup when you measure it out. Blend everything on medium speed until smooth.
2. Pour shake into a 16-ounce glass, add a straw and serve it up. Pop the shake into the freezer for 10 to 15 minutes to firm it up, if necessary.

- MAKES 1 SERVING.

• • • •

STARBUCKS FRAPPUCCINO (BOTTLED VERSION)

This clones Starbucks' "Lowfat Creamy Blend of Coffee & Milk" that you find in the 9½-ounce bottles in most stores. Those little suckers will set you back at least a buck, but this *Top Secret Recipes* version costs a mere fraction of that. The recipe requires espresso, but don't worry if you don't have an espresso machine. Check out the Tidbits below for a way to clone espresso with a standard drip machine and ground coffee.

½ cup fresh espresso, chilled
2½ cups lowfat milk (2 percent)

¼ cup granulated sugar
1 tablespoon dry pectin*

Combine all of the ingredients in a pitcher or covered container. Stir or shake until sugar is dissolved. Chill and serve cold.

• MAKES 24 OUNCES.

*This is a natural thickener found in fruits that is used for canning. You can find it in the supermarket near the canning supplies. It is used in this recipe to make the drink thicker and creamier, and can be found in the original recipe. It does not add to the flavor and can be excluded if you don't care so much about duplicating the texture of the real thing.

To make the "Mocha" variety: Add a pinch ($\frac{1}{16}$ teaspoon) of cocoa powder to the mixture before combining.

To fake espresso with a drip coffee maker and standard grind of coffee: Use $\frac{1}{3}$ cup ground coffee and I cup of water. Brew once then run coffee through machine again, same grounds. Makes about $\frac{1}{2}$ cup fresh espresso to use in the above recipe. Run a pot of water through machine, without grounds, to clean.

•   •   •   •

STARBUCKS CARROT CAKE

There's nothing like a freshly baked slice of carrot cake with cream cheese frosting and a tall glass of cold milk. And a hot latte ain't such a bad chaser either. I suppose that's why Starbucks is where you'll find some of the best carrot cake around. It's moist and flavorful, packed with nuts and golden raisins. Starbucks makes sure its tasty baked goods are fresh by contracting with local bakeries to produce cakes and scones and muffins from the coffee chain's top secret specs. Now *TSR* has some secret specs too with this formula for a carrot cake clone that tastes like it came from your crowded local coffee house.

1 ½ cups all-purpose flour
2 teaspoons baking powder
1 teaspoon baking soda
2 teaspoons ground cinnamon
½ teaspoon salt
¼ teaspoon ground nutmeg
¼ teaspoon ground allspice
1 ½ cups dark brown sugar

1 cup vegetable oil
3 eggs
¼ teaspoon vanilla extract
1 cup shredded carrot (1 large carrot)
¾ cup chopped walnuts
½ cup golden raisins
vegetable shortening

FROSTING
8 ounces cream cheese, softened
1 tablespoon milk

1 teaspoon vanilla extract
3 cups powdered sugar

OPTIONAL GARNISH
⅓ cup chopped pecans

1. Preheat oven to 350 degrees.
2. Sift together flour, baking powder, baking soda, cinnamon, salt, nutmeg and allspice in a large bowl.
3. Use an electric mixer to combine brown sugar and oil. Add the eggs and vanilla and beat on high speed for about a minute.
4. Combine the wet mixture with the dry stuff. Mix on low speed until all ingredients are incorporated then crank up the speed and blend on high until batter is smooth.
5. Add shredded carrot, walnuts, and raisins and mix by hand. Pour batter into a 9x13-inch baking pan that has been generously greased with shortening.
6. Bake for 40 to 50 minutes or until a toothpick stuck in the center comes out clean. Allow the cake to cool completely.
7. Make the frosting by mixing softened cream cheese, milk, and vanilla in a large bowl with an electric mixer. Add the powdered sugar, one cup at a time, and blend well until frosting is smooth.
8. When the cake has cooled, frost the top with the entire bowl of cream cheese frosting. Sprinkle the pecans over the frosting. Slice into 12 pieces to serve. Cover the leftover cake and store it in the fridge.

• MAKES 12 SERVINGS.

• • • •

STARBUCKS
IMPROVED
CRANBERRY BLISS BAR

Each holiday season Starbucks brings out one of its most beloved dessert recipes: A soft triangle of white chocolate and cranberry cake, covered with delicious creamy lemon frosting and dried cranberries. But, when the holidays leave us, so do the Cranberry Bliss Bars. Since this is such a popular item, I decided to go back and improve the recipe that was first published as a bonus recipe in the QVC book, *Best of Top Secret Recipes*. When I tasted the original again (a frozen sample from last X-mas), I noticed chunks of ginger in the cake that I didn't see before—crystallized ginger. Making the recipe with this ingredient rather than powdered ginger greatly improved the quality of the clone. You can find crystallized ginger in bottles next to the herbs and spices in your supermarket. I also felt that my earlier version was much too buttery and included too much white chocolate. With this new reduction in white chocolate it becomes a more convenient recipe since you only have to buy one bar of Ghirardelli white chocolate (if that's the brand available in your market—if not, any white chocolate bar will do) rather than buying two bars and only using half of one. If you've tried the previous version of this recipe (and even if you haven't) I think you'll really dig this update which makes 16 delicious cake bars, each at a fraction of the cost of the original.

CAKE

¾ cup butter, softened (1 ½ sticks)

1 ¼ cups light brown sugar, packed

3 eggs

2 tablespoons minced crystallized ginger

1 ½ teaspoons vanilla extract

¼ teaspoon salt

1 ½ cups all-purpose flour

½ teaspoon baking powder

¾ cup diced dried cranberries

4 ounces white chocolate, cut into chunks

FROSTING

4 ounces cream cheese, softened

3 cups powdered sugar

4 teaspoons lemon juice

½ teaspoon vanilla extract

¼ cup diced dried cranberries

DRIZZLED ICING

½ cup powdered sugar

1 tablespoon milk

2 teaspoons vegetable shortening

1. Preheat oven to 350 degrees.
2. Make cake by beating butter and brown sugar together with an electric mixer until smooth. Add eggs, ginger, vanilla, and salt and beat well. Gradually mix in flour and baking powder until smooth. Mix ¾ cup diced dried cranberries and white chocolate into the batter by hand. Pour batter into a buttered 9x13-inch baking pan. Use a spatula to spread the batter evenly across the pan. Bake for 35 to 40 minutes or until cake is light brown on top. Allow cake to cool.
3. Make frosting by combining softened cream cheese, 3 cups powdered sugar, lemon juice and vanilla extract in a medium bowl with an electric mixer until smooth. When the cake has cooled, use a spatula to spread frosting over the top of the cake.
4. Sprinkle ¼ cup of diced cranberries over the frosting on the cake.

5. Whisk together ½ cup powdered sugar, 1 tablespoon of milk, and shortening. Drizzle icing over the cranberries in a sweeping motion or use a pastry bag with a fine tip to drizzle frosting across the top of the cake.
6. Cover the cake and let it chill out in the fridge for a couple hours, then slice the cake lengthwise (the long way) through the middle. Slice the cake across the width three times making a total of eight rectangular slices. Slice each of those rectangles diagonally creating 16 triangular slices.

• MAKES 16 BARS.

•   •   •   •

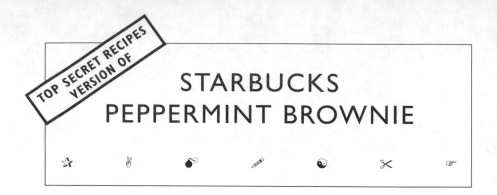

STARBUCKS
PEPPERMINT BROWNIE

Here's a great one for the holidays (or for any time of the year): It's a mint chocolate brownie with mint buttercream frosting on top, and creamy chocolate frosting on top of that. And to simplify the cloning process a bit, we start with a common fudge brownie mix. By changing the required ingredients listed on the brownie mix box, and adding some other modified steps, we can improve on the finished product. Rather than oil, use a stick of melted butter in your brownies for a richer, better flavor. And cook the brownies at a slightly lower temperature so that they come out moist and chewy. Since this recipe is for peppermint brownies, adding just a bit of peppermint extract will do the trick. The peppermint brownies from Starbucks have red and white frosting drizzled lightly across the top. To save time, you can skip this mostly cosmetic step. Or you can buy pre-made red and white frostings that come in little cans (with tips included).

BROWNIES

1 19.8-ounce box fudge brownie
   mix (Betty Crocker Fudge
   Brownie Mix is best)
½ cup butter, melted (1 stick)

¼ cup water
2 large eggs
¼ teaspoon peppermint extract

PEPPERMINT BUTTERCREAM FROSTING

½ cup butter, softened (1 stick)
1½ cups powdered sugar
1 tablespoon milk

¼ teaspoon peppermint extract
¼ teaspoon vanilla extract

CHOCOLATE FROSTING

⅓ cup whole milk
¼ cup butter (½ stick)
1 12-ounce bag semi-sweet
   chocolate chips

1 teaspoon vanilla extract
1 cup powdered sugar

OPTIONAL DECORATIVE ICING

1 can white frosting (with fine tip)   1 can red frosting (with fine tip)

1. Preheat the oven to 325 degrees, then prepare a 9x9-inch baking pan by spraying it with a light coating of non-stick spray. Cut a piece of parchment paper or non-stick aluminum foil to the same width as the bottom of the pan, but make it much longer than the pan so that the left and right ends go up and out of the pan on the left and right sides. This will create a "sling" that will help you lift the brownies out of the pan after they've baked.
2. Make the brownie batter by first sifting the box of ingredients. This will remove the clumps. Add the melted butter, water, eggs and peppermint extract and mix the batter by hand just until all the dry stuff is mixed in. Pour the batter into your prepared baking pan and bake it for 50 to 55 minutes, or until a toothpick stuck in the center comes out clean. Allow brownie to cool before frosting.
3. Make the peppermint buttercream frosting by beating together 1 cup of powdered sugar and the softened butter in a medium bowl with an electric mixer. Mix in another ½ cup of powdered sugar, then add 1 tablespoon of milk, and the peppermint and vanilla extract. Mix for about 1 minute

to make the frosting smooth. Add an additional ¼ cup of powdered sugar if the frosting is too thin and light. You want a frosting that can be spread easily, yet it should be firm enough to hold up the layer of chocolate frosting that's coming next. When the brownie has cooled, use a spatula to spread the frosting evenly over the top. Put the brownie in the fridge to firm up the buttercream frosting.

4. Make the chocolate frosting by bringing ⅓ cup whole milk and ¼ cup butter to a boil in a small saucepan over medium heat. Pour the chocolate chips into a heat-safe bowl. When the milk and butter comes to a boil, pour the mixture over the chocolate chips and let it all just sit there in the bowl for a couple minutes. Add the vanilla extract to the mixture and whisk until smooth. Use an electric mixer to beat in 1 cup powdered sugar until the frosting is smooth. Spread the chocolate frosting over the white frosting on the brownie.

5. To add the decorative red and white icing if you decide to go for it: First apply the white icing to the top of the cake in a sweeping motion diagonally across the top of the entire cake, then add the red icing over the white in the same sweeping motion in the same direction.

6. Stick the brownie back in the fridge for about an hour before removing it from the pan and slicing it into 9 equal portions. The leftovers will keep well for several days covered in the refrigerator.

- MAKES 9 BROWNIES.

• • • •

STARBUCKS
PUMPKIN SCONE

During the holiday months you'd better get over to Starbucks bright and early if you want to get your teeth around a delicious pumpkin scone. These orange triangles of goodness are made with real pumpkin and pumpkin pie spices, and they quickly vanish out the door when fall rolls around. Each scone is generously coated with a simple plain glaze and then spiced icing is drizzled over the top for the perfect finishing touch. But good scones are more than just good flavor. To get the flaky texture we'll cut cold butter into the dry ingredients, either with a pastry knife and some elbow grease, or by pulsing away at it with a food processor, until all the butter chunks have been worked in.

2 cups all-purpose flour
7 tablespoons granulated sugar
1 tablespoon baking powder
½ teaspoon salt
½ teaspoon ground cinnamon
¼ teaspoon ground nutmeg

¼ teaspoon ground cloves
¼ teaspoon ground ginger
½ cup canned pumpkin
3 tablespoons half-and half
1 large egg
6 tablespoons cold butter (¾ stick)

PLAIN GLAZE
1 cup plus 1 tablespoon
   powdered sugar

2 tablespoons whole milk

SPICED ICING

1 cup plus 3 tablespoons
    powdered sugar
2 tablespoons whole milk
¼ teaspoon ground cinnamon

⅛ teaspoon ground nutmeg
pinch ground ginger
pinch ground cloves

1. Preheat oven to 425 degrees.
2. Combine flour, sugar, baking powder, salt, ½ teaspoon cinnamon, ½ teaspoon nutmeg, ½ teaspoon cloves, and ½ teaspoon ginger in a large bowl.
3. In a separate medium bowl, whisk together pumpkin, half-and-half, and egg.
4. Cut butter into cubes then add it to the dry ingredients. Use a pastry knife or a fork to combine butter with dry ingredients. Continue mixing until no chunks of butter are visible. You can also use a food processor: Pulse butter into dry ingredients until it is the texture of cornmeal or coarse sand.
5. Fold wet ingredients into dry ingredients, then form the dough into a ball. Pat out dough onto a lightly floured surface and form it into a 1-inch thick rectangle that is about 9 inches long and 3 inches wide. Use a large knife or a pizza wheel to slice the dough twice through the width, making three equal portions. Cut those three slices diagonally so that you have 6 triangular slices of dough.
6. Bake for 14 to 16 minutes on a baking sheet that has been lightly oiled or lined with parchment paper. Scones should begin to turn light brown.
7. While scones cool, prepare plain glaze by combining ingredients in a medium bowl with an electric mixer on medium speed. Mix until smooth.
8. When scones are cool, use a brush to paint a coating of the glaze over the top of each scone.
9. As that white glaze firms up, prepare spiced icing by combining ingredients in another medium bowl with an electric mixer on medium speed. Drizzle this thicker icing over each

scone and allow the icing to dry before serving (at least 1 hour). A squirt bottle works great for this, or you can drizzle with a whisk. You can also create a makeshift pastry bag by spooning the icing into a plastic storage bag, then snipping a corner off the bag to make a very small opening through which you squirt the icing.

- MAKES 6 SCONES.

• • • •

STARBUCKS VANILLA ALMOND BISCOTTI

This gargantuan coffee chain has local bakers whip up many of the pastries and baked goods you see displayed behind the glass. That means everything gets to the stores real fresh, but we also find slight variations in many of the products at Starbucks in different cities. This particular flavor of biscotti, however, comes from a central location, all wrapped up in plastic. That's okay for biscotti, since it's a crispy cookie and doesn't need to be enjoyed bakery fresh. And a good biscotti is a great coffee companion. The thin profile and crispy nature of this cookie makes it perfect for dunking in hot cup of joe. But how does it get that shape? The dough is first baked as one giant rectangular cookie loaf, then the loaf is removed from the oven while it's still soft, and it's sliced. These slices are arranged on a baking sheet and cooked once again until crispy. ("Biscotti" is Italian for "twice baked".) These biscotti are best on the second day after they completely dry out, and they'll keep for several weeks. Happy dunking.

3 tablespoons butter	3 tablespoons buttermilk
⅔ cup granulated sugar	1¾ cups all-purpose flour
1 egg plus 1 egg white	2 teaspoons baking powder
½ teaspoon vanilla extract	1 teaspoon baking soda
¼ teaspoon salt	½ cup finely chopped almonds

1. Preheat oven to 350 degrees.
2. Cream together the butter and sugar in a large mixing bowl until smooth. Add egg and egg white and continue beating

until creamy, then add the vanilla, salt and buttermilk and mix until combined.

3. Sift the flour, baking powder, and baking soda together into a medium bowl. Add the dry stuff to the wet stuff in the mixing bowl, but do it a little at a time. When all the flour's in, toss in the finely chopped almonds, but save a couple tablespoons of the nuts for something we'll do later. Don't mix this dough too much or it might toughen up; you only want to mix it enough to get all the ingredients incorporated, and then you'll have tender biscotti. You may want to use your hands to work everything together as the dough thickens.

4. Form the dough into a rectangular loaf on a lightly greased or parchment paper-lined sheet pan. The dimensions of the loaf should be somewhere around 10 inches long and 5 inches wide, and about an inch thick in the middle. Sprinkle the leftover almond bits over the top of the loaf, then bake it for 30 to 35 minutes or until the top has turned light brown. Remove this now puffed-up loaf from the oven and let it cool for 5 minutes or as long as it takes for it to be cool enough to handle and slice.

5. When it's cool, move the biscotti loaf to a cutting board. Use a long serrated bread knife to slice the dough across its width. Make slices that are approximately ¾-inch thick. Keep the slices standing up and move them back to the sheet pan. Position them in rows on the pan so that they aren't touching, then pop the whole pan back into the oven for 10 to 15 minutes or until the cookies are crisp on the outside. When you remove the cookies from the oven, keep them out on the sheet pan for several hours or overnight so that they completely dry out. A good biscotti is a crispy biscotti.

• MAKES 20 BISCOTTI COOKIES.

• • • •

SUBWAY CHIPOTLE SOUTHWEST SAUCE

Everyone hip on Subway's sandwiches knows the key to cloning the flavor of many of the chain's top-sellers is about recreating the secret sauces. For example, Subway's Sweet Onion Chicken Teriyaki Sandwich is nothing without the Sweet Onion Sauce. And one of Subway's newest creations, the Chipotle Southwest Cheese Steak, is just a cheese steak sandwich without the Chipotle Southwest Sauce. Now, with this simple sauce clone, you can recreate the slightly sweet, slightly sour, and a little bit smoky sauce at home to take any of your home sandwich creations on a trip to the spicy Southwest. But you don't have to stop at sandwiches. This sauce also makes an amazing dressing for a zesty Southwestern salad. You'll need to pick up some ground chipotle chile pepper (smoked jalapeno) in the spice section of your market. McCormick makes good stuff.

½ cup mayonnaise
2 teaspoons lime juice
1 teaspoon granulated sugar
1 teaspoon minced cilantro
½ teaspoon paprika
½ teaspoon white vinegar
½ teaspoon water

¼ teaspoon salt
¼ teaspoon garlic powder
¼ teaspoon ground chipotle chile
    pepper
pinch dried thyme
pinch ground cumin

Combine ingredients in a small bowl. Cover and chill for at least 1 hour before using.

• MAKES ½ CUP.

• • • •

TOOTSIE ROLL MIDGEES

How would you react if your dentist suddenly whipped out a giant Tootsie Roll for you to bite down on so that he could make a mold of your teeth? Ask patients of a dentist in Philadelphia who does just that. This is just one of the many facts that you learn researching the history of the Tootsie Roll, which, by the way, was named after the inventor's five-year-old daughter. Leo Herschfield created the chewy chocolate candy in his small store in New York in 1896. In those days, the candy was hand rolled and delivered to customers by horse-drawn carriage. Over one hundred years later, more than forty-nine million Tootsie Rolls in a variety of sizes are produced each day from operations all over the world. Even though this clone recipe duplicates the tiny bite-size versions of the candy, you're free to make yours any size you like. The technique here is a tweaking of the previous secret formula that was featured in *Low-Fat Top Secret Recipes*, and it includes several upgrades. I found that more cocoa, plus the addition of salt and butter to the mix improve the flavor quite a bit. I also found that bringing your sweet bubbling mixture to the firm ball stage (250 degrees—yes, you're going to need a candy thermometer for this), and then stretching and pulling the candy like taffy (fun!) as it cools, will give you a finished product more like the real deal.

1 cup sugar
½ cup light corn syrup
¼ cup salted butter
¼ cup cocoa

¼ cup condensed skim milk
2 tablespoons water
½ teaspoon vanilla extract
⅛ teaspoon salt

1. Combine all ingredients in a small saucepan and set it over medium/low heat.
2. As ingredients begin to warm, whisk well to combine. Add a candy thermometer to the pan and closely monitor the temperature. You want the candy to reach 250 degrees (known as the firm ball stage).
3. As candy is cooking, rub a light coating of butter on a baking sheet. If you have a silicone non-stick pad, that also works well. Lay the pad down onto a baking sheet and rub a coating of butter on it.
4. When the candy reaches 250 degrees, pour it onto the buttered surface. Allow it to cool for 7 to 10 minutes. As the candy cools enough to be handled, fold the edges over onto the center. Eventually you will be able to pick up the ball of candy, and, with buttered hands, twist and pull the candy for a good 10 minutes or until it begins to turn lighter in color. Let the candy rest for an hour or so, then pull and twist it again for about 5 minutes. This process will work air into the candy so that it develops the consistency of the real thing.
5. When the candy has become an even lighter shade of brown, divide it into three or four chunks and roll those into ropes that are about ½-inch thick. Cut into 1-inch pieces. Wrap these pieces in wax paper that has been cut into 2x3-inch rectangles, and twist the ends to seal.

• MAKES 75 BITE-SIZE CANDIES.

•　•　•　•

WENDY'S
WILD MOUNTAIN BACON
CHEESEBURGER

The real secret to duplicating the taste of this new Wendy's product is in recreating the spicy Southwestern pepper sauce, and that secret recipe is right here. That's easy enough. And, if you want to stay true to the original burger, you'll have to get yourself some marbled yellow and white colby/Jack cheese. Look for it in the deli section—I used Tillamook brand. Cook up some bacon, slap it all together and you'll have one of the best homemade hamburgers on the planet.

SOUTHWESTERN PEPPER SAUCE

⅓ cup mayonnaise
¾ teaspoon paprika
¼ teaspoon ground cumin
¼ teaspoon minced garlic
¼ teaspoon lemon juice

⅛ teaspoon cayenne
    pepper
⅛ teaspoon dried oregano
pinch salt
pinch granulated sugar

3¼ ounces ground beef
1 kaiser bun (no seeds)
1 slice colby/Jack cheese
2 slices cooked bacon

1 leaf iceberg lettuce
2 tomato slices
2 red onion rings

1. Make the Southwestern pepper sauce by combining ingredients in a small bowl. Cover and chill the sauce until it's needed.
2. Form the ground beef on wax paper into a square patty that is slightly bigger than the diameter of the bun. Put the patty into the freezer for at least 30 minutes so that it will firm up. This prevents the ground beef from falling apart as it cooks.
3. When you're ready to make the burger, heat up a large skillet over medium heat. Brown the faces of the kaiser bun on the skillet. When the faces of the bun are light brown, use the skillet to cook the beef patty. Add a sprinkle of salt and pepper to the meat, then cook it for 2 to 3 minutes per side or until done.
4. Assemble burger by positioning the patty on the bottom bun. Place the slice of cheese on the beef, followed by the slices of cooked bacon. Place the lettuce leaf on the bacon, than add the tomato slices and onions. Spread about 1 tablespoon of Southwestern sauce on the face of the top bun. Flip the top over onto the rest of the sandwich and serve.

- MAKES 1 BURGER.

TIDBITS

Wendy's also serves this sandwich with two patties. If you like your burgers thick, just add another beef patty onto the first one (on top of the cheese), followed by another slice of colby/Jack.

• • • •

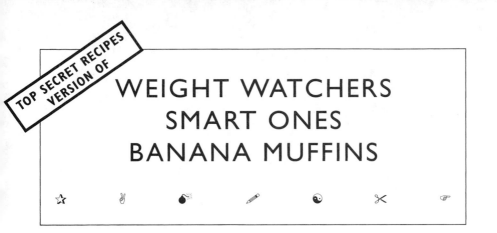

WEIGHT WATCHERS
SMART ONES
BANANA MUFFINS

These easy muffin clones are modeled after the low-fat product found in the freezer section of your market from one of the first brands to make low-fat food hip and tasty. Muffins are notorious for their high fat content, but in this recipe mashed banana and egg substitute provide moisture and flavor. Now you can satisfy a muffin urge without counting fat grams.

1 ¼ cups granulated sugar
½ cup mashed banana
½ cup milk
⅓ cup buttermilk
1 tablespoon egg substitute
1 teaspoon vegetable oil
1 teaspoon vanilla extract

½ teaspoon banana flavoring
¼ teaspoon lemon extract
1 ½ cups all-purpose flour
½ teaspoon baking soda
½ teaspoon baking powder
¾ teaspoon salt

1. Preheat oven to 350 degrees.
2. Combine sugar, banana, milk, buttermilk, egg substitute, oil, vanilla, banana flavoring and lemon extract in a large bowl. Mix well with electric mixer on high speed.
3. In a medium bowl combine flour, baking soda, baking powder, and salt.
4. Mix the dry ingredients into the wet ingredient with the electric mixer.

5. Pour batter into muffin cups in a muffin pan until each cup is about ⅔ full.
6. Bake for 25 to 30 minutes or until muffins turn light brown on top.

• MAKES 12 MUFFINS.

•　•　•　•

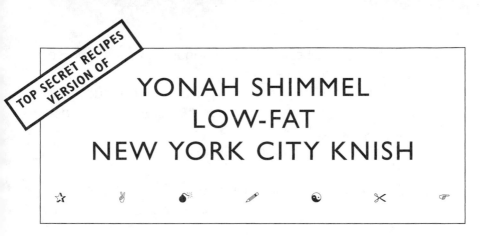

YONAH SHIMMEL LOW-FAT NEW YORK CITY KNISH

Here's a recipe came about from a challenge issued by the New York *Daily News*. They wanted to find out if a West Coast boy could duplicate the taste of an authentic New York City knish. But, mind you, not just any knish. This knish comes from one of the oldest knisheries in the Big Apple; a place which also takes pride in the low fat content of its knishes, versus the popular deep-fried variety. When I tasted the famous Yonah Shimmel knish (the first knish I had ever sampled), I realized that not only could a simple clone recipe be created, but that the fat gram count could come in even lower. The *Daily News* even went so far as to have a lab analyze the fat content of not only the original knish and the clone, but also the fat grams in a street vendor knish and a supermarket knish, just for comparison. The lab results are listed following the recipe.

6 medium russet potatoes
¼ minced onion
2½ tablespoons low-fat butter
3 tablespoons fat-free chicken
    (or vegetable) broth
½ teaspoon salt, or more to taste

⅛ teaspoon ground black pepper,
    or more to taste
seasoning blends, chives or pepper
    flakes to taste (optional)
6 sheets phyllo dough

1. Peel, halve and boil potatoes until tender, 15 to 20 minutes. Mash potatoes in a large bowl.
2. Sauté onion in 1½ tablespoons butter until translucent but not brown. Add to mashed potatoes with broth, salt, pepper and spices. Stir well.
3. Melt remaining tablespoon of butter. Pre-heat oven to 375 degrees.
4. Layer 3 sheets of phyllo dough and cut in half. Repeat with remaining 3 sheets. Spoon 1 cup of potato mixture on each section of phyllo, mold into a large ball and position off-center at one end of strip of dough. Roll ball along the length of phyllo, folding dough over bottom of filling and leaving some filling poking through the top. (Trim and discard excess dough.)
5. Brush melted butter over edges of knish to seal the seams and press down onto an ungreased baking sheet. Repeat with other knishes. Bake 30 to 40 minutes, until golden brown.

• MAKES 4 KNISHES.

HOW THEY STACK UP

Top Secret Recipes knish—Price: 40 cents, Weight: 6.75 ounces, Fat: 3.63 grams

Yonah Shimmel knish—Price: $1.50, Weight: 11.27 ounces, Fat: 7.01 grams

Street vendor knish—Price: $1, Weight: 4.35 ounces, Fat: 4.53 grams

Supermarket knish—Price $1.50, Weight: 9.89 ounces, Fat: 11.27 grams

• • • •

TRADEMARKS

Applebee's is a registered trademark of Applebee's International, Inc.

Arby's and Horsey Sauce are registered trademarks of Arby's, Inc.

Baja Fresh is a registered trademark of Fresh Enterprises.

Benihana is a registered trademark of Benihana, Inc.

Bennigan's is a registered trademark of S&A Restaurant Corp.

Best Foods and Hellman's are registered trademarks of Unilever.

Big Boy is a registered trademark of Waffle House, Inc.

Buffalo Wild Wings is a registered trademark of Buffalo Wild Wings Grill & Bar

California Pizza Kitchen is a registered trademark of California Pizza Kitchen, Inc.

Carrabba's is a registered trademark of Carrabba's Italian Grill, Inc.

The Cheesecake Factory, Sweet Corn Tamale Cakes, Bang-Bang Chicken & Shrimp, and White Chocolate Raspberry Truffle are registered trademarks of The Cheesecake Factory, Inc.

Chevys is a registered trademark of Chevys, Inc.

Chili's, Romano's Macaroni Grill, and Penne Rustica are registered trademarks of Brinker International.

Claim Jumper is a registered trademark of Claim Jumper Restaurants LLC.

Cracker Barrel Old Country Store is a registered trademark of Cracker Barrel Old Country Store, Inc.

Del Taco is a registered trademark of Del Taco, Inc.

Denny's is a registered trademark of DFO, Inc.

Hard Rock Cafe is a registered trademark of Hard Rock Cafe International, Inc.

Hooters is a registered trademark of Hooters of America.

Houston's is a registered trademark of Hillstone Restaurant Group.

IHOP, Country Griddle Cakes, and Harvest Grain 'N Nut are registered trademarks of IHOP Corp.

Islands is a registered trademark of Islands Restaurants.

Jacquin's is a registered trademark of Jacquin's.

Jason's Deli is a registered trademark of Deli Management, Inc.

Joe's Crab Shack is a registered trademark of Landry's Restaurants, Inc.

Kraft and Miracle Whip are registered trademarks of Kraft Foods.

Lincoln Snacks and Poppycock are registered trademarks of Lincoln Snacks.

Lone Star Steakhouse is a registered trademark of Lone Star Steakhouse & Saloon, Inc.

INDEX